A CULTURAL HISTORY OF WESTERN EMPIRES IN THE MODERN AGE

A Cultural History of Western Empires
General Editor: Antoinette Burton

Volume 1
A Cultural History of Western Empires in Antiquity
Edited by Carlos Noreña

Volume 2
A Cultural History of Western Empires in the Middle Ages
Edited by Matthew Gabriele

Volume 3
A Cultural History of Western Empires in the Renaissance
Edited by Ania Loomba

Volume 4
A Cultural History of Western Empires in the Age of Enlightenment
Edited by Ian Coller

Volume 5
A Cultural History of Western Empires in the Age of Empire
Edited by Kirsten McKenzie

Volume 6
A Cultural History of Western Empires in the Modern Age
Edited by Patricia M.E. Lorcin

A CULTURAL HISTORY OF WESTERN EMPIRES IN THE MODERN AGE

Edited by Patricia M.E. Lorcin

BLOOMSBURY ACADEMIC
LONDON • NEW YORK • OXFORD • NEW DELHI • SYDNEY

BLOOMSBURY ACADEMIC
Bloomsbury Publishing Plc
50 Bedford Square, London, WC1B 3DP, UK
1385 Broadway, New York, NY 10018, USA
29 Earlsfort Terrace, Dublin 2, Ireland

BLOOMSBURY, BLOOMSBURY ACADEMIC and the Diana logo are
trademarks of Bloomsbury Publishing Plc

First published in Great Britain 2018
Paperback edition published 2023

Copyright © Patricia Lorcin and Contributors, 2018

Patricia Lorcin and Contributors have asserted their right under the Copyright,
Designs and Patents Act, 1988, to be identified as Author of this work.

Cover design: Raven Design
Cover image: Global Culture GHY, Mumbai, India © Joe McNally/Getty Images

All rights reserved. No part of this publication may be reproduced or transmitted in any form or by any means, electronic or mechanical, including photocopying, recording, or any information storage or retrieval system, without prior permission in writing from the publishers.

Bloomsbury Publishing Plc does not have any control over, or responsibility for, any third-party websites referred to or in this book. All internet addresses given in this book were correct at the time of going to press. The author and publisher regret any inconvenience caused if addresses have changed or sites have ceased to exist, but can accept no responsibility for any such changes.

A catalogue record for this book is available from the British Library.

A catalog record for this book is available from the Library of Congress

ISBN: HB: 978-1-4742-4263-9
PB: 978-1-3503-5826-3
ePDF: 978-1-3502-9043-3
eBook: 978-1-3502-9042-6

Series: The Cultural Histories Series

Typeset by RefineCatch Limited, Bungay, Suffolk
Printed and bound in Great Britain

To find out more about our authors and books visit www.bloomsbury.com
and sign up for our newsletters.

CONTENTS

ILLUSTRATIONS vii
GENERAL EDITOR'S PREFACE xi

   Introduction 1
   Patricia M.E. Lorcin

1 War 21
   Richard Fogarty

2 Trade 47
   David Lynch

3 Natural Worlds 69
   Robert Rouphail

4 Labor 93
   Daniel Bender

5 Mobility 115
   Jessica Namakkal

6 Sexuality 137
   Anna Clark and Elizabeth Williams

7 Resistance 155
   Roland Burke

8   Race   177
    Bruce Hall

NOTES   195
FURTHER READING   201
NOTES ON CONTRIBUTORS   229
INDEX   233

ILLUSTRATIONS

INTRODUCTION

0.1 Detroit Industry, fresco on the South wall, 1932–3, by Diego Rivera (1886–1957), Detroit Institute of Arts, Michigan, United States of America. Credit: DeAgostini/Getty Images.   4

0.2 *King Kong* (1933). Credit: Hulton Archive/Getty Images.   7

0.3 President Eisenhower speaking at a function to celebrate the admission of Alaska and Hawaii to the Union. Credit: Abbie Rowe/PhotoQuest/Getty Images.   11

0.4 Animal rights demonstration at McDonald's restaurant in Sao Paulo. Credit: Cris Faga/NurPhoto via Getty Images.   13

0.5 Berlin, Germany, 2017. Model wearing American apparel. Credit: Christian Vierig/Getty Images.   19

CHAPTER 1

1.1 A Berber fighter during the 1924–5 Rif War. Credit: ullstein bild via Getty Images.   29

1.2 The Rif War against France and Spain. A French military airfield at Fez, June 1925.   30

1.3 British soldiers wade upriver through the jungle on patrol in 1957 during the Malayan Emergency. Credit: Horace Abrahams/Keystone Features/Getty Images.   38

1.4 French soldiers detain suspected nationalist fighters in the Aurès Mountains in 1955, during the Algerian war. Credit: Michel DESJARDINS/Gamma-Rapho via Getty Images. 40

1.5 September 4, 1965: Vietnamese children at the Phu Thuong Orphanage near Da Nang taste ice cream for the first time, brought to them by US Marines, as part of a goodwill mission during the Vietnam War, Vietnam. Credit: US Marine Corps/Getty Images. 44

1.6 A US special forces soldier monitors Iraqi forces advancing toward Mosul airport on February 23, 2017. Credit: AHMAD AL-RUBAYE/AFP/Getty Images. 45

CHAPTER 2

2.1 A wood chip mountain for export in Puerto Montt, southern Chile. Credit: Julio Etchart/ullstein bild via Getty Images. 48

2.2 Weighing cotton in Mumbai. Illustration from the magazine *The Illustrated London News*, Volume XLI, October 11, 1862. Credit: De Agostini/Biblioteca Ambrosiana. 51

2.3 A woman farmer taps dripping resin from a rubber tree in a plantation on Pulau Langkawi Island, Malaysia. Credit: In Pictures Ltd./Corbis via Getty Images. 53

2.4 Empire Marketing Board 1927–33 poster. Credit: British National Archives. 55

CHAPTER 3

3.1 French Foreign Legion postcard, 1952. Credit: Art Media/Print Collector/Getty Images. 76

3.2 Irrigation channels for sugar cane crops, Mauritius. Credit: Kate Hopper. 83

3.3 Nigeria. Bomu, Kpor, Ogoni Area—ecological destruction due to petroleum. Credit: Markus Matzel/ullstein bild via Getty Images. 86

3.4 A Fairchild C-123 Provider cargo plane sprays Agent Orange over a forest in North Vietnam. Credit: Bettmann/Contributor. 90

ILLUSTRATIONS ix

CHAPTER 4

4.1	Mounted Police patrol the South African mine region during the Rand Revolt. Credit: Bettmann/Contributor.	98
4.2	Alexander Bustamante leads a march of striking dock workers and other laborers in Kingston, Jamaica, 1938. Credit: Bettmann/Getty Images.	102
4.3	African soldiers take part in the Battle of France, 1940. Credit: Galerie Bilderwelt/Getty Images.	106
4.4	Demonstrators protest Nike's sweatshop production. Credit: Alan Dejecacion/Getty Images.	112

CHAPTER 5

5.1	Mexican men being registered to work as braceros in 1951. Credit: PhotoQuest/Getty Images.	118
5.2	Western tourists take pictures of destroyed military vehicles in the Golan Heights. Credit: Morse Collection/Gado/Getty Images.	129
5.3	Ugandan Asians arrive at Stansted Airport on a charter flight after being expelled from Uganda, September 18, 1972. Credit: Keystone/Getty Images.	131
5.4	Protestors at Raleigh-Durham International Airport protesting the Muslim travel ban, January 29, 2017. Credit: Leo Chin.	135

CHAPTER 6

6.1	Postcard of the colonies of the Netherlands, *c.* 1900. Credit: Culture Club/Getty Images.	140
6.2	*Mui tsai*, child slave. Credit: Anti-Slavery International.	143
6.3	A scene from the film "The Sheik," in which Rudolph Valentino (1895–1926) embraces Agnes Ayres. Credit: Hulton Archive/Getty Images.	146
6.4	Josephine Baker posing with a tiger rug, *c.* 1925. Credit: Hulton Archive/Getty Images.	146
6.5	A man sits in front of OAS graffiti in Algeria, *c.* 1962. Credit: Dominique Berretty, Gamma-Rapho Collection/Getty Images.	150

CHAPTER 7

7.1 Dr W.E.B. DuBois of the United States, after his speech before the World Congress of Partisans of Peace in Paris. Credit: Bettmann/CORBIS/Bettmann Archive. — 157

7.2 Vietminh poster celebrating the victory of Dien Bien Phu. Credit: Photo by Apic/Getty Images. — 160

7.3 Gamal Abdul Nasser of Egypt (center left) talking with Jawaharlal Nehru of India during the Bandung Conference. Credit: Howard Sochurek/The LIFE Picture Collection/Getty Images. — 166

7.4 Victory of Robert Mugabe in Rhodesia, 1980. A supporter of Robert Mugabe holding a cock, symbol of the Zanu Party. Credit: Keystone-France/Gamma-Keystone via Getty Images. — 168

7.5 Four starving Biafran children sit and lie around a bowl of food in the dirt during the Nigerian-Biafran civil war. Credit: Hulton Archive/Getty Images. — 172

7.6 UN Human Rights Conference in Vienna. Credit: Leopold Nekula/Sygma via Getty Images. — 174

CHAPTER 8

8.1 Black Brazilian women protest. Credit: EVARISTO SA/AFP/Getty Images. — 181

8.2 A dalit with a poster of Dr Ambedkar in Chennai. Credit: Claude Renault/Getty Images. — 184

8.3 An Arab prisoner being questioned and jailed in camps during the Zanzibar revolution by local African revolutionaries led by John Gideon Okello, January 12, 1964. Credit: STRINGER/AFP/Getty Images. — 192

Every effort has been made to trace copyright holders and to obtain their permission for the use of copyright material. The publisher apologizes for any errors or omissions and would be grateful if notified of any corrections that should be incorporated in future reprints or editions of this book.

GENERAL EDITOR'S PREFACE

Histories of empire have been transformed in the last three decades by a combination of new methods, new archives, and a new generation of scholars who have come of age in a postcolonial world. The impact of these historical forces on how imperialism is understood has been remarkable. For decades the province of geopolitics, diplomacy, and the "official mind," imperial history is now just as likely to be told from the bottom up as from the top down. The rise of cultural history has played a significant role in how we think about and narrate imperialism from the ancient world to the twentieth century. With an emphasis on evidence drawn from literature, the arts, life-writing, and a host of fragmentary sources, cultural historians think through patterns of representation and experience that shape the conditions in which histories of all kinds—economic, political, social—happen. They investigate often overlooked subjects and offer new angles of vision on familiar topics through a cultural lens. The ambition of *A Cultural History of Western Empires* is to advance conversations about the work of culture in shaping how empire took root, took shape, was maintained, and faced challenges whether its regimes were of long or short durée. Indeed, no thoroughgoing histories of the subject can afford to ignore the influence that culture has had on the shape of empires in local, regional, and global contexts.

The geographical remit of *A Cultural History of Western Empires* is indicated in its title. As compelling a topic as the wide variety of imperial formations is, and as interconnected as west and non-west have been along the axis of empire from Greece to Beijing and back again, the authors in this volume explore empire's cultural histories in a broadly western European setting. And while the differences between French and German and English imperial experiences are often notable, what is equally striking are the features that cultures of labor, trade, sexuality, race, war, mobility, natural worlds, and resistance share across imperial locales. Even allowing for specificities of time and place, there is a value to taking a very long view of the concept and practice of *imperium*—not simply to note commonalities or differences but to be able to discern through lines across such widely distinctive terrains as the Frankish kingdoms and the world of the post-Versailles settlement. In no small respect, attention to cultural forces, identities, rhetorics, tropes, relationships, and imaginaries make this kind of discernment possible. Reading for culture—which is to say, developing the capacity to plumb a variety of sources and archives for evidence of how meanings and forms were constantly made and struggled over across a range of domains—reveals the work of historical forces that have undergirded and, at times, have redirected or undone imperial power. Empire simply cannot be understood in all its limits and possibilities without an analysis of its cultural histories.

This is a work of scholarly synthesis rooted in the original scholarship and intellectual vision of the volume editors and their contributors. Its audience is students seeking a comparative, interdisciplinary, and evidence-based account of how empires worked at multiple scales. Readers will get a sense, then, of the cultural impact of large-scale territorial expansion and hegemony *and* of the meaning and experience of conquest and colonization in more intimate environments. Contributors have written their essays to make available a broad overview of their theme or topic. Each one draws on a range of materials and case studies to make a larger argument about the history of cultural formations and influences that pertain to their subject. The series is structured around six time periods: Antiquity, The Medieval Age, The Renaissance, The Enlightenment, The Age of Empire, and the Modern Age. These are conceptual and pedagogical, signaling a periodization that modern Western imperialism itself has played an important role in shaping and sustaining. Casting Rome as an imperial touchtone and colonized territories as "ancient" or "medieval" in temporal terms remains an important cultural resource for contemporary empire-building, and it draws on a long cultural legacy that contributors both address and challenge. Each volume takes up the chronological parameters assigned in critical conversation with the historical evidence, allowing readers to see the pros and cons of thinking about empire itself as a maker—and breaker—of time periods. Of equal significance, each volume is organized with the same chapter titles so that readers can either follow a theme across time frames—mobility in the Enlightenment as compared to the twentieth century, for example—or read through a single period by exploring the range of thematic lenses on offer. This combination of diachronic and synchronic affords us a unique opportunity to cultivate comparisons that are as deep as they are broad, and to appreciate the indispensability of cultural history to practically all aspects of imperial regime making and unmaking across this particular swath of the global past.

Such a purposeful focus on culture at this juncture in the history of the historiography of empire is worth remarking on. As an object of historical inquiry, culture is arguably the carrier of a number of historical forces that attention to politics or economics alone cannot capture. Though embedded in and constitutive of every aspect of imperial geopolitics, race, gender, and sexuality were long invisible to the historians' eye because they were considered trivial, or at best inconsequential, to the workings of real power. Cultural history practices, which bring new forms of seeing and reading as well as new subjects to our sightline, open up the imperial archive to aspects of the past, which, in turn, shed new light on old paradigms. Thinking with and through culture also reorients our gaze, pulling us toward sources—diaries, images, discursive motifs—in a diverse array of formations and spaces that illuminate dimensions of hegemony and power otherwise invisible: dismiss-able, even, as immaterial because they are ostensibly "only cultural." What the collective example of this series accomplishes is to suggest how, why, and under what conditions culture has been a maker of imperial history—indeed, that empires have been done and undone by the cultural forces they sought to control but which were not always completely in their grasp. As twenty-first-century forms of imperial power emerge, claiming historical newness and relying on past models of conquest and occupation all at once, we need narratives that insist on the power of histories attuned to the ideological and material work of culture more than ever.

Culture is at the dynamic heart of all imperial histories. It operates in spaces of high command and conjugal intimacy; in ceremony and in ordinary life; in military documents and botanists' texts; at court and on the plantation; through trade routes and refugee settlements; in the pronouncements of empresses and the movements of the lowly beetle; in the signing of treaties and the violence of the battlefield and the inner workings of the household. Thinking through cultures of empire, in turn, throws us back on the protocols and presumptions of the discipline by encouraging us to be ever vigilant about where—in what spaces and through what repertoires—history happens. Empire is not, perhaps, unique in this regard. The irony is that while imperial ambition and self-regard have often been steeped in convictions about the power of culture to conquer and colonize, imperial narratives on a grand scale are often the most impervious to the argument that culture matters. What follows is a wide-ranging and lively set of arguments about how and why that has been incontrovertibly so from antiquity to modern times.

Introduction

PATRICIA M.E. LORCIN[1]

> Only Americans have the sense of mission and gall to engage in benign, but energetic global cultural advocacy. We are the most potent cultural imperialists in history.
>
> —Ben Wattenberg (quoted by Mirrlees 2006: 203)

When the Treaty of Versailles took effect on January 1, 1920, the stature of the Western empires, hitherto seemingly firmly grounded, was undermined.[2] The misleading triumph of the war's endgame for the Allies, which saw the demise of four empires—the Austro-Hungarian, the German, the Russian, and the Ottoman—held the seeds of the undoing of the remaining European empires and the rise to prominence of that of the United States. To be sure, in the war's immediate aftermath the Belgians were mandated Rwanda-Urundi while the British and French acquired the colonial spoils of Germany in sub-Saharan Africa and procured mandates in the Middle East, thus temporarily endorsing their imperial hegemony. But, by coming to the aid of the Allies during the war, the Americans gained a theoretical toehold in Europe that would lead, throughout the twentieth century, to increasing influence both on the continent itself and eventually in Europe's disintegrating overseas empires. As the century progressed, the cultural imperialism, championed by Wattenberg, would be matched by an overseas military culture that was geared to protect US strategic and economic interests. By the end of the twentieth century, it was the only empire remaining. As Irving Kristol aptly put it in the *Wall Street Journal* in 1997, ". . . the United States has come to dominate the world militarily and culturally."

Prefiguring these developments, President Woodrow Wilson, one of the three foremost leaders presiding over the Treaty negotiations, believed that, in the wake of the war's tragedy, it was incumbent on the United States to assume a prominent role in the regulation of world affairs (Reynolds 2014: 9). In his January 1918 speech, Wilson outlined his fourteen points and advocated, among other things, free trade, democracy, and self-determination. The speech appeared to target not only the Continent but also the Continent's colonial powers, whose territories had neither free trade, democracy, nor self-determination. Point five, furthermore, actually pertained to the colonies and was ambiguous enough to suggest an endorsement of the idea of equal rights for the colonized peoples.[3] David Lloyd George and Georges Clemenceau, the leaders of the two largest European colonial empires, inevitably were skeptical of Wilson's idealism. More to the point, however, was their desire to implement the agreement conceived by Mark Sykes and François Georges-Picot in 1916, which set out the potential British and French spheres of cultural and economic influence in Asia Minor, once the war was over and the "Palestine question" could be satisfactorily resolved.[4] The compromise reached in response to Wilson's idea of a new world order in which annexation or colonization was to be discouraged, was the mandate system. As perverse as it may now seem, the mandate system was deemed to be a trusteeship during which, according to the prevailing conceit, the strong would protect the weak (MacMillan 2003: 98–106). In theory, it was unlike bone fide colonization; in practice, there was little difference (see Pedersen 2015). The feature that set the mandates apart from longer standing colonies, was the absence of a substantial settler base. The ideological underpinning of the strong protecting the weak was merely a reiteration, in a new guise, of the British sociologist, Benjamin Kidd's (1858–1916) mantra of the Europeans as the "trustees of civilization."

The Mandates were established under Article 22 of the Covenant of the League of Nations, which came into being in January 1920, with the finer details being determined at the Cairo Conference of 1921 (Wallach [1996] 2005: 294–301). If the British and French leaders were wary of Wilson's ideas for a new world order, intellectuals in the colonies were hopeful that the League of Nations was a path to more equality or, better still, eventual independence. With this in mind, individuals like Emir Khaled, the grandson of Abd al-Qadir, the nineteenth-century leader of the opposition against the French conquest of Algeria, wrote to Wilson requesting Algerian representation at Versailles in the hope that the "Algerian question" would be placed before the League of Nations (McDougall 2008: 46). Although Khaled's intention was geared to seek allies in his quest for Algerian autonomy, or even independence, it nonetheless was an early indication of the gradual overshadowing of the European empires by the United States. US imperialism preceded the twentieth century, of course, but the events of the twentieth century led to its development into the leading western imperial power.[5]

THE INTERWAR YEARS

The interwar period was, paradoxically, the high point of European colonialism while simultaneously being the swansong of its empires. The war had sapped European strength, morally and financially, and any hope that the colonies could provide succor was soon undercut by the emergence of structured anticolonialism and the impact on settler societies of the Great Depression. In the immediate aftermath of the war, however, the colonial offices of the metropoles did not see the potential unravelling of their hegemony. Rather, they looked to the colonies to solve some of the problems that the war had created. The acquisition by the British of the German East African lands meant that the British East African Protectorate was divided up into territories that became colonies in their own right. In order to try and populate areas like the newly established colony of Kenya, where settler population was low, the British government implemented a Soldier Settlement Scheme for demobilized military personnel and made 2.54 million acres (1.03 million hectares) of land available for white settlement, most of which came from the African reserves.

In 1922, Lord Frederick Lugard published *The Dual Mandate in British Tropical Africa*. Influenced by his service as High Commissioner of the protectorate of Northern Nigeria, he advocated indirect rule or collaboration between native chiefs, their underlings, and colonial administrators. It was essential, he wrote, "that democracy should take an intelligent and well-informed interest in questions which affect the Empire of which it is the inheritor and trustee" (Lugard 1922: 7). Lugard was conscious that the Great War had undermined European social and political structures and greatly weakened its participants, but was confident that, with proper guidance, the imperial territories had the potential to help the metropoles back on their feet. Similarly, the Netherlands announced "a new approach to colonial management" in the Dutch East Indies whereby they would improve relations through increased agricultural output, expand the education of vernacular languages, and provide the wherewithal to improve Indonesian living standards (Booth 2012: 1148). Although the Dutch were not motivated by the same impulse as Lugard, having remained neutral during the war, their interest was to make the colony pay for itself, rather than sap their healthy GDP. Indeed, similar initiatives were taken in several parts of colonized Asia and Africa as European business enterprises invested heavily in their colonies (Abernethy 2000: 113; Booth 2012: 1147). Companies such as Société Commerciale de l'Ouest Africain (SCOA) and the Compagnie Française de l'Afrique Occidentale (CFAO) in French sub-Saharan Africa and the United Africa Company (UAC) in British West Africa, which had been established in some form prior to the war, fanned out across the colonial territories and this in spite of the Depression. UAC, for example, originally a merger of the African and Eastern Trading Corporation and the Niger Company, encountered serious economic difficulties

FIGURE 0.1: Detroit Industry, fresco on the South wall, 1932–3, by Diego Rivera (1886–1957), Detroit Institute of Arts, Michigan, United States of America. Credit: DeAgostini/Getty Images.

during the Depression, but these were resolved with its takeover in the thirties, by Unilever, the Anglo-Dutch trading company. With the growth of the automobile industry (Figure 0.1), furthermore, rubber became a prized commodity. As cultural and social enthusiasm for the automobile grew, rubber plantations were established and flourished in a number of colonies, most notably in British Malaya, French Indochina, and the Belgian Congo.

In spite of these developments and the seeming opportunities that they could offer the local population, it was the colonial establishment that continued to reap the benefits. Thus, the notion that improved relations and increased rights for the colonized peoples might help to create a cooperative workforce that could mitigate the disasters—both economic and human—of the war, or ensure that the colony paid for itself, was not always accompanied by the sort of democratic impulse that Lugard or the Dutch were advocating.

In the Belgian Congo, for example, unlike plantation-produced rubber, the Belgians had focused on the harvesting of wild rubber. As accessible areas were depleted and the Belgians pushed their labor force further and further into the hinterland, it led to inhuman cruelty on a massive scale. The journalist and politician, E.D. Morel first castigated Belgian methods in *Red Rubber* (1906). Two decades later, André Gide's *Voyage au Congo* (1927) raised similar concerns. Nothing was done to improve the situation where workers' rights were entirely overlooked.

In Algeria, where the French notions of liberty, equality, and fraternity could have led to a more equitable situation, the 1930 centenary celebrations of the conquest were held amidst impolitic colonial grandstanding with little consideration for Algerian sensibilities. Six years later, the Blum-Violette Bill, which sought to grant a select group of Muslims access to French citizenship and hence the vote, was quashed by the settlers. To disappointments such as these was added the disillusionment throughout the European empires that the colonized subjects, who had fought in large numbers for the colonial powers during the war, were presented with little more than medals. Furthermore, the relentless bloodletting of the war had undermined the image and ideological underpinning of the civilizational superiority proffered by the Europeans.

The interwar years in the colonies were thus characterized by increasing unrest. In India, Britain's foremost colony, the Indian National Congress, first formed in 1885, was already a well-organized movement. In conjunction with Mahatma Gandhi's 1909 tract *Hind Swaraj* (Home Rule), anticolonialism in India developed throughout the post-First World War period into a non-violent mass movement, which eventually led to independence in 1947. Protest in other colonies was not as peaceful. In French Indochina, for example, the short-lived 1930 Yên Bái revolt was met with brutal reprisals, triggering a peasant uprising that took a year to suppress and prompting Ho Chi Minh to form the Indochinese Communist Party. Throughout the European empires, in Africa and Asia, protest movements of various strengths and ideological hues struggled to attain autonomy or independence (Isaacman and Isaacman 1983; Clayton 1994; Cooper 1996b; Thomas *et al.* [2007] 2015; Shipway 2008; Thomas and Curless 2017). In Indonesia, in spite of Dutch attempts to improve relations with the local population, by 1927 Sukarno had formed the Indonesian Nationalist Party (PNI). The rapid expansion of its membership prompted the Dutch into action imprisoning Sukarno and curtailing PNI action (Dahm 1969; Legge 1972). In spite of these developments, most colonial administrations appeared oblivious or chose to ignore the changes resonating among their subject populations. The sapping of European imperial power was also evidenced by the fact that diplomatic and financial concessions, which had been obtained from the Ottomans and Chinese during the nineteenth and early twentieth centuries, were abrogated. At the instigation of Kemal Ataturk, the 1923 Lausanne Treaty abolished the Capitulations, granted by the Ottomans. The "unequal treaties" between the western powers (including the United States) and the Chinese—the result of the Opium Wars—were abolished in stages, first at the 1922 Washington Conference when the Chinese managed to curtail foreign governments' jurisdiction over their nationals residing in China and completely by 1930 (Abernethy 2000: 111).

Of all the western nations, only the United States was to consolidate its existing imperial power and, beginning in the interwar period, was to start its gradual move toward the position of dominant global power. The nineteenth century had witnessed US expansionism into the Pacific, South America, and the Caribbean, but it had remained an essentially regional player. Coming to the aid of Allied Forces during the First World War was not only decisive militarily for the Allies, it was also symbolic of the US move from regional to global involvement not just militarily but also economically. Starting in the interwar period, aspects of American popular culture started to take hold in Europe, the beginning of what Victoria de Grazia (2005) has dubbed "the irresistible empire." The First World War had swept away the European hierarchical certainties of the prewar period and mass mobilization had had a radicalizing impact on the populace. The Russian Revolution, the failed Sparticist revolt, and the waves of strikes throughout Europe in the immediate aftermath of the war signaled a desire for change among the populations at large that would respond to the innovations of American mass culture.

It was the emerging cultural product from Hollywood—feature films—that would become the most effective means of spreading US culture throughout the world and help to transform it into the leading imperium (Figure 0.2). John Trumpbour (2002), among others, has demonstrated the political wrangling that went on between the United States and European countries, in particular, Britain, France, and Belgium, over the distribution of Hollywood films in their respective countries. European elites, whether political or cultural, were alarmed at the potential erosion of their national values, which the messages of the films and the lifestyles of their stars epitomized. The endorsement of mass culture that the film industry symbolized represented both a potential disruption of established hierarchical values in the metropole but also suggested a more devastating unraveling of such values in the European colonies. Coca-Cola, hamburgers, and jeans would eventually become the symbols of American cultural dominance, but it was the film industry, which had an insidious cultural, social, and eventually political influence that served as a counterculture to Europe and its empires. Its importance as a tool for the spread of American influence is suggested by the involvement of the US State Department in negotiating agreements rather than leaving it to the Commerce Department, as would normally be the case (Trumpbour 2002).

US cultural penetration was not without its opponents, however, and the thirties saw a conservative backlash against "Yankee culture." In France, where extreme right and fascist groups were much in evidence, American art forms were denigrated as "judeo-negro-américane" jazz and "Israëlite cinema." The backlash was even harsher in Germany where Hitler and his cohorts closely associated it with a "decadent" Weimar Republic and Goebbels labeled American jazz as "the art of the subhuman" (Trumpbour 2002: 231; Wipplinger 2017).

FIGURE 0.2: *King Kong* (1933). Credit: Hulton Archive/Getty Images.

Nonetheless, such opposition was unable to stop the appeal of American culture for the general population. In addition to jazz, the popularity of performers such as Josephine Baker or "new-fangled" dances such as the Charleston, suggested that American culture provided a form of escapism from the haunting horrors of the Great War and from the values of the hidebound societies of the prewar past. In much the same way as US troops had come to the rescue of the war-weary Allied troops during the war, American culture was now helping to alleviate Europe's war-weary societies.

THE SECOND WORLD WAR AND THE CLASH OF EMPIRES

If the interwar period was characterized by intimations of the emergence of US global hegemony, the Second World War was the decisive factor in tipping the balance from the European form of imperialism toward that of the United States. The war itself was, in many respects, a second clash of empires pitting the western imperial forces against those of Germany and Japan. During the war, Germany's short-term imperial interests were restricted to occupying the continent and battling the Allied forces in and around the Mediterranean, but had the war's outcome been otherwise the colonies of the occupied countries would, no doubt, have been part of the victor's spoils. The Japanese, meanwhile, were marching through the European colonies in Asia and in 1941 attacked the American naval base at Pearl Harbor to prevent the Americans coming to the aid of Europe's beleaguered Asian colonies. The US decision to enter the war and, in particular, the choice to privilege the European arena before the Asian, was a decisive factor in the war's outcome. At the war's end, two potential empires—the German and the Japanese—were shattered and European imperialism was in tatters.

The overrunning of the European colonies by the Japanese during the war hastened their independence. Although India had escaped the Japanese onslaught, it gained its independence in 1947, followed by its blood-stained partition into two countries. Independence for the remaining British Asian colonies followed shortly after: Ceylon (Sri Lanka) and Burma (Myanmar) in 1948, while Malaya (Malaysia) would follow in the wave of decolonizations that occurred in the late 1950s and early 1960s.[6] In 1945, Indonesian nationalists declared independence from the Netherlands, as did Ho Chi Minh in Vietnam from France. Whereas the Dutch, after a brief struggle, accepted the inevitable and acknowledged Indonesian sovereignty in 1949, the French did not, waging a nine-year war, which ended in their ignominious defeat at Dien Bien Phu in 1954. Although the Americans nominally watched from the sidelines offering help at strategic moments, it signaled the beginning of their involvement in Vietnam and the consolidation of first its image, and then its position, as a twentieth-century imperial power (Karnow 1983; Shipway 1996; Hunt and Levine 2012; Miller and Wainstock 2013). The "winds of change," as Harold Macmillan was to put it in 1960, were reshaping twentieth-century imperialism.

THE BENIGN HEGEMON

As the ideological and hegemonic positions of European empires shrank, that of the United States gained in stature. The European economies were in ruins. In spite of being the only non-occupied Allied power, Britain's international position was greatly weakened. In contrast to the aftermath of the First World War, the government no longer had illusions of its colonies as an economic succor. The other leading imperial power, France, had not suffered in quite the same way as Britain, as its infrastructure was largely intact, but it too was economically weakened and one of its leading colonies, Indochina, had been occupied by the Japanese. The Americans came to Europe's rescue, yet again, militarily and, as important, economically. The Bretton Woods Agreements of July 1944 removed international currencies from the gold standard and pegged them to the dollar, thus stabilizing exchange rates in an effort to avoid the galloping inflation of the interwar years. The move made the dollar the global currency and endowed the US with global financial power, a step that would eventually lead to the anchoring of US capitalist culture worldwide. The Agreements, furthermore, established the World Bank and the International Monetary Fund, which handled the much-needed loans that would put Europe back on its feet economically and provide an important market for the Americans whose wartime economy had boomed, providing the US population with a commensurate standard of living (Chua 2007: 255). The 1947 Marshall Plan, meanwhile, provided the necessary technical support that would hasten the rebuilding of a strong Europe, an important adjunct to the success of the Truman Doctrine. The creation of the European Coal and Steel Community, the first step toward what would become the European Union, and the establishment of the North Atlantic Treaty Organization (NATO), both at the instigation of and with encouragement from the United States, were significant to its strategic and economic aims. US aims may not have been imperial at the time, but the institutions and measures taken to buttress the ravaged western European economies and create a strong allied bloc against Soviet incursion, laid the groundwork for the emergence of the United States as the rising western imperial power.

At the same time as these developments in Europe, in a gesture as much symbolic as realistically necessary, Great Britain informed the United States that it was neither economically in a position to contain the ongoing Greek civil war (1946–9) by continuing to support the royalists against the communist insurgents, nor able to maintain a viable presence in Palestine.[7] In 1947, the Americans took over in Greece and a year later Britain withdrew from Palestine, opening the way for the founding of the state of Israel. The new state was immediately recognized by the United States. This would lead to a close partnership that provided the Americans with a strategic position in the Middle East. In 1952, Turkey entered NATO providing a vital base for troops in the area. As the dust from the war settled, the United States emerged as the strongest western power militarily and economically.

THE COLD WAR YEARS

Of the significant developments during the Cold War that were landmarks of sorts on the US road to imperial stature, only three will be mentioned. The first was the decolonization of the European colonies, most of which had obtained their independence by the end of the 1970s. During the fifties, the United States had remained largely neutral with regard to Europe's colonies, but as the Cold War developed there was a realization that such support could counter US interests by pushing the nationalists into the Soviet camp. This prompted the United States to encourage decolonization. Two examples of this are the Suez

Crisis (1956) and the Algerian War of Independence (1954–62). Although Egypt had gained its freedom from British occupation in 1922, British and French economic and shipping interests remained closely bound up with the Suez Canal. The Crisis was provoked as a result of the Canal's nationalization by Gamal Abdel Nasser, thus jeopardizing British and French interests. When diplomatic negotiations failed and Britain and France invaded, following on Israel's march into Egypt, a US-sponsored UN resolution forced their withdrawal. Nasser emerged triumphant, and went on to assume an important role in the decolonization process. The withdrawal of the French and British troops was also a serious loss of prestige to what had hitherto been the two most important imperial powers. The denouement in Egypt was especially pertinent with regard to events in Algeria. The war had started two years earlier and by 1957 Radio Cairo was regularly broadcasting pro-nationalist messages across Africa. Nor was the humiliation that France had suffered in Egypt lost on the leadership of the FLN (Front National de Libération), who were starting to curry favor in diplomatic circles. The Americans had initially supported the French in their struggle to keep Algeria French, but in July 1957 John F. Kennedy, then a junior senator, addressed Congress urging them to take a moral stand on colonialism, and declaring that it was important to show the colonized that "we are a freedom loving people who want all people free." He criticized President Eisenhower for refusing to condemn what was going on in Algeria, for by doing so he was aligning the United States with French colonialism. Kennedy's views were initially condemned by both Congress and the national press, but with the escalation of the war the Americans became concerned about the weakening of NATO forces due to the deployment of so many French troops to Algeria (O'Brien 2005: 357–8). When it became obvious that it was in the US Cold War interests to eschew the colonial line, Congress came around (Wall 2001; Connelly 2002). Furthermore, the Civil Rights movement had led high-profile African-Americans, such as Richard Wright and Malcolm X, to sites of decolonization in West Africa, in particular Ghana, where they critiqued western colonialism linking it to US treatment of African-Americans and the need for civil rights (von Eschen 1997; Gaines 2006). The United States thus distanced itself from European imperialism and gained in international prestige.

A second development that bears mentioning was the shoring up of US strategic footholds around the world to ensure that Communism was contained. Korea, freed from Japanese occupation in 1945, became an early pawn in the Cold War leading to the Korean War (1950–3). Twenty-one of the UN member states participated, but it was the Americans who provided the bulk of the troops. Although the war's outcome may not have ended with the United States gaining the whole of the peninsula, it provided the Americans with an ally in the area south of the 38th parallel, even though pro-American sentiments were not always consistent. Two other strategically important territories in, or bordering on, the Pacific were Hawai'i and Alaska. Both had been under the aegis of the United States since the nineteenth century, but after the attack on Pearl Harbor in 1941 the US built substantial military fortifications in each. In Hawai'i, military personnel during the war expanded from 43,000 to over a million men (Whitehead 2004: 82–3). As part of the United States' nineteenth-century colonial empire, Hawai'i remained under the inequality of territorial rule until after the Second World War (Bell 1984: 7; Saranillio 2010). As the decolonization of the European territories proceeded, the US acted accordingly with its own territories. In much the same way as France retained some of its overseas departments and territories (DOM/TOM), following the decolonization of its African and Asian territories, the US followed suit by creating incorporated (Hawai'i and Alaska) and unincorporated territories (e.g. Guam, Virgin Islands, Puerto Rico). In spite of lukewarm enthusiasm in the United States, both in Congress and among the American people, by the end of the fifties Alaska and Hawai'i had become the forty-ninth and fiftieth state respectively (Figure 0.3).

The Cold War may have remained "cold" between the United States, its Allies, and the Soviet Union, but it did not preclude crises and actual warfare when US or Allied interests were at stake. Nor did it prevent dangerous

FIGURE 0.3: President Eisenhower speaking at a function to celebrate the admission of Alaska and Hawaii to the Union. Credit: Abbie Rowe/PhotoQuest/Getty Images.

brinkmanship, as the Cuban Missile Crisis of 1962 demonstrated. Kennedy's calling of Khrushchev's bluff as Soviet nuclear-armed ships steamed toward Cuba enhanced US international stature as the guardian of global security. A quite different outcome transpired during the Vietnam War (1955–75)—or Second Indochinese War as it was sometimes called. The war is significant in that it was the first US defeat since the Second World War, with a great cost to lives and long-lasting ordnance damage to Vietnam, Cambodia, and Laos, the countries that made up French Indochina. Furthermore, US activities in Cambodia during the war contributed to ushering in the genocidal Khmer Rouge at war's end. The Vietnam syndrome, as it has been dubbed, alludes to American humiliation as a result of this defeat and the resulting impact on US foreign policy in El Salvador and Iraq (Simons 1998). But it was also a reinforcement of the increasingly held view that the United States was more aggressively imperialist than it claimed to be. No longer seen as mere cultural imperialists, it had acquired the mantle of the world's leading imperial power.

US military activity in Africa, during the Cold War, was initially restricted to the presence of bases in North Africa, especially in Morocco. Its relations in sub-Saharan Africa were ostensibly limited to its efforts to introduce democratic practices and provide economic assistance. In fact, it was just as concerned about Soviet encroachment in the area, as it was elsewhere. Until 1986, when Congress passed the Comprehensive Anti-Apartheid Act (CAAA) and it joined the international community in imposing sanctions, the United States maintained economic relations with South Africa not just to keep the Soviets at bay but also to avoid losing an important trading partner. By 1986, however, the Soviet Union under Mikhail Gorbachev was showing a different face. To paraphrase Margaret Thatcher, he was a man "with whom one could do business." The Cold War was winding down and three years later the Soviet Union would collapse, symbolically expressed with the dismantling of the Berlin Wall. If American triumphalism at the end of the Cold War seems disingenuous today, more mindful individuals were conscious of the hubris in Fukuyama's concept of the "end of history" whereby western liberalism had at last triumphed (Fukuyama 1992). By the end of the twentieth century, the world was a much more complicated place than it had been in the immediate aftermath of the Second World War.

The third dimension that I want to raise in the development of US hegemonic interests and power is its conquest of consumer society. Although American consumer goods and artifacts had started their global penetration after the First World War, it was only in the boom period of the late fifties and sixties that conspicuous consumption *à l'americaine* really took off. The impact on the global economy, which its promotion of mass market commodities had, whether in the form of clothing (Levis, mass-produced garments), household goods, electronics, cultural products (films, TV series, pop art), or comestibles (Coca

FIGURE 0.4: Animal rights demonstration at McDonald's restaurant in Sao Paulo. Credit: Cris Faga/NurPhoto via Getty Images.

Cola, McDonalds, fast food), provided the United States with a high profile and an exemplar of easy living (Figure 0.4). Kristen Ross has demonstrated how, following decolonization, the French espoused American consumer culture, thus reshaping their traditional agriculturally based society into a more consumption-oriented one (Ross 1995). De Grazia (2005) has documented the impact of US consumerism on European society in extensive detail. Although the degree of soft imperialism of this development can be debated, and it cannot be compared with the imposition of economic interests in the nineteenth century as a result, for example, of the Opium Wars, it nonetheless is comparable to the way trade often preceded the flag in earlier times. In short, it prepared the terrain for the more aggressive forms of imperialism, developed later.

THE EU AND AN IMPERIAL LEGACY

While the United States was establishing its super power status, the former European imperial powers, in particular France and Britain, did not walk away from their colonies without looking back, nor indeed did they stop economic or military involvement, particularly in Africa. In the immediate years after independence, companies like SCOA, CFAO, and UAC continued to trade profitably in Africa. By the mid-1970s, Africanization was adopted by most of these large companies, all of which persisted in some form until the end of the century.[8] Investment in former colonies also continued. In the Ivory Coast, for example, during the economic boom of the late sixties and early seventies—"the Ivorian miracle"—French investment and presence far exceeded that of the colonial period. Encouraged by then president Felix Houphouet-Boigny, the French population in the colony increased to 60,000, double the 30,000 of the colonial period (Lorcin 2014: 146). Britain, too, maintained its imperial and economic links, establishing the British Commonwealth with those of its former colonies who were interested in joining (now known as the Commonwealth of Nations, it comprises 52 member states, many of which were not former colonies), while France and most of its former African colonies created close ties in what came to be known as *Françafrique* (this too has expanded and now includes all Francophone Africa and beyond). Both France and Britain have maintained military bases in some of their former colonies, France more extensively than Britain. Furthermore, as Véronique Dimier has pointed out, former European colonial powers in the European Economic Community (EEC; now the European Union, EU) were "at the heart of European Development Policy." The French politician, Claude Cheysson, who took up a position as commissioner for development in the EEC in 1973, stated that when he arrived at the Commission, "the style was very colonial indeed" (Dimier 2009: 251). At the end of the twentieth century, former imperial powers, now in the EU, were still embroiled in trade disputes relating to the economic interests of former colonial territories. The "Banana Wars" of the nineties between the United States and the EU is one such example. In a measure introduced in 1993, bananas from former ACP countries (i.e. the former African and Caribbean colonies of EU members) were exempt from import duty, whereas bananas from elsewhere were not. In appearance, disputes such as these may be par for the course in the process of globalization, but they nonetheless had echoes of earlier economic squabbles between imperial powers.

Economic factors were not the only throwback to the past. The Falklands Crisis of 1982, when Margaret Thatcher stormed across the Atlantic to counter the Argentinian invasion and make "Britain great again," won her increased popularity at the polls and demonstrated an aspect of the imperial legacy (Lorcin 2013a: 100). Similarly, French interventions in Africa, such as in Chad in 1986 and in Mali in 2013, reinforced the ties of *Françafrique* even though they were at the behest of the leaders of the countries in question and with the sanction of the UN. There is, however, a difference between British and French activity: the political leaders of the former closely associate their governments with the United States or its overseas activities, whether it was Tony Blair's quasi-obsequious relations with George W. Bush, especially during the second Iraq war, or Theresa May rushing to be the first European head of state to visit President Trump in the wake of the Brexit referendum. On the other hand, French presidents, with the exception of Nicolas Sarkozy, have tried to pursue their own agendas by distancing France from the United States, as did General de Gaulle in 1966 by withdrawing from NATO and closing down the US military bases in France, or François Mitterrand in 1986 by forbidding the US to fly over French airspace when attacking Libya, or even Jacques Chirac in 2003 ruling out the participation of French troops in the Iraq invasion, earning the opprobrium of the US whose press labeled them "cheese-eating surrender monkeys" while liquor stores poured quantities of French wine down the drain. The simplification of the Anglo-American relationship as an Anglo-Saxon axis, or more pejoratively "Britain riding on US coattails," fails to take into consideration earlier imperial aspirations and activities. Although both Britain and France exploited their colonies economically, Britain was primordially an economically motivated empire with prestige following in its wake, whereas for France maintaining its international prestige, or rivaling that of other imperial powers, in particular Britain, was as important a motor of its nineteenth-century empire—if not more so—as were its economic interests. The cultural dimensions of all the Western empires lay in the spread of the specific attributes of what they considered their national values, whether it was the administrative and legal frameworks of the British, the elite "civilization" of the French, or the consumerism of the Americans, to name but three significant examples.

By the end of the twentieth century, America's image as a "benign hegemon" had been eclipsed by a more hardnosed consumerism. The emergence of the EEC/EU as an economic force, concurrently with Japan and later south-east Asia, coupled with their espousal of American-type consumerism, gave rise to competitive forces that provoked a more cutthroat US stance. The emulation of American culture in these new consumer societies was accompanied by an increased reliance on a transport system that was largely dependent on oil.

THE OIL CULTURE AND ITS WARS

Throughout the twentieth century, as oil replaced coal as the fuel of industrialization and its myriad by-products (e.g., the many forms of plastic, solvents, synthetic materials) became an essential part of consumer society, its pricing and the control of its extraction became all-important (Price-Smith 2015). As the century progressed, the demand for oil increased exponentially due to increases in population and escalating globalization and, with it, consumerism. Although oil had been exploited in the Caucasus and North America since the nineteenth century, the proliferation of oil reserves in the twentieth century—particularly its discovery in Iraq (c. 1908), Saudi Arabia (1938), Algeria (1948), Syria (1956), and in what are now the Arab Emirates (late 1950s and 1960s)—focused attention on these areas and made them important sites of contention among imperial powers. The belief that the area encompassing Iraq and Syria contained enormous reserves of oil was among the motives behind the Sykes-Picot agreement in 1916, as important, no doubt, as the dismembering of the Ottoman empire at the war's end. In the interwar period, oil production in the mandates was limited to Iraq, but the French excavated for oil in Syria throughout their mandate. During the Second World War, the motivation for Operation Barbarossa, Hitler's invasion of the USSR, was to access the oil of the Caucasus in order to supplement his depleting wartime reserves. That Barbarossa failed contributed to the Allied victory.

The Cold War was marked by a series of oil crises, which highlighted potential bellicosity connected to the stakes involved. The first postwar oil crisis occurred in 1951, when Iran nationalized its oil industry in the hope of obtaining a fairer share of the profits. The result was a coup orchestrated by the American and British secret services, which were fearful of the influence of the USSR (Marsh 2002). To try and maintain some sort of control of their resources, in 1960 five of the non-US oil-producing countries, of which four were in the Middle East, banded together to form the Organization of the Petroleum Exporting Countries (OPEC). Its aim was to unify petroleum policies while providing a steady income to producers. It did not herald the end of the crises, nor did it stop western powers from meddling in them. The 1967–70 Nigerian civil war or Biafran war, for example, pitted the Nigerian government against the Ibos, who lived in the oil-rich area of the former colony, with Britain supporting the former and France the latter. Whereas the lack of human rights and mistreatment of the Ibo people was at the heart of the conflict, the strategic and economic interests were about maintaining the control of the rich oil reserves in the area. A series of crises in the seventies, most notably that in 1973 when OPEC introduced an oil embargo in response to US involvement in the Yom Kippur war, sent oil prices soaring and increased tensions between western powers and oil-producing countries, particularly those in in the Middle East.

The end of the Cold War did not improve the situation. Of particular note were the Gulf War of 1990–1, which followed Iraq's invasion of Kuwait, and the 2003 US-led invasion of Iraq, which morphed into a war that dragged on until 2011. As this volume goes to press, American troops are still present in the area. In the intervening period between these two American-led wars in Iraq, the Twin Towers fell due to the brutal Al-Qaeda attack of September 11, 2001. (One of their many grievances against the West was their cultural insensibility, as evidenced by US violation of territory sacred to Islam by stationing their troops in Saudi Arabia.) Did this event prime the Bush regime psychologically to act precipitously in marching into Iraq in 2003, or was terrorism just the excuse to invade and have access to the oil fields? Unlike the Gulf War, which responded to Saddam Hussein's belligerence, the justification in 2003 was the erroneous allegation, made by the Bush and Blair regimes, of the presence of weapons of mass destruction. None were ever found. The Ba'ath Party was destroyed and Saddam Hussein, who had once been supported by the United States in its war against Iran (1980–8), was executed. Iraq was left in ruins. Halliburton, the oil company from which Dick Cheney allegedly resigned when he became vice-president, profited greatly from the invasion, emphasizing the capitalist culture that framed the invasion. The belligerent stance of the US and the UK, as instigators of the war, was initially condemned by UN weapons inspectors. In 2016, the long-delayed Chilcott report on Tony Blair's role in the lead-up to the war, was equally condemnatory, stating that Blair had totally misled his people. The final irony—or perhaps calculation—is that the allies will probably benefit from the eventual rebuilding of the devastation that the war has wrought on Iraq. Was the Bush decision to invade Iraq imperialism as evidenced by the prevailing capitalist culture? Or was it just gross miscalculation and relative ignorance of the situation in the Middle East in gauging where the invasion would lead? However one chooses to answer these questions, it was the point when the idea of the Americans as mere propagators of cultural imperialism was finally laid to rest.

ARE WE ROME?

In a book published five years after the Iraq invasion of 2003, Cullen Murphy, the author and former editor of *Atlantic Magazine*, asked the question *Are We Rome?* (Murphy 2008). It was a question the nineteenth-century empires had also wrestled with (Lorcin 2002, 2013b). In his study of US activities in the Middle East, the historian Rashid Khalidi highlights certain parallels. Since the end of the Cold War, he states, unlike Britain and France in the nineteenth century, US domination encompasses the whole world and in this it resembles premodern empires such as the Roman empire, Tang China, and the Mongols (Khalidi 2004: 153). The exemplar of Rome is not new in US history, nor is Murphy the only recent author to have reclaimed it (Lorcin 2013b: 416–19). Whereas the connection to Rome provides a certain eminence to the concept of US imperialism and raises the specter of possible decline, scholars have preferred to look at its distinctions, suggesting that US imperialism is a "new imperialism," a "soft imperialism," a "humanitarian imperialism," or "the Empire in new clothes" (Hardt and Negri 2000; Harvey 2003; Passavant and Dean 2004; Bricmont 2006; Mirrlees 2006; Mooers 2006). Are these "types" of imperialism any different in form from what went before? Certainly, Hardt and Negri think so, pointing out that "in contrast to imperialism, Empire establishes no territorial center of power and does not rely on fixed boundaries or barriers" (2000: xii). Their work, which provoked considerable debate, was published before 9/11 and the subsequent wars in Afghanistan and Iraq, a time their argument may have made more sense. But, whatever the era, can one really have empire (the situation) without imperialism (the process)?

In considering what imperialism means, the two concepts of colonialism and imperialism are often elided. Observers who make this association overlook the fact, the absence of settlers or a colonial administration—in other words, the physical territorial imprint of earlier empires—does not mean that such disruption cannot take place without that presence, or indeed that the cultural impositions of imperialism are absent. To be sure, the difference between US imperialism and the nineteenth-century western imperialisms is the lack of settler colonization, but many of the military bases that the United States has around the world have large numbers of military personnel. Even though they do not qualify as settlers, their presence impinges—for better or worse—on the local culture, economy, and society. This can lead to as much local dissatisfaction and resentment as any European settler colony. The June 2016 demonstrations against the US military presence (and its culture) in Okinawa are a case in point. Nonetheless, military colonization is an established fact of US imperialism. In an article that appeared in *The Nation*, David Vine (2015) claimed that there are 800 US military bases of varying sizes around the world. The US Department of Defense is more circumspect about broadcasting the number of their overseas bases, but the fact remains that the number is in the many hundreds. As other empires before it, the United States establishes its overseas bases for strategic and economic reasons. Strategically during the Cold War as a bulwark against a communist threat and since the 1990s against terrorism and what it sees as rogue states, such as North Korea. Economically, as Ellen Wood has aptly described it, the US "has maintained a so-called informal empire, imposing market forces and manipulating them to the advantage of US capital ... this would have been impossible without the support of military power, but that power has not been generally used ... [for] capturing and holding colonial territories" (2006: 13).

If US economic and strategic interests are sometimes obscured when discussing the military presence, the notion of a *Pax Americana* is not. As Harvey has pointed out, for those individuals who admit to the notion of US imperialism, they feel that the US must "establish a Pax Americana that can bestow the same benefits upon the world as the Pax Britannica secured in the last half of the nineteenth century" (2003: 4). Pro-imperial observers, such as the late Ben Wattenberg, or the historian, Niall Ferguson, openly encourage(d) the US to take up the imperial mantle (Wattenberg 1991; Ferguson 2003). Both Ferguson and Khalidi compare the British and American empires, but whereas Ferguson imagines the US as a possible continuation of British imperial achievements, Khalidi, who only focuses on the Middle East, chides the United States for its total lack of political or social understanding of the area. Although he in no way condones imperialism, he contrasts the US diplomats and politicians with interwar imperialists such as Gertrude Bell, T.E. Lawrence, and Percy Cox, all of whom were either Arabists or had a sophisticated grasp of local culture, politics, and society, allowing them to maneuver with less heavy-handedness than their American counterparts, who have left the Middle East in ruins (Khalidi 2004: 161). In short, cultural and social differences shape political and diplomatic developments.

CONCLUSION

The ideological principles of spreading democracy and human rights, which are called upon to justify invasion and interference, like all ideologies of empire, are suited to their particular epoch. Although the notion of imposing democracy (rather than introducing it gradually) is a throwback to Lugard's idea of the need for democratic principles, Wood argues that the essence of US democracy is "the coupling of formal democracy with substantive class rule, the class rule of capital" (2006: 19). The propping up of the numerous autocratic rulers that the United States supported over the twentieth century, or CIA involvement in

FIGURE 0.5: Berlin, Germany, 2017. Model wearing American apparel. Credit: Christian Vierig/Getty Images.

deposing democratically elected leaders such as President Allende of Chile in 1973, belie a genuine intention to spread democracy to areas where it is lacking. This type of selectivity is, of course, a hallmark of imperialism and its socioeconomic cultures. Similarly, upholding human rights as a justification to use military force to invade can be seen as a modern manifestation of the "civilizing mission." Jean Bricmont has elaborated the way in which human rights has justified the promotion of imperialism. His intention is not to highlight US or western hypocrisy, but rather to demonstrate that Left-leaning individuals, whether politicians or intellectuals, can be as implicated in present-day imperialism as the neo-conservatives or those on the traditional Right (Bricmont 2006). In this it is no different from the nineteenth century when left-wingers were implicated in imperialism in much the same way as they are today. Whether it is the civilizing mission, the introduction of modernity, of democracy or of human rights, the conceit of western imperialists over time has been that they will swap improvement of the societies they inhabit for the exploitation of territorial resources and all will benefit as a result.

For over two millennia, western imperialisms have affected history, directly or indirectly. They have transformed the society, culture, economy, and politics of the areas they have invaded, conquered, or colonized, and influenced the territories on their peripheries (Figure 0.5). In turn, they too have been transformed, economically, culturally, and morally. In the name of cultural concepts such as "civilization," "progress," and "modernity," they have exploited natural resources and dragooned the labor to extract them. In the process, more often than not, they betrayed the values they had committed to extend.

CHAPTER ONE

War

RICHARD S. FOGARTY

In his *The Wretched of the Earth* ([1961] 2004), psychiatrist and anticolonial activist Frantz Fanon analyzed the "reactionary psychoses" that he found in colonial subjects living through the wars of decolonization so prevalent after 1945. Understanding these mental disorders required giving "special priority to war understood in its totality and in its particularity, to colonial war. After the two great world wars, there has been no shortage of publications on the mental pathology of soldiers engaged in combat and of civilian victims of evacuations and bombings. The unprecedented features of some of the psychiatric descriptions presented here confirm, if confirmation were still necessary, that colonial war is distinctive even in the pathology that it produces" (Fanon 1974: 179–80). Although Fanon was interested in the particularities of the colonial situation and colonial warfare, his statement highlights the two critical foci for an analysis of war in the cultural history of Western empires in the modern age: "big" wars such as the Second World War, and the "small" wars that fractured and dissolved the formal western colonial empires built up during the nineteenth and early twentieth centuries. Both conventional wars waged between states, in large part by uniformed militaries organized along traditional lines, and numerous "irregular" or "asymmetrical" wars waged within states or colonies by partisans or guerillas, often loosely organized and inextricably integrated into civilian populations, implicated the politics and resources of empires in profound, often fateful ways. Surveying this history requires attention to both kinds of wars, as well as to the many ways distinctions between them often broke down. Moreover, one of the clear lessons that viewing the modern history of Western empires through the lens of war can teach is that colonial violence, and perhaps colonialism itself, is truly war without end.

EMPIRE, WAR, AND VIOLENCE

Fanon insisted on the distinctiveness of "colonial war," which he argued took on "the character of a real genocide" (1974: 179). And it is precisely this totalizing quality that necessitates a focus on the culture of colonialism, and culture more broadly, when attempting to understand the history of war and empire in the modern age. Fanon was most famous for analyzing the role of violence in colonialism, for arguing that colonialism "is violence in its natural state" (1974: 25). This violence was not limited to battlefields, even the often unconventional battlefields of colonial conquest—with its massacres, burning of villages, dislocation of peoples and expropriation of lands, indiscriminate killing of men, women, and children to sow terror and demonstrate overwhelming power—and of colonial resistance—with its massacres, bombings of cafés and other public places, assassinations of representatives of the colonial order, and murder of civilian colonists. Fanon himself documented all of this incisively to demonstrate that the violence of colonialism bred the violence of anticolonialism, and indeed only the latter could cure the former. This was all the more true because modern empires sustained their rule through cultural violence, waging war on ways of life and beliefs, establishing the culture and even the skin color of the colonizers as the standard against which all of indigenous culture would be measured and found wanting (Fanon 1974; see also Fanon 1952).

Yet this focus on culture to understand colonial violence and war is not unique in the field of the history of warfare. In fact, a cultural approach to the history of war has predominated in much of the writing about the subject for the last several decades. In 1976, John Keegan published his seminal work, *The Face of Battle*, which made the "immediate and personal" experiences of ordinary soldiers central to military history ([1976] 1978: 342). The same year saw Michael Howard call for historians to provide an understanding, "not simply of the wars themselves but of the societies which fought them." For military historians, there is "literally no branch of human activity which is not to a greater or lesser extent relevant to his subject. He has to study war not only, as Hans Delbrück put it, in the framework of political history, but in the framework of economic, social and cultural history as well. War has been part of a totality of human experience, the parts of which can be understood only in relation to one another. One cannot adequately describe how wars were fought without giving some idea of what they were fought about" (Howard 1976: ix–x). Since this time, though there is still some debate about the nature and role of military history in the academy, historians of both war and culture have taken up these approaches in earnest and the so-called "new military history" is no longer so new (the literature on the subject is large, but for useful overviews, see Paret 1991; Lynn 1997, 2007; Citino 2007; Evans 2008; Biddle and Citino 2014).

Such an approach is tailor-made for understanding colonial warfare, and scholars have expanded Fanon's insights into the violence inherent in all aspects of colonialism to consider what terms such as war and violence really mean in colonial contexts. The prolific historian of European colonialism H.L. Wesseling has, like Fanon, argued that colonial wars are in fact distinct from war as commonly understood. War aims in colonial wars were absolute, with permanent subjection of entire populations as their chief goal. Victory in these wars was hard to define, since this absolute aim was difficult—often impossible—to achieve. For indigenous peoples, these conflicts involved the entire population, since physical and cultural survival was at stake. In this existential struggle, conquerors sought not merely battlefield victory, but the winning of the "hearts and minds" of entire peoples—in effect not merely waging war against indigenous culture, but expressly *for* western culture. War was total for indigenous peoples, but means were always limited for the conquerors, who often sought empire on the cheap (costs measured both in western lives and money). In these sorts of wars, the usual dichotomy between war and peace was difficult to discern and maintain, with constant resort, even after formal conquest, to "police actions," "pacification," suppression of revolts, and violent displays of authority and power. In the end, all of colonial rule, from conquest to governance, and indeed to decolonization was a form of "structural violence" that makes the history of colonialism and the history of war synonymous (Wesseling 1997: 3–11).

A recent volume edited by historian of French colonialism Martin Thomas explores this idea more expansively. He makes clear that modern empires provide the contexts for some of the clearest examples of what French sociologist Pierre Bourdieu called "symbolic violence," a hegemonic project substituting the social values and standards of the colonizer for those of the colonized (Thomas 2011: xvii). In the end, Thomas comes to the same conclusion as Wesseling: "Whether or not colonial control stemmed directly from military conquest, it seems reasonable to suggest that violence was integral to the structures of colonialism: its economic foundations, its institutions, and its governing precepts" (2011: xviii). What this means for an analysis of war in the cultural history of empires since the end of the First World War is that the focus must be not merely on large conventional conflicts waged in the course of expanding, maintaining, or challenging imperial rule—the Second World War, the wars in Algeria and Vietnam, for instance. The focus must also be on the violence, sometimes explicitly militarized and sometimes not, of everyday colonialism (on violence and everyday colonialism, see Moyd 2014).

In his 1896 analysis of colonial warfare, British Colonel Charles Callwell famously called western armies' operations in the building and maintenance of empire "small wars," a term which ever since has distinguished colonial violence from supposedly more conventional interstate warfare. Small wars are "all campaigns other than those where both the opposing sides consist of regular troops" (Callwell [1896] 1906: 21). Callwell and other professional soldiers since have taken these conflicts seriously, but recognized that they were different and called both for different analysis and for military approaches that diverged from those western soldiers developed with fighting each other in mind. Though they differed from Callwell and the so-called British school, who leaned more heavily on vigorous force and intimidation in what has come to be called counterinsurgency, French military figures also recognized the very different circumstances colonial war presented. In the nineteenth and early twentieth centuries, generals such as Thomas-Robert Bugeaud, Joseph Gallieni, and Hubert Lyautey certainly did not shrink from violence, even extreme violence, but they made political maneuvering and supposedly humanitarian efforts to bestow upon indigenous peoples the benefits of enlightened colonial rule an explicit part of their strategies for erecting stable French control (Porch 1986; Wesseling 1997: 20–4; Finch 2013). They recognized what Fanon would later also highlight: that colonial rule itself was a sort of war against native populations, a total war that encompassed all aspects of political, social, economic, and cultural activities. So not only were the wars of colonial conquest, "a series of real wars comparable in intensity and magnitude with many of the major wars in European history" (Wesseling 1997: 19), but any attempt to grapple with the history and meaning of war in modern imperial and colonial contexts must take account of the systemic violence that was the "very essence" of modern empires (Thomas 2011: xiv). Accordingly, the survey that follows will proceed chronologically, beginning with the aftermath of the First World War, and will give due attention to the large-scale conflicts that punctuate the history of empire in this period, but will also take care to note the "smaller," though often no less significant and deadly, episodes that scholars must consider as part of imperial wars without end.

THE APOGEE OF WESTERN COLONIAL EMPIRES: THE VIOLENT STATUS QUO, 1920–39

Two brief spasms of violence in British India in 1919 can stand as representative of the two kinds of "war" that would characterize the history of Western empires in the aftermath of the First World War. In early May, the British Indian government declared war on Afghanistan, in response to a cross-border incursion. Thus began the three-month Third Anglo-Afghan War, which pitted against each other uniformed armies acting on behalf of states, included pitched battles and skirmishes, as well as the use of air power, and concluded with a formal peace treaty. Scarcely three weeks before the outbreak of these formal hostilities, hundreds of peaceful protesters and religious pilgrims gathered in the Jallianwala Bagh, a park in Amritsar in the province of Punjab. They were there in contravention of a recent official prohibition of public meetings, and so the local commander ordered his Gurkha troops to fire on the crowd. Largely trapped in the walled confines of the park, and under fire that was deliberately aimed at preventing escape and inflicting maximum damage, at least 379 men, women, and children were killed, and over 1,000 wounded. Although the use of force aimed at dampening political unrest and anticolonial feeling, the carnage radicalized Indian politics and stands as one of the landmark events leading to eventual independence (Draper 1985).

Central to both events was the figure of Reginald Dyer. A colonel temporarily promoted to brigadier general, Dyer commanded the Gurkhas at Jallianwala Bagh and personally directed their murderous fire. He hoped, he said, to make a sufficient impression on the local population to prevent an anti-British uprising. A few weeks later, he was posted to the Afghan frontier, and led a brigade in significant combat there (Collett 2006). It is true that Dyer's actions at Amritsar proved deeply controversial, and many condemned the barbarism of his orders that day. But it is also true that he had many defenders, and many of these praised him for having "saved" British India from violent revolt. And what is eminently clear is that he and others saw his actions that spring and summer, both in the Punjab and the North-West Frontier, as part of his primary duties as a soldier responsible for militarily upholding British colonial rule. At base, this was not merely a technical question of firepower and military maneuver, but also a cultural question of "prestige." As scholar V.G. Kiernan has noted of European thinking about colonial war, "Everything, or almost everything, could be tolerated if it was deemed necessary for the upholding of prestige" (Kiernan 1998). It was not accidental that the ostensible reason for the Jallianwala Bagh massacre, in addition to a generalized fear of revolt, was an earlier attack by Indians on a British woman. European women in the colonies were the repositories and emblems of white status and authority, and as such their preservation from harm or even contact with indigenous populations was a primary duty for male colonizers (Chaudhuri and Strobel 1992; Clancy-Smith and Gouda 1998; Stoler 2002). The masculinity embodied in the military uniform positioned men like Dyer as particularly aggressive guardians of gendered and racialized honor and prestige. He himself declared that, for the British, women were "sacred," and this explained both his murderous actions at Jallianwala Bagh and his later order that Indians wishing to cross the street in which the British woman had been attacked must crawl on "on all fours" or be whipped (Lal 1993). Dyer's service in the Afghan war, and mention in dispatches there, only further emphasized his embodiment of masculine European superiority and right to empire. In his actions in 1919, we can see clearly how the violence of everyday colonialism (even if the massacre of hundreds of civilians represents a grotesque extreme) and the violence of conventional war could be linked and were a critical part of the war story of empire during this period.

From some points of view, the anxiety of Dyer and other colonial officials about prestige and the dangers of indigenous challenges to European authority appears curious. At the end of the First World War, European overseas empires appeared to be at the very height of their power and stability. They certainly reached their greatest physical extent. The victorious powers that emerged from the First World War expanded their imperial holdings, with the two largest empires—the British and the French—adding significant former Ottoman and German territories as League of Nations mandates. The interwar period saw spectacular displays of imperial confidence and triumphalism, most notably the British Empire Exhibition of 1924 and the Paris Colonial Exposition of 1931, which attracted tens of millions of visitors to witness the grandeur of European power and efforts to "civilize" the world's peoples. The technological, economic, and military power of the West was never more secure, even overwhelming, and anticolonial resistance, whether in the form of demands for greater rights or for independence, was muted and ineffectual compared with what emerged after 1945. For many in the West, the First World War had proved that empire "paid," since colonial material and manpower resources contributed notably to the global war effort (Sarraut 1923). The empires that had won the "Great War for Civilization" remained confident in their right and duty to uphold that civilization and continue its spread and development through imperialism, and they retained the means to do so.

Yet viewed from other perspectives, the aftermath of the First World War showed the first signs that the Western empires built up over the course of the eighteenth and nineteenth centuries were in trouble, and that ideas and events were beginning to destabilize the very idea of empire itself. First of all, the war saw four of the world's largest empires go down to defeat and dissolution. By 1918 or very soon thereafter, the German, Austrian, Russian, and Ottoman empires were no more. Great Britain and France expanded their imperial holdings, often at the expense of these defeated empires, but both nations were exhausted and relatively weakened by the effort required to win the Great War. Moreover, the "mandates" under which these two powers (as well as Belgium, Japan, South Africa, Australia, and New Zealand) came to rule the possessions of their defeated enemies resided formally under international control through the League of Nations. This stemmed from impulses that ran counter to the idea of foreign imperial rule, in particular Wilsonian rhetoric of national self-determination. American President Wilson himself balked at extending his ideas, developed as an antidote to the imperial machinations that he believed had helped bring on the war, to non-western (and non-white, for he was a white supremacist) peoples. But many of these peoples enthusiastically took up Wilson's ideals to challenge imperialism and colonialism. In a "Wilsonian Moment," anticolonial movements and uprisings developed across the globe in 1919 (Manela 2007). In addition, the ideas that underwrote the mandate system suggested that the end goal of imperial control was to confer on the colonized the right to self-rule, since the mandatory powers were to relinquish power and claim over the territories once their populations had developed the capacity for self-determination. This begged the question of why the same logic should not apply to all areas and instances of imperial rule, and perhaps implied that the end of empire was only a matter of time. At the Versailles Peace Conference in 1919, Japan formally, if unsuccessfully, challenged the supposed racial superiority that undergirded western imperial rule, while the emerging powers of the United States and the Soviet Union showed themselves largely ideologically opposed to and politically unwilling to support "old-fashioned" European colonialism (even though they themselves arguably constituted their own particular kinds of empire).

All of this is to say that colonial violence and war in the interwar period (and beyond) took place against the backdrop of increasing challenges to imperial control and legitimacy and the growing destabilization of empires on both the practical and ideological levels. Seen in this light, displays of imperial confidence such as the British Empire Exhibition and the Paris Colonial Exposition might well have been efforts to mask increasing anxieties and doubts. Nonetheless, expressions of confidence in the aftermath of the First World War were rooted in a real sense that the war had proven the utility of empire. Contemporaries understood the conflict as a war of empires, and so increasingly have historians (Gerwarth and Manela 2014b; Jarboe and Fogarty 2014). Great Britain mobilized its vast imperial resources, including not just armies and materials from its white-ruled Dominions but also over a million Indians as soldiers and laborers, and hundreds of thousands of Africans to fight and carry supplies. France mobilized more than 500,000 colonial subjects to fight in Europe, and some 200,000 to labor there as well. Along with material resources, these figured prominently in the French war effort and the nation's *culture de guerre*. The German, Ottoman, Austro-Hungarian, Russian, Belgian, Portuguese, Italian, Japanese, US, and even Chinese war efforts saw significant colonial involvement and implications. Notorious episodes in the aftermath of the war—such as widespread race riots in Britain in 1919, provoked by resentment against the presence of men of color engaged in war-related work, and the international scandal of the so-called "Black Shame," which saw the flowering of racist anxieties in response to the French use of troops from the colonies to occupy the Rhineland in defeated Germany—demonstrated that the culture of empire, and its ever-present basis in racism and white supremacy, helped define the culture of war (Bland 2005; Van Galen Last 2015).

Violence and continued warfare were prevalent in many areas around the globe after the ostensible end of the Great War in 1918, and much of this was attributable to the effects of empire. Most immediately and perhaps most spectacularly, Russia, eastern and southern Europe, and the Middle East suffered endemic violence throughout the early 1920s. Historians have designated these "shatter zones of empires," as peoples there sought to rearrange and reconstitute political arrangements in the wake of the dissolution of the Russian, Austro-Hungarian, and Ottoman empires (Eichenberg and Newman 2010). The Russian Civil War ended only in 1922 with the solidification of Communist control over what remained of the empire of the tsars, and after the loss of millions of lives. Millions more were displaced, and the rulers of the new Soviet Union would remain resentful and covetous of the newly independent states that split off from the Russian empire (Finland, the Baltic states, Poland). The Balkans had begun to shatter even before 1914, as the Ottomans lost control of Bulgaria, Greece, Serbia, and Montenegro, and this was of course the violent nationalist ferment that ultimately brought on the Great War. Violence continued in the region well into the 1920s. This stretched into the Ottoman heartland itself as the empire collapsed after 1918, and the emergence of a new Turkish nation-state brought with it intense violence, pitched campaigns involving Turkish resistance and French, British, Armenian, and Greek forces, and population transfers between Greece and Turkey. Great Britain secured mandatory authority over Iraq, Transjordan, and Palestine, while French mandates included Syria and Lebanon. Syria in particular saw violence during this period, with France waging a fierce counterinsurgency struggle there until 1923. This had devastating effects upon the entire social order (Thompson 2000). The British faced indigenous resistance in Iraq as well, which they crushed by using air power to deadly effect, and later even more serious revolts in Palestine, first of Arabs in 1936 and then of Jews in 1939.

Violence also marked the life of empires outside the so-called shatter zones. Notably, the British faced a serious threat to imperial control within the United Kingdom. After armed struggle including paramilitary activity and civil war, the Irish Free State exited the UK in 1922, and the Republic of Ireland emerged in 1937. France faced violent revolt against imperial control as well during this period. In 1928, rural people in French Equatorial Africa and French Cameroon (mandated to France from Germany after the First World War) rebelled in the face of forced labor and abusive exploitation by colonial administrators and private concessionary companies. Although the revolt made little impression on the French public at the time, colonial and military authorities repressed the violence only with great difficulty in 1931. During the same period, the French colonial state faced revolt on the other side of the world. In 1930, at Yen Bay in French Indochina, indigenous soldiers under French command mutinied. The violence spread quickly, and for a little over a year French authorities faced persistent violence coordinated by organized and ideologically driven nationalist and communist militants. French colonial control survived, but that the cost of empire was constant resort to violence was increasingly clear (Thomas 2005).

War in the context of Western empires in the 1920s and 1930s often combined traditional police actions and "pacification" in the face of indigenous resistance, which had been common for over a century, with approaches more characteristic of large-scale, formal, conventional warfare. As early as 1920, for example, Winston Churchill directed British forces in Iraq to use air power extensively and with devastating effect to put down resistance to the imposition of mandatory control (Fromkin 1989). One of the largest conflicts of the interwar period took place in Morocco. In 1920, Spanish forces sought to expand *de facto* control in the Rif region, over which they had *de jure* authority but little real power. The mountainous area had always been recalcitrant to imperial authority, and its Berber peoples had mounted fierce resistance to both Spanish and French incursions. In 1921, Riffian forces under the command of Abd el-Krim inflicted a humiliating and crushing defeat on the Spanish in the Battle of Annual, killing some 8,000 Spanish soldiers, following up the victory with further advances over the next several years. Emboldened, Abd el-Krim's forces attacked the French zone of control as well in 1925, inflicting serious casualties.

France and Spain joined forces to secure control over their respective possessions in Morocco, and by the middle of 1926 the Europeans had prevailed. The conflict marked an important development in colonial warfare. The "disciplinary columns" and "pacification" through the deployment of light infantry that had characterized Europeans' approach to security in their empires

FIGURE 1.1: A Berber fighter during the 1924–5 Rif War. Credit: ullstein bild via Getty Images.

FIGURE 1.2: The Rif War against France and Spain. A French military airfield at Fez, June 1925.

now yielded to the deployment of the full weight of mass assaults using the latest military technology. General Hubert Lyautey, the archetype of the soldier-administrator who sought to impose colonial control through civilizing efforts and political cooperation, now stood aside as Marshal Philippe Pétain, hero of the Western Front, made use of air power, artillery, and large numbers of infantry to end a revolt led largely by irregular guerilla forces (Thomas 2005: 212–13). Spanish forces used chemical weapons, often dropped from airplanes and often targeting civilians (Balfour 2002). Spanish and French forces numbered nearly a quarter of a million troops, outnumbering the Riffians over two to one. In the climactic battle in May 1925, European forces outnumbered Abd el-Krim's forces ten to one, and included overwhelming air power (Pennell 1986). Henceforth, Western empires showed themselves more willing to deploy the techniques and technologies they had developed to wage modern, industrialized war against each other in Europe.

Colonial war also began to have important effects on events in Europe. Morocco was a "nursery of reaction" for Spanish officers, who could have freer rein and gain promotion more quickly on colonial service, and it was these *africanistas* who began the Nationalist rebellion against the Spanish Republic in 1936. Francisco Franco's Nationalist forces during the Spanish Civil War included important contingents of native Moroccan troops, or "moors," and the colonial context of this harbinger of the Second World War is critical (Kiernan 1998: 204–5). Mussolini's Fascist Italy was an important player during the Spanish Civil War, but the Italians had earlier launched another armed conflict in Ethiopia that had clear implications both for colonial warfare and for the coming violence of the Second World War. Mussolini had already completed the conquest of Libya, begun before the First World War, with a decade of extremely violent repression, including the use of air power and bombing, chemical weapons, concentration camps, and deportations. Just after Libya was thus "pacified," in the words of its governor Marshal Pietro Badoglio, in 1932, Mussolini turned his attention to the conquest of Ethiopia (Aldrich 2007: 271). One of the very last territories in Africa not yet colonized by Europeans, Ethiopia had earned its independence by humiliating an earlier attempt at Italian conquest at the Battle of Adwa in 1896. In October 1935, after three years of preparation, Mussolini's forces invaded. Making particularly effective use of air power and chemical weapons, the Italians added Ethiopia to their colonial empire seven months later. The war demonstrated the ineffectiveness of the League of Nations to regulate international relations in a world of empires and imperial expansion, and contributed to the breakdown of diplomacy that helped bring on the Second World War.

Large-scale violence, whether in pursuit of colonial conquest or the maintenance of colonial order, was thus common in the history of Western empires between the world wars. Yet the structural violence of everyday colonialism was also prevalent and shaped the cultures of empires both in the colonies and the metropoles. For instance, Italian efforts to "pacify" Libya focused on the cultural suppression of the Senussi Sufi order through arrests, confiscation of property, and closure of religious schools. After resistance ended, Italian policy encouraged European settlement and the expropriation and development of Libyan land. The same was true in Ethiopia, and the destruction and transformation of physical environments, the rending of social fabric, the disruption of economic life, and the suppression of indigenous culture accompanied overt and often extreme physical violence (Ben-Ghiat and Fuller 2005).

The case of Syria under French mandatory rule is another good example of the multiple levels on which colonial violence operated during this period. Advocates of France's expansion in the Middle East hoped for a peaceful transition to French control in Syria, but the recently enthroned King Faisal contested the new mandatory authority. French forces won the conventional military conflict decisively at a pitched battle at Maysalun in July 1920, but less-organized resistance persisted (Andrew and Kanya Forstner 1981). Thereafter, until French control ended in 1946, colonial authorities resorted constantly to violence and coercion to maintain order. Military and police action on the ground and from the air was common, but structural coercion played an important role as well. Urban planning and political initiatives aimed at undermining resistance, and cultural initiatives in education, language, art, propaganda, and youth movements also sought to strengthen French political control (Dueck 2010; Neep 2012).

In fact, though Republican France and Fascist Italy had little in common politically at home, their renewed and vigorous attempts to make empire "stick" or "pay," to solidify the bases of colonial control, economic exploitation, and imperial power, were similar. And their attempts to do so via overt military means and the subtler social and cultural displacement of a mission to civilize (civilizing and disciplining the peoples and the lands) were typical of Western empires in general during this period. For instance, in Belgium and its lone, though huge, imperial possession of the Congo, the years after the First World War saw the development of a more conscious empire-building and imperialist identity, as well as a renewed commitment to exploiting the resources of the region more effectively (Aldrich 2007: 233–5; Jarboe and Fogarty 2014: 23–48). Though the violence of Belgian control over the Congo under the personal rule of Leopold II is justly notorious, violence continued to be the salient feature of imperial control for many Congolese. The same was true in Portuguese Africa. The conditions of the Great War in Africa for both Portuguese soldiers and native Africans were appalling, largely through official ambition and incompetence, and the postwar period saw continued suffering (Gerwarth and Manela 2014b: 179–96). Efforts to exploit colonial resources intensified—all with absolute minimum cost to the metropole since that was official policy under the dictator Salazar—which included stricter arbitrary legal control, forced labor, and population relocation. In the end, the colonial framework was "authoritarian and increasingly coercive" and "seems to have been more violent and oppressive than that of neighboring colonial regimes" (Aldrich 2007: 89). At the same time, the government more zealously promoted the cultural, civilizational mission of Portugal in Africa as a point of patriotic pride and domestic political unity.

Thus, an intensified commitment to colonial exploitation in many Western empires after the First World War meant that colonial subjects of these empires suffered an intensified level of structural violence. Developments such as the renewed French commitment to *mise en valeur* (rational economic exploitation) and increased resort to measures such as forced labor in West Africa may appear as less the story of "war and empire" than does the military conquest of the territory during the late nineteenth century (Conklin 1997). But for colonial subjects living through what Fanon called "violence in its natural state," this constant presence of physical force and coercion rendered larger spasms of violence, whether suppression of anticolonial resistance or participation in the world wars, more as intensifications of the status quo than as real deviations from the norm.

Fanon was not the only figure who recognized the centrality of violence to the essence of colonialism. Mahatma Gandhi did as well, though he came to very different conclusions about the form anticolonial resistance should take. Gandhi understood British rule of India as a sort of war, an everyday violence perpetrated upon colonial subjects, and he understood too that the colonized needed to win back their self-esteem in order to free themselves and to constitute a new society and nation. But the strategy he used was non-violent resistance. Gandhi urged a non-violent response even to the appalling massacre at Jallianwala Bagh in 1919, but the incident was instrumental in convincing him definitively that British control over India had to end and that Indians had to achieve *swaraj*, or self-rule (Judd 1996: 258–72). Thus, violence in its multifarious forms was never far away from the most important and decisive events in the history of Western empires during the interwar period.

FROM GLOBAL WAR TO "DIRTY WARS," 1939–75

On May 8, 1945, German forces surrendered unconditionally to the Allies, ending the Second World War in Europe. Globally, the war had been one in which empires were implicated in every imaginable way. The Western empires of the United States, Great Britain, France, and the Netherlands struggled with imperial Japan for control of territories in Asia and the Pacific. The Nazi empire, built in a relatively brief spasm of violent expansion, clashed titanically with the Soviet empire, as well as with the United States and the imperial powers of western Europe. All of these imperial powers mobilized the human and material resources of their global empires on an unprecedented scale, waging total conventional war. But May 8 also witnessed an event that suggested that other forms of colonial violence and war still had a central place in Western empires. During a parade in the Algerian town of Sétif celebrating the end of the war, French police intervened forcefully when native Algerians displayed anticolonial banners and called loudly for independence. Rioting ensued, and several people on both sides of the dispute were shot. Over the next several days, Algerians massacred more than 100 European settlers with extreme brutality, torturing and mutilating their victims. The French response was no less brutal, as troops moved in to restore order. Police actions by regular soldiers, vigilante attacks by settlers, and even air raids by French aircraft and shelling from a French battleship caused mass and indiscriminate casualties. The French army put the number of men, women, and children killed at 10,000 to 15,000, while Algerians and their sympathizers claimed up to three times this figure (Clayton 1992; Planche 2006). Clearly, even an imperial state such as France, exhausted and divided and traumatized by its own suffering in the cataclysm of the Second World War, was still willing and able to deploy overwhelming force in defense of the integrity of its empire.

In many ways, the roughly four decades that spanned the Second World War through the bulk of the process known as decolonization was one during which overtly militarized violence eclipsed the subtler forms of structural colonial violence. Yet these latter forms never disappeared, of course, and in fact the "dirty wars" of decolonization—so called because they were often more diffuse, seemingly more confusing, and more asymmetrical than many of the most salient aspects of the total global war that began the period—can appear as conspicuous blends of conventional warfare and the insidious and entrenched forms of fear, contempt, hate, and violence that characterize colonial situations. It is important not to overdraw the distinctions between colonial and conventional war during this period. The Second World War was a war of empires and colonial empires figured importantly in its history, and it is hard to imagine wars dirtier than, say, the racial, internecine, and partisan wars on the Eastern Front, or the Nazis' war against the Jews, the exterminatory impetus of which was cultural and racial. And the wars of decolonization often featured uniformed soldiers, pitched battles, and many of the other accoutrements of conventional warfare. In the end, analysis of the history of war and empire in this period must maintain the dual focus—on war as conventionally understood and on structural violence—that is so necessary to understanding the role of war and violence in earlier colonial contexts.

Yet the period did indeed begin with a conventional conflict waged largely by uniformed militaries, supported by high technology and machines, over vast battlefields on land, on water, and in the air. Residents of the belligerents' colonies participated extensively, much as they had done in the Great War. The British Empire's white Dominions provided several million troops for the war effort, as did India and the African colonies (Killingray 2010). French forces in 1940 included a large proportion of colonial subjects in uniform, and sixty percent of the Free French forces that helped liberate the metropole at the end of the war was made up of soldiers from North and sub-Saharan Africa (Wieviorka 2010; Jennings 2015). The territories of the Western empires became battlefields as well, with troops from the colonies and from Europe fighting in places such as North Africa (from Morocco to Egypt), East Africa, West Africa, Iraq, Syria and Lebanon, Iran, Burma, Malaya, Singapore, Madagascar, and throughout the Pacific and Indian Oceans. The navies and air forces that were so critical to acquiring and maintaining the empires of the West ranged the whole globe, and made this second worldwide conflagration a "world" war and a war of empires even more fully and explicitly than the Great War.

Another way in which the Second World War marked an intensification of the imperial characteristics that marked the First was the full emergence of the United States, the Soviet Union, Germany, and Japan as the empires that would dictate the shape of the war and, eventually, of the postwar world. Great Britain and France remained the two largest Western overseas empires in terms of formal territory and foreign populations directly controlled and ruled, but the four newer players would determine among themselves what role empire would play after 1945. One signal of this new reality is that one can argue that the Second World War did not really begin in Europe. Although Hitler's aggression in Europe transformed the conflict into a truly global war, Japan's aggression in Asia brought the rising imperial power into conflict with the United States' imperial interests in the Pacific region, as well as the interests of Great Britain, France, and the Netherlands, all of whom maintained large colonies in Asia and the Pacific. Long before the bombing of Pearl Harbor in 1941 brought the United States and Japan into open conflict, tensions had been building, and the region was embroiled in armed conflict since at least 1937, when Japan invaded China. Japan's actions throughout the period aimed explicitly at building a colonial empire, complete with racially based hierarchies, and the war with the US was a "race war" that bore many of the classic hallmarks of earlier colonial wars (Dower 1986). The Unites States prevailed in this struggle, and that victory would set the stage for the emergence of the nation as a global imperial power and, by the end of the twentieth century, a global hegemon.

The other imperial power to emerge, despite immense sacrifice during the war, in a strengthened geopolitical position was the Soviet Union. Not only had the USSR by the early stages of the war (before the Nazi invasion of 1941) reconstituted much if not all of the Russian empire of the tsars, but eventual victory over Germany, which brought with it dominance in eastern Europe, and a share in the victory over Japan meant that the Soviet Union could act as a serious rival with the United States for colonial control and global influence (Hasegawa 2006). These two powers and their rivalry would decisively shape life even in territories they did not control, the processes of decolonization, and the postcolonial world.

Japan and Germany did not have the opportunity to shape the postwar world in the same ways, since both empires were of relatively short lifespan and came to shattering ends in defeat in 1945. Japan was not technically a "Western" empire, but the influence of western models of development, politics, economy, and imperial control were important in the whole enterprise from the late nineteenth century onwards (Myers and Peattie 1984). And though there is debate about how much Japanese colonial practices differed from those of other contemporaneous empires, many practices of economic exploitation, racial hierarchy and discrimination, and structural violence meant that the experiences of Japanese colonial subjects were very similar to those living under other colonial regimes (Uchida 2011; Booth and Deng 2016). And in fact, the conditions of total global war only enlarged and intensified the presence of violence in everyday life. But nowhere in the history of modern empire did violence have a larger and more intense presence than in the German empire of the Second World War. In the 1950s, anticolonial writer Aimé Césaire and political theorist Hannah Arendt both identified Nazi expansionism as consistent with—and even an extension of—European imperialism and colonialism of the nineteenth and twentieth centuries (Césaire 2000 [1950]; Arendt 1968 [1951]). More recently, Mark Mazower has noted that the Nazi empire and the waging of war were synonymous, and that they reflected "the modern European will to power" that built the West's global empires. Yet though Germans under Hitler's regime were "heirs to this tradition," they took the unprecedented steps of trying to build their empire in Europe itself and to do it at a radically accelerated pace over just a few years (Mazower 2008: xxxix). This helps explain the extreme violence and destructiveness of Nazi empire-building and colonial rule, even as many elements were squarely within the broad conventions of western expansionism.

One of the Nazis' spectacular failures as colonial rulers was their inability, largely because of inflexible and extreme racism, to recruit or coopt the helpers from among the conquered and colonized on which Western empires traditionally depended. Illustrative of this failure were efforts to enlist the help of the world's Muslims as soldiers to build and defend Hitler's New Order. Wilhelm II's war effort during the Great War had also included a concerted attempt to raise the Muslim world against the other colonial powers of the West (Germany's enemies Great Britain, France, and Russia ruled over millions of Muslim subjects) and recruit them for an anticolonial "jihad" (McMeekin 2010; Jarboe and Fogarty 2014: 136–58). This campaign seemed logical to its advocates because Europe's colonial powers had all long sought to instrumentalize Islam for their own purposes, and to recruit Muslims to serve imperial political and military interests. The Nazis followed in this tradition and they recruited several hundred thousand Muslims to serve in the Wehrmacht and SS, but their efforts ultimately foundered on the same essentialist stereotypes of Islam and Muslims that plagued earlier efforts, in addition to the Nazis' chaotic prosecution of the war effort and their rigid adherence to racist policies. In the end, as elsewhere in Hitler's New Order, colonial subjects might have the opportunity to serve their masters' interests, but the ruled would never share even a little bit in the status and privileges of the rulers (Motadel 2014). This flexibility existed, even if often severely circumscribed, in other Western overseas empires, and gave some suppleness and longevity to, for instance, France's and Great Britain's empires.

The spectacular militarized violence of the Second World War should not obscure the continued importance of structural violence in imperial situations during the same period and after. The everyday violence of Germany's empire was grotesque in its extremity, and there is a limit to how much the term "structural" illuminates policies of racial extermination, intentional starvation, brutal and indiscriminate reprisals, mass killing, and the abjectly murderous conditions of POW, concentration, and death camps. Yet, as with so many aspects of Hitler's empire, only the scale and depth of depravity was unprecedented, and Western empires had already inflicted most of these types of violence on peoples outside Europe. After the war ended, the structural violence of the Western empires that remained would continue in the form of discrimination, arbitrary arrest, abuse, excessive police force, restrictions on movement and other freedoms, differential legal regimes and punishments—the whole panoply of colonial control. These would intensify under the pressures of decolonization, and mix with more lurid forms of militarized violence such as that witnessed at Sétif in Algeria in May 1945. Yet decolonization would develop and continue apace, beginning immediately after the end of the war. Western metropoles were exhausted from the war, Soviet communism and US liberal capitalism were both hostile to traditional, "old" European empires (even as the two new superpowers were very obviously empires of a different sort), and colonial populations had tired of fruitlessly agitating for greater rights within imperial frameworks, now turning to demands for national independence.

Nonetheless, imperial centers proved themselves willing to deploy violence to maintain empire. Winston Churchill famously paired the fight for national survival in the face of the Nazi menace with a fierce determination to maintain the British Empire. Yet efforts to keep India contributing to the war effort and prevent its conquest by the Japanese laid the foundations for Indian independence in 1947, and partition and the legacies of British colonial policies led to mass violence in the process and repeated wars in the region ever since, as India, Pakistan, and Bangladesh have struggled to work out what a postcolonial status quo will look like in the region. As far as direct British involvement, though, India's decolonization was notable for an absence of imperial violence and war. Not so in other places, whether controlled by the British or other western colonial powers. Even as negotiations were ending and resulting in Indian and Pakistani independence, Great Britain became embroiled in open warfare on the Malay peninsula. In 1948, the Malayan Communist Party began an insurgency against British rule, even as the British were taking steps to loosen colonial control over the region. Yet typical of processes of decolonization during the Cold War era, particularly militarized processes, western leaders were keen to ensure a non-communist future for newly independent states. So British forces waged war on their guerilla opponents, making use of air power and other elements of conventional tactics, as well as approaches developed earlier in the history of western colonialism: forced relocation, concentration camps, punitive raids, destruction of infrastructure, and political and humanitarian initiatives aimed at "winning over" the indigenous people on whose support the guerilas depended. These were successful, insofar as they prevented the communists from coming to power at the time and later when the new nation of Malaysia came into being. But the violence was extreme and protracted, ending only in 1960 and leaving tension throughout the region in its wake (Stubbs 2004; Barber 2007).

FIGURE 1.3: British soldiers wade upriver through the jungle on patrol in 1957 during the Malayan Emergency. Credit: Horace Abrahams/Keystone Features/Getty Images.

The British experience in Malaya serves in many ways as a typical example of the wars of decolonization. First of all, officials declined to call it a war, labelling it instead the "Malayan Emergency." Western empires often referred to these wars by such euphemisms, the better both to distance themselves from international agreements pertaining to the ethical conduct of war, and to delegitimize their enemies. This tendency operated colloquially as well. Even when the French, for instance, called their war in Indochina by its proper name, they added a qualification: it was *la sale guerre*, or "the Dirty War." And so the military and colonial history of the period is filled with "emergencies," "conflicts" (as Americans used to refer to the Vietnam War), "insurgencies," "insurrections," "revolts," "uprisings," "rebellions," and the like, all distinct from "legitimate" or "real" war between states that recognized each other as such. These terms have the virtue of highlighting the unusual nature of colonial wars, which did have some singular characteristics, and they indicate a political and cultural shift from emphasizing clashes between nation-states and conventional warfare to more amorphous and shifting confrontations within empires, nations, and societies. But such terms also elide or sublimate the many, many ways that colonial wars were, in fact, "war."

The Cold War structured many of these wars, as the West (and especially the United States) vied with the Soviet Union for influence across the globe. Thus, the peculiar mix of structural and conventional violence that characterized colonial wars, and the asymmetry between the defenders of imperial control and their opponents, give the wars of decolonization their distinct place in the histories of both war and empire. The French empire provides good examples. In Indochina, the French government sought to reassert its colonial authority in the face of a nationalist and communist resistance emboldened and empowered by turmoil both in France—first conquered and occupied by the Germans and then busy with reconstructing the nation in Europe—and in south-east Asia itself—which saw the ebbing and flowing of the Japanese empire. Embroiled in an unpopular counterinsurgency war that it could ill afford in many senses, the French effort was in the end sustained by very large doses of US moral and material support. This did not stop the French from losing the war, tellingly in a pitched battle at Dien Bien Phu in 1954. Prior to this, the United States' anticommunism had outweighed its hostility to traditional European empires, and then after 1954 the Americans began to defend their own particular brand of global hegemony in a war effort that would last two more decades and cost both Vietnam and the US dearly (Lawrence 2005; Statler 2007; Logevall 2012).

A second example, again involving France, was the Algerian War of Independence, which posed such uncomfortable questions for the French and their empire that it came to be known as "the war without a name" in the metropole (Talbott 1980). Beginning in 1954 and lasting for eight years until the French colonial administration and army left, along with hundreds of thousands of European settlers, all parties waged the war in particularly brutal fashion. As Algerian nationalists relied on assassinations, bombings, terror, and other tactics that addressed their relative weakness in the means of violence, the French colonial state responded with indiscriminate and extrajudicial killing, widespread and systematic torture, and the use of overwhelming force. The war was a confusing maelstrom of splits among Algerians themselves, among French metropolitan and colonial officials, within the French army, between European settlers and those tasked with defending their interests, and among different factions of French society in France itself and in Algeria. If any war lived up to the descriptive "dirty," this was it. And the legacy of the violence has haunted both Algeria and France ever since (Horne 2006; Shepard 2006).

There are many examples that illustrate the distinct aspects of the wars of decolonization, but two final and less well-known examples can stand as symbols of the kinds of violence millions of people witnessed and suffered as

FIGURE 1.4: French soldiers detain suspected nationalist fighters in the Aurès Mountains in 1955, during the Algerian war. Credit: Michel DESJARDINS/Gamma-Rapho via Getty Images.

formal Western empires collapsed after the Second World War. The two largest remaining overseas empires were those of the British and the French. The French proved willing to deploy significant—even extreme—violence in a failed attempt to maintain imperial status and control not only in Indochina and Algeria, but also in a far-flung corner of empire in the Indian Ocean. In 1947 in Madagascar, the French colonial administration and military suppressed what they termed an "insurrection" led by nationalist militants. Coordinated attacks on French military targets and plantations eventually elicited an overwhelming response, and official French estimates at the time put the number of Madagascans killed at over 80,000 in the space of little more than a year. Events in Madagascar paralleled those in other areas of Western colonial empires during the era of decolonization in terms of violence levels, repressive military tactics, and death tolls. But what is remarkable is how little known the episode is outside of Madagascar, where it plays an important role in the national historical memory (Tronchon 1986).

Violence in British Kenya was until recently similarly less well known outside the area of its occurrence. Between 1952 and 1960, British colonial authorities confronted what they called by the usual euphemisms of "uprising" or "rebellion" among Kikuyu peoples in Kenya. The so-called rebels came to be called Mau Mau, and targeted both white European settlers and perceived political and ethnic enemies among the indigenous population. To the British, Mau Mau came to be synonymous with unreasoning savagery and violence, but the grievances that propelled the violence were clearly rooted in the economic and land policies of colonial rule. British military and legal repression was severe, and probably some 20,000 Kenyans died in what recent historians have called Britain's "Dirty War" (Anderson 2005) and "Britain's Gulag" (Elkins 2005a). The story is unremarkable when viewed in the wider context of colonial violence during the period and, as historian David Anderson has pointed out, the violence in Kenya was more characteristic of even British decolonization than imagined by those who see that empire as having managed the process more magnanimously and peacefully than other imperial powers (Anderson 2005: 5).

The warfare between anticolonial forces and the defenders of empire was distinctive enough to spawn numerous and influential theorists on both sides of the divide. Mao Zedong was the most influential anticolonial thinker on war, as he struggled to liberate China from what he never failed to characterize as western (and Japanese) imperialism, and he articulated very clearly the different approaches that wars of decolonization necessitated. These approaches were most notable for the ways they integrated political and military imperatives, and indeed put first the political imperative of gaining and keeping the support of the masses of people among whom anticolonial guerrilla forces had to live and fight. His first point in the list of priorities laid out in his classic 1937 book *On Guerilla Warfare* is, "Arousing and organizing the people," followed by, "Achieving internal unification politically" (Mao [1937] 1978: 41). Only then does he address purely military matters. Yet Mao thought precisely and clearly about the technical problems of war, and his list of principles for effective fighting included in another classic text, "The Present Situation and Our Tasks" (1947), begins with an admonition to, "Attack dispersed, isolated enemy forces first; attack concentrated, strong enemy forces later," and goes on to give very practical advice about waging the sort of wars in which anticolonial forces around the world found themselves involved (Mao 1961: 161–2). This, along with Mao's victories and ultimate success, helps explain the global influence of his thinking on war.

If Mao and the many fighters and writers he inspired wrote about and acted out insurgency, a significant body of thinking, writing, and practice arose in opposition as well. Writers connected to France and its modern colonial wars, such as David Galula and Bernard Fall, were very influential more broadly, particularly as American soldiers tried to make sense of, and prevail in, their own similar military effort in Vietnam (Fall 1964; Galula 1964). Tellingly, as the United States carried out wars in the twenty-first century that bore many similarities to these earlier conflicts, a new generation of counterinsurgency theorists would seek to build upon this body of work (Nagl 2005; Kilcullen

2010). In fact, the US experience of war and empire, and the experience of people around the world who had to contend with America's empire and its wars, came to be of overriding importance as the era of decolonization wound down in the older European empires in the 1970s. Che Guevara, the anticolonial revolutionary active in Latin America and Africa, wrote about and practiced guerilla warfare in the mold of Mao Zedong, and like Frantz Fanon preached the value of violent struggle not only in defeating western colonialism, but in reconstituting the self-worth of subjugated populations. In 1967, the year of his death, he wished for a "bright future" in which "two, three or many Vietnams" would "flourish throughout the world with their share of deaths and their immense tragedies, their everyday heroism and their repeated blows against imperialism" (Guevara 1998: 175). Yet as scholar Martin Thomas has noted, the violence of colonial states and their agents was "an insecure foundation on which to build a supposedly better society" (Thomas 2011). If this was true, it begged the question not only of whether the United States could build a better future through nearly constant warfare in defense of its new, peculiar form of empire, but also whether the violence that figures such as Guevara and Fanon called for in opposition to this new kind of imperialism could lead to the bright, emancipated future of anticolonialists' dreams. The fifty years that have passed since Guevara's death may not yet have clarified the issue.

CONCLUSION: WAR WITHOUT END, 1975–PRESENT

In 1975, one of the West's oldest overseas empires all but ceased to exist. After a 1974 revolution that ended authoritarian rule in Portugal, the process of decolonization accelerated in an empire that had originated over five and a half centuries earlier. Colonial war was critical to the entire process, since fighting to maintain control of imperial holdings was a priority for the ruling *Estado Novo*, and indeed exhaustion from fighting wars against independence movements in Africa was a critical factor in bringing on revolution in the metropole. The new regime first recognized the independence of Guinea-Bissau, then Mozambique, São Tomé and Principe, and Angola, and so by the end of 1975 colonial wars that had raged for over 13 years came to an end (MacQueen 1997). Yet violence did not end in the newly independent nations, and Angola immediately descended into civil war, while the former Portuguese colony of East Timor, which had declared independence in November 1975, suffered invasion and occupation by Indonesia before the year was out. The Portuguese empire was virtually extinct (it would relinquish its last remaining territory, Macau, to China in 1999), but the legacy of colonial violence lived on, as it would in many former colonial possessions of the Western overseas empires.

The year 1975 also saw another process whereby a process of decolonization came to completion through war, and once again the aftermath saw yet more violence as part of the legacy of empire. Yet whereas events in Portuguese Africa signaled the exit of a western imperial power from the modern story of war and empire, events in Vietnam exemplified the continuing importance of the United States as the world's most prominent imperial power, and as a central player in many episodes of global imperial violence. On April 30, the South Vietnamese capital of Saigon fell to invading North Vietnamese troops. The last US troops and political personnel fled the former client-state as it crumbled, ending a two-decade effort to prevent the unification of Vietnam under communist control. The communists, for their part, proclaimed this their final victory in the war to decolonize Vietnam and free it from foreign imperial control (Goscha 2016). Yet war was far from over, and skirmishing with neighboring Cambodia began immediately. These clashes escalated steadily, culminating in Vietnam's invasion of Cambodia in 1978. A good deal of the friction between the two nations stemmed from the presence in Cambodia of the murderous and erratic Khmer Rouge government, whose way to power was paved by US destabilization of the country in the early 1970s, carried out as part of American efforts to prevail in the Vietnam War (Young 1991). The twisting course of instability and violence in south-east Asia is deeply complex, but the role of the United States is clear and critical. And though US policy in the region culminated ignominiously and symbolically with a chaotic evacuation from the rooftop of the American embassy in Saigon, the United States has remained the central actor in the global history of war and empire in the late twentieth and early twenty-first centuries.

This is not to say that other actors and events were not important during the period. France has maintained very close military, political, economic, and commercial ties with many of its former colonies in Africa. This is a deliberate policy choice, and is distinct and well-known enough to have a name, *Franceafrique*. France intervenes militarily in Africa more than any other former colonial power, and the presence of troops from former colonies in July 14 and Armistice Day ceremonies highlights the ways empire, war, and the fraternity of arms continues to link France with its former colonies. Great Britain's approach is not so obvious in many ways, but its willingness on occasion to fight to retain control of the last remnants of empire that remain does stand out. The two-month Falklands war of 1982 may have seemed a curious anachronism and an odd sideshow, but one of the world's wealthiest and most powerful nations mobilized a huge and technologically advanced naval, air, and ground force and conducted serious military operations to maintain control of a few islands and a few thousand residents almost 8,000 miles away from London.

Even as the last stages of decolonization continued with the end of white minority rule in South Africa in 1994, and the return of outposts like Hong Kong and Macau to China in the late 1990s, then, the violent afterlives of empire punctuated the history of the late twentieth century. Often these events were evidence of neoimperialism and neocolonialism—names for processes by

FIGURE 1.5: September 4, 1965: Vietnamese children at the Phu Thuong Orphanage near Da Nang taste ice cream for the first time, brought to them by US Marines as part of a goodwill mission during the Vietnam War, Vietnam. Credit: US Marine Corps/Getty Images.

which former colonial powers maintained predominant positions in business and finance, and interfered in newly independent nations' politics to exercise a control that smacked of older imperial and colonial hierarchies. And violence or the threat of violence, structural or in the form of open warfare, was never very far out of the picture. Even the fall of communism in eastern Europe in 1989 and the demise of the Soviet Union in 1991, which arguably constituted very large-scale processes of decolonization (certainly the Soviet empire came to an end), had some roots in imperial war. In 1978, the Soviet Union invaded Afghanistan in order to restore a client regime on its southern border. The protracted quagmire that ensued has prompted comparisons with the Vietnam War ever since, and played a role in weakening the Soviet army and state in the years leading up to the collapse of 1989–91 (Braithwaite 2011).

But it is the United States' role in the world that ensures the story of war and Western empire is still ongoing in the twenty-first century. The US most directly stood in for, or "replaced," old-style European imperial power when it took responsibility from France for maintaining a non-communist South Vietnam. It

FIGURE 1.6: A US special forces soldier monitors Iraqi forces advancing toward Mosul airport on February 23, 2017. Credit: AHMAD AL-RUBAYE/AFP/Getty Images.

is clear that Americans and their leaders do not see themselves as building and maintaining an empire along the lines of previous Western empires, ruling over peoples and territories directly. For instance, in the early years of the twenty-first century, Secretary of Defense Donald Rumsfeld routinely went out of his way to assure the world that despite US military action in the Middle East, the United Sates had "no aspiration to occupy or maintain any real estate in that region."[1] The nature of US hegemony and its status as an empire is a subject of intense debate, but those who describe the United States as an empire, whether approvingly or disapprovingly, rarely confuse it with the territorial empires of earlier centuries. The United States usually exercises imperial influence and control indirectly, via culture, economic weight, and neoimperial and neocolonial relationships. The United States also maintains empire through the military and war, force, and violence. And all of these methods can mix together simultaneously, as when the United States carries out the kinds of "hearts and minds" campaigns of economic and humanitarian aid that have been an overt part of military and political strategies ever since at least the Vietnam War, strategies that would for instance be very familiar to earlier architects of the French republican colonial empire such as Gallieni and Lyautey.

The United States enforces what many call an informal empire via repeated military interventions (historically most notably in Latin America), larger-scale wars (most recently in the Persian Gulf, Afghanistan, and Iraq), and a network of over 700 military bases in dozens of countries around the world. Since the terrorist attacks of September 11, 2001, the United States has been involved in major military operations—in a word, war—continuously in Afghanistan and Iraq. The so-called "war on terror" of which these are ostensibly a part also embraces smaller-scale operations that involve the deployment of troops, drone strikes, and many other forms of militarized violence around the world in an effort to preserve American interests, which amount to an effort to preserve American hegemony. It is difficult to see this as anything other than violence in defense of empire, whether or not the United States is interested in formally acquiring colonial "real estate," and it is the sort of violence that moves back and forth between the two poles that have defined the history of war and empire since 1920: everyday structural violence and open conventional warfare. Certainly, peoples around the world on the receiving end of American force in defense of national interests often experience American power as a structural pressure, frequently taking cultural forms, in their everyday lives. These same peoples also often experience this power as a deadly and concrete reality. This is nothing new, because imperial violence and war have been a constant, seemingly endless presence in the lives of many of the world's peoples during the whole history of modern Western empires. And, not coincidentally, many of the peoples affected by American imperial violence experienced it historically at the hands of other, earlier empires. Nearly a hundred years after the empires of the West concluded a global war that caused the collapse of several of them, and unleashed forces that would erode others, it seems clear that empire and war remain alive and well and intertwined, and there is no end in sight.

CHAPTER TWO

Trade

DAVID LYNCH

THE EPIC STORY OF TRADE

Trade in and since the twentieth century has expanded massively in its volume, variety, complexity, and geographic scope. The countries at the forefront of this expansion were the early industrializers, which is to say the western imperial powers such as Great Britain, the United States, France, and Germany. During this era, the imperial powers lost their colonies, but much of the colonial relationship continued in what some have called informal imperialism in which military and economic power inequities continue despite newly independent countries' political sovereignty[1] (Baumgart 1982: 6–7).

The expansion of trade has brought with it societal changes both celebrated and vilified. Early industrializers experienced unimaginable levels of wealth, dramatically more urbanization, and celebrated the free trade they believe got them there. Yet trade has been castigated by those harmed or threatened by it. In former western colonies, the trade patterns developed in the colonial era have, too often, continued after formal colonialism's end: primary products are exported from developing former colonies to the industrialized former colonial powers where they are transformed, with greater value added, into final products. Advances into more industrial production by former colonies have been hindered by developed countries' tariff escalation: low tariffs on primary products and higher tariffs on intermediate or finished articles. Because tariff escalation includes low or no tariffs on primary products used in industrial production—the very thing many former colonies have specialized in since colonialism—the situation seems helpful to them (Figure 2.1). The return on investment in developing nations is therefore altered to favor primary products,

FIGURE 2.1: A wood chip mountain for export in Puerto Montt, southern Chile. Credit: Julio Etchart/ullstein bild via Getty Images.

"... while the high protective rates levied on manufactured goods pose a significant entry barrier for any developing nation wishing to compete in this area" (Carbaugh 2015: 115).

Despite this, some former colonies, such as Brazil, Indonesia, Mexico, Malaysia, and Singapore, have become more industrialized as investment from developed to developing countries has increased industrialization. Low wages are a competitive advantage, as is so-called competition in laxity in which developing nations attract investment by lowering environmental or other standards. To critics this is a "race to the bottom," draining the capacity of governments to function in developed and developing countries.[2] There is discontent within developed economies as well. Industries that face greater competition from imports and thus declining market shares, profits, wages, and jobs are likely to fight against more trade liberalization. In the 1970s and 1980s, for instance, textile and apparel production in developed countries was under dramatic price competition from imports in developing countries, many of which were former colonies. The former colonies and other developing countries have come to dominate textile and especially apparel production, with only niche or very high-end production surviving in metropole and other developed countries.

These battles are not new. A particularly dramatic set of events associated with trade, economic liberalization, and, more broadly, globalization, has led to a dominant narrative among scholars in a number of fields and among policymakers in many countries, including the industrialized countries that continue to dominate the major international economic institutions. This dominant theme celebrates the rise of the West and suggests development in former colonies, and other developing countries, should be based on open trade and investment policies. W.W. Rostow, a US economist and key advisor in the Kennedy and Johnson administrations, identified five stages of economic growth, which he believed countries could move through more rapidly than early industrializers had done because it was now clear what needed to be done. Countries could advance from the traditional to the transitional stage through specialization of primary products. Income from primary product specialization would then be invested in a few leading industries. As these initial steps in industrialization met with success, the country would urbanize and the economy's industrial base would widen. The country would then enter the take-off stage in which "growth becomes . . . [society's] normal condition," investment having now become entrenched in the economy with technological innovation becoming increasingly important as the economy would mature and, lastly, the country would reach the mass consumption stage in which services would become a larger aspect of the economy (Rostow 1960: 4–11). That mass consumption would be held up as the ultimate goal of economic development toward which there should be a normal progression demonstrates the assumed tacit acceptance of US-promulgated market-oriented cultural practices. The United States proselytized pro-market and pro-consumption values to Europe and then to the rest of the world. These consumptive values and concomitant market orientation were at the core of what Victoria de Grazia calls the United States' dominance of the Market Empire in which US imperial influence was an empire without borders and "a great imperium with the outlook of a great emporium" (2005: 3). The key to its ascendance were the legions of mass marketers who inculcated much of the world in the culture of brands, identity through consumption, and other hallmarks of a consumer culture, which ultimately would come to see open markets as the proper order.

Just as there are sometimes local backlashes against a homogenizing culture, some were skeptical that colonial and other developing countries would experience the steady economic trajectory toward prosperity suggested by Rostow and others. Raúl Prebish, sometimes called Latin America's Keynes, had been an economic liberal, but increasingly saw the shortcomings of applying market solutions to the developing world. Competition between developed countries and monetary policies in dominant markets could roil currency markets and thus harm developing countries. Markets did not operate as advertised he thought, particularly in developing countries. In essence, agricultural and other primary product prices dropped relative to imported industrial goods. This was later known as the theory of unequal exchange.

Scholars associated with the concept had different ideas about what drove inequality in the exchange between rich and poor countries, but what they agreed upon was that the relationship's unfairness harmed colonial and other developing countries (Love 1980: 45, 64). These voices would emerge as a partial corrective to the standard liberal view of trade and globalization, but have not become the dominant story.

This dominant story of trade in and since the twentieth century is often told as an epic—there are heroes and villains, setbacks and doubt along a journey of growth. The telling and retelling of such epics establishes widely held cultural myths, such as the belief that developed countries industrialized with few barriers to foreign competition (and thus so too should former colonies). Myths further community solidarity and imbue storytellers and listeners with societal and cultural norms such as individual sacrifice for the greater good. The epic story of trade, along with its related liberalizing force, investment, helped make industrialized countries wealthy well beyond prior generations' imaginations and deepened the wealth and power gap between industrialized countries and the rest of the world to unprecedented levels. The tale as it has been commonly told includes a utopian past—before the First World War when the fruits of economic liberalization were supposedly enjoyed by many—ruined by the villain of excessive nationalism that ultimately led to the First World War. While trade and investment levels were indeed high before the First World War, it should be noted that the dominant narrative contained in this epic is itself contested. Some argue that facts have been misremembered in order to promote the "correct" lesson; one prominent critic has called the "official history of globalization" a misleading fable (Chang 2008: 21–6). The utopian past of pre-First World War globalization did, in fact, include substantial economic interdependence and increasing liberalization, but it also included very high tariffs in many industrial economies, including the world's largest at the time, the United States. Before 1913, US tariffs on industrial goods averaged 44 percent. In 1913, they dropped to 25 percent, but were raised again during the First World War (Chang 2008: 54). Moreover, this globalization era, so celebrated in the narrative, included considerable non-voluntary participation. Colonialization was a key part of pre-First World War globalization, including the exploitation of colonial populations and economies to the point of altering global trade and investment patterns: colonial economies were shaped to ensure a steady supply of raw materials would flow to industrialized metropole economies. For instance, the Indian textile industry was once more advanced than that of Britain (Figure 2.2), but collapsed in the face of British restrictions on internal Indian textile production and sales, and on Indian textile exports to Britain (Nehru [1946] 1985: 298–9, 331). British textile mills did not have to compete with Indian mills for access to Indian cotton.[3]

FIGURE 2.2: Weighing cotton in Mumbai. Illustration from the magazine *The Illustrated London News*, Volume XLI, October 11, 1862. Credit: De Agostini/ Biblioteca Ambrosiana.

The dominant narrative regarding trade in the twentieth century downplays the coercive and antiliberal aspects of the colonial past. This narrative is part of an overarching narrative regarding the role of markets in history and what led to Europe's take-off. Historian Kenneth Pomeranz exams the roots of what he calls "the great divergence," the title of his book examining Europe's rise. While there is no single nor simple answer to why Europe took off economically, he notes scholarly literature's overemphasis on market forces as having led industrialization in Britain and in Europe more broadly. As historians looked to previous centuries for the seeds of the West's rise, which germinated in the nineteenth and twentieth centuries, he argues, "... the more market dynamics appear even amid supposedly hostile medieval culture and institutions, the more tempting it has been to make market-driven growth the *entire* story of European development, ignoring the messy details and mixed effects of numerous government policies and local customs" (Pomeranz 2000: 5).

Pomeranz also notes that—like the story of trade examined in this chapter— the historical narrative explaining western Europe's rise serves a current purpose: "... an increasingly exclusive focus on private initiatives has not only provided an enviably clear story line, but a story line compatible with currently predominant neoliberal ideas" (2000: 4).

ECONOMIC LIBERALISM BEFORE THE FALL

The dominant narrative, focusing on trade and investment liberalization, thus skims over these substantial caveats. After all, there are dramatic events to describe: beneficial and expanding globalization cut short by cataclysmic war, only to rise again, falling to the Great Depression and the Second World War, and then redemption: globalization's spread and with it, prosperity. Due to the rapid increases in transportation and communication technologies in the nineteenth century (ever more efficient steam ships, the expansion of trains, the dissemination of telegraph and then telephone technology), the world had shrunk to a degree not possible in previous eras.

Many but all not major economies followed more liberalized trade and investment policies.[4] Despite caveats about continued trade barriers, the world had shrunk in terms of transportation, communication, and tariff policy. John Maynard Keynes captured the spirit of the pre-First World War era of globalization—liberalism before the fall—as it has been mythologized.

> The inhabitant of London could order by telephone, sipping his morning tea in bed, the various products of the whole earth, in such quantity as he might see fit, and reasonably expect their early delivery upon his doorstep; he could at the same moment and by the same means adventure his wealth in the natural resources and new enterprises of any quarter of the world, and share, without exertion or even trouble, in their prospective fruits and advantages; or he could decide to couple the security of his fortunes with the good faith of the townspeople of any substantial municipality in any continent that fancy or information might recommend ... But most important of all, he regarded this state of affairs as normal, certain, and permanent, except in the direction of further improvement, and any deviation from it as aberrant, scandalous, and avoidable (Keynes 1920: 6).

Keynes' point was, of course, that this did come crashing down with the First World War and that he foresaw the structural problems from the coming prosperity: namely burdening Germany with reparations that would ruin its economy.

Keynes' arguments against reparations had already failed to change the minds of policymakers when he raised them as an official in the British Treasury Department while Britain negotiated the terms of the peace. He resigned when he could not convince his government that requiring Germany to pay reparations far in excess of its ability to pay would be ruinous. His book, *The Economic Consequences of the Peace*, written in 1919 and published in 1920, was intended to highlight what to him was clearly folly. The book made Keynes a well-known figure, and his wisdom about German war reparations was later shown to be prescient. This set him on the path to being the most important economic figure of the century.

A RETURN TO NORMALCY?

But his book's cautions about reparations did not prevent the prosperity of the 1920s from creating societal amnesia about globalization's fragility. The recovery from the war in the 1920s seemed genuine to most contemporary observers and expanding economic levels of trade and investment seemed like a "return to normalcy," to borrow a slogan from Warren Harding's successful 1920 presidential campaign. Part of that normalcy, to observers at the time, was the continued close economic relationship between western colonial powers and their colonies, former colonies, or some other imperial arrangement, such as the mandates. Much of that economic relationship consisted of primary products exported to the metropole countries for industrial production. Cotton and rubber are two prominent examples (Figure 2.3).

FIGURE 2.3: A woman farmer taps dripping resin from a rubber tree in a plantation on Pulau Langkawi Island, Malaysia. Credit: In Pictures Ltd./Corbis via Getty Images.

Economic relations between colonial and other dominions and the metropole remained important and indeed, at least for the Allied victors of the First World War, had expanded. Germany's West and East African colonies were transferred through the League of Nations' mandate system, as were the holdings of the Ottoman empire first envisaged by Sykes-Picot in 1916, into largely British and French authority. Their authority over these "new" lands was nominally with the intent of independence, but in reality remained quite colonial, to the dismay of many living there who hoped for more rapid independence. Oil had been discovered in commercially viable amounts in Iran in 1901 (Gasiorowski 2017: 292). While there were hopes for commercial oil in the Levant and in the Arabian Peninsula, commercially viable amounts of oil would not be discovered there until the 1930s.[5] British oil interests in Iran would be facilitated by a British military presence in the Levant. This Levantine British presence would also secure trade with India, which was seen as more commercially important to Britain than was the Middle East.

Metropole countries had been quite reliant on their trade with their colonies and it was widely perceived that this would continue, despite lip service about self-determination. Why would it change? After all, colonization was widely perceived in metropole countries as being good for both sides and these holdings were important economically for the metropole countries. John Ravenhill notes:

> For the early European industrializers, trade with their colonies, dominions, or with other lands of recent European settlement, such as Argentina, was more important than trade with other industrialized countries. For the United Kingdom, a larger share of imports was contributed by Argentina, Australia, Canada and India together than by the United States, despite the latter's importance in British imports of cotton for its burgeoning textiles industry. These four countries also took five times the American share of British exports in 1916. Similarly, Algeria was a larger market for French exports in 1913 than was the United States (2011: 10).

The British government wanted the public to view their colonies as beneficial, as the British Empire Marketing Board's 1927 poster "Jungles To-day are Gold Mines To-morrow" attests, complete with stereotyped representations of indigenous Africans—presumably traders—and a list of trade values under the heading "Tropical African Colonies in Account with the Home Country" (Figure 2.4). In case the viewer missed the banner declaring "growing markets for our good," the trade values for 1895, 1905, 1910, 1915, and 1925 are listed. In four of the five years, Britain had a trade surplus with these colonies and over the thirty-year period, the nominal value of trade went up ten-fold (British National Archives, n.d.).

FIGURE 2.4: Empire Marketing Board 1927–33 poster. Credit: British National Archives.

The economic growth and expanding economic liberalism that passed for normalcy in the 1920s would later seem like an aberration. The Great Depression, the rise of trade and monetary nationalism, the spread of fascism, and, of course, the Second World War made it clear. The epic of free trade goes to great lengths to show that the all-too human response to economic crisis—trade protectionism—was flawed. It was the largest economy in the world and the largest trader, the United States, which set rising protectionism into motion.

SINS AGAINST FREE TRADE

The Great Depression generated an existential challenge to many domestic producers. Agricultural prices dropped substantially, proving disastrous to farmers in both colonial and metropole economies. Industrial prices also dropped as demand evaporated. This increased pressure on the US Congress to limit the damage done by imports. The Tariff Act of 1930, better known as the Smoot-Hawley tariff act (or simply Smoot-Hawley), so named after its congressional co-sponsors, raised tariffs in order to protect struggling US farmers and manufacturers from low prices. The bill began with the aim of protecting farmers—global wheat and sugar prices, for instance, were depressed—but was logrolled into protecting a wide swath of US agriculture and industry. In the Senate alone, there were some 1,200 amendments to the bill and the public record of the hearings on the bill was nearly 20,000 pages long (Eichengreen 1986: 5). This gave US trading partners sufficient warning that their fragile economies were about to be harmed by the United States. Australia, Canada, Cuba, France, Italy, Mexico, New Zealand, Portugal, Spain, Switzerland, and others moved toward protectionism in the wake of the law (Irwin 2011: 168–70; Carbaugh 2015: 183). In Canada, Smoot-Hawley became a campaign issue in the 1930 election before it had been signed into law in the United States. It helped the protectionist Conservative Party come to power and it subsequently raised tariffs (McDonald *et al.* 1997: 803). The US lurch toward protectionism led twenty-five other countries to respond with higher tariffs of their own (Carbaugh 2015: 183). Moreover, other trade developments damaged world trade in this era. Some countries simply turned away from the United States by extending trade preferences to select other countries. For instance, Great Britain and its former colonies met in Ottawa in 1932 and agreed to reduce tariffs between one another. "Although imperial preferences were not established in direct retaliation against the United States, the international climate against the Smoot-Hawley tariff helped give rise to it" (Irwin 2012: 18).

Smoot-Hawley and the retaliation it inspired had the collective effect of raising taxes on consumers during a depression. To be sure, this was the wrong policy to help alleviate the Great Depression, but the negative economic effects of Smoot-Hawley have long been exaggerated. The Smoot-Hawley tariff act raised tariffs marginally, from approximately 38 percent to 45 percent on dutiable items[6] (Eichengreen 2015: 120–2). Tariffs, in other words, were already quite high and Smoot-Hawley is thought to have had only minor investment repercussions. Its damage was more nuanced. It increased international friction, engendered retaliation instead of conciliation, and ended the prospects for coordinating responses to reverse the economic decline just when international coordination was most desperately needed (Eichengreen 2015: 120–2).

What is not exaggerated is the scar this left on economic policymakers. The lesson that protectionism dangerously led to more protectionism and that it ultimately benefits no one became as entrenched as the belief that it was a mistake to appease Hitler at Munich. Even though trade's collapse in the Great Depression cannot be correctly blamed on Smoot-Hawley, a global trade decline of approximately two-thirds between 1929 and 1934 was a searing event and policymakers had a Pavlovian response (Winham 2009: 13). The socialization regarding Smoot-Hawley became so embedded in economic policy lore that in 1993, sixty-three years after Smoot-Hawley's passage, Smoot-Hawley was the defining moment in a showdown debate over the North American Free Trade Agreement (NAFTA) between Democratic Vice President Al Gore and third-party presidential candidate Ross Perot. During the debate, Gore gave Perot a photograph of Smoot and Hawley as a gift, explaining to the audience that

Perot's opposition to NAFTA was akin to Smoot and Hawley's disastrous protectionism. Whether the parallel was true was immaterial; Perot had been painted with the negative connotations of protectionism by the comparison. The role of Smoot-Hawley in the epic story of trade is cautionary and remains powerful. Barry Eichengreen, who persuasively argues that Smoot-Hawley's economic impact is exaggerated, also notes its continued socializing role for policymakers everywhere.

> Thus the textbook assertion that Smoot-Hawley worsened the Depression in the United States is bad history in the service of good policy. Although there is no evidence that the tariff had a significant negative impact on the American economy, its ritual invocation helped policy makers resist the protectionist temptation in 2009. That in turn made it easier to mount an internationally coordinated response (2015: 122).

The Group of 20 (G20)—whose members include the EU and nineteen of the most significant national economies—pledged not to engage in trade protectionism in the face of the Great Recession. To facilitate this, the G20 has the WTO issue a report every six months listing all restrictive trade measures the G20 members have taken. This is not foolproof, of course, and in the 2017 G20 meeting in Germany, the Trump administration successfully pressed the G20's communique to weaken its free-trade pledge by removing language about the G20 goal being to "avoid all forms of protectionism" (Buergin *et al.* 2017; G20 2017: 1).

REDEMPTION

Indeed, it was the perceived evils of the Smoot-Hawley tariff act, the subsequent lack of coordinated international response to end the Great Depression, and the view that economic collapse strengthens political extremism (e.g., Weimar Germany's economic chaos assisting Nazism's rise) that led policymakers to meet at Bretton Woods, New Hampshire in 1944. They proposed economic institutions to facilitate economic cooperation and coordination after the war. They sought cooperation and coordination sufficient to gain the benefits of capitalism—innovation and efficiency—while tempering capitalism's unacceptable instability. Thus the major post-Second World War economic institutions were born: the International Monetary Fund (IMF), the International Bank for Reconstruction and Development (IBRD), better known as the World Bank, and, after a proposed International Trade Organization (ITO) could not make it through the US Congress, the General Agreement on Tariff and Trade (GATT).[7] The GATT was supposed to be a temporary mechanism to reduce tariffs and was intended to be subsumed within the more expansive ITO once the ITO wound its way through the ratification process (Drache 2000: 7; Irwin *et al.* 2008: 112). Instead, it became permanent and in 1995, a few years before turning fifty, the GATT evolved into the World Trade Organization (WTO). These institutions fit into the larger attempt by (especially) the United States and Britain of creating a strong global economy to make extremism (communism) less attractive. Of course, there were commercial interests too; the institutions were complementary in that access to (initially US) capital would help countries rebuild and thus revert to being customers again. Stable foreign exchange markets fostered by the IMF, anchored to the US dollar, would also facilitate trade, a direct reaction against the currency wars that further hobbled trade during the Great Depression. These institutions were clearly dominated by the western industrial powers, especially the United States. Membership was open, but decision-making in them remained in the West. To economic liberals, these institutions underpinned cooperation that led to the strong economic growth throughout the Cold War. Even other western powers—despite their own privileged position in these institutions—had reservations that the already substantial US economic power was growing. For example, former French President Valéry Giscard d'Estaing famously said the US dollar acting as the anchor in the Bretton Woods system gave the United States an "exorbitant privilege." The view from former colonies, many of which became newly independent in this timeframe and had no privileged position in these institutions, was more critical. There, the institutions came to be seen as proxies for the US approach to economic development: that poor countries should develop with less government intervention in the economy.

The epic story of trade describes the Bretton Woods Conference and the institutions it established as redemption against the sins of the interwar beggar-thy-neighbor policies. They further point to the "saintly" John Maynard Keynes—a major influence at Bretton Woods—being vindicated. His advice about German war reparations after the First World War, which policymakers ignored in 1919 to disastrous effect, instead largely became policy at end of the Second World War and has been viewed as having helped heal and unite Europe after the war. Indeed, it has become part of the larger story that Keynes helped save capitalism from its own worst excesses.[8] The story also includes a largely benevolent United States serving as a market of last resort, a lender of last resort, and a guarantor of military security. The United States was benevolent in the sense it kept the trading system largely open and stable since the Second World War. This benevolence did not help everyone and it certainly coincided with US self-interest by bolstering anticommunist governments and creating customers for US producers. However, the Bretton Woods institutions coupled with the Marshall Plan had another effect: it bought the western colonial powers time and, more importantly, money, to delay the independence of their colonies. Exhausted from the Second World War, western colonial powers struggled to retain their colonies. The United States was publicly calling on them to decolonize, but also handing colonial powers financing that allowed colonialism to continue. So, too, did direct US aid for specific colonial holdings in the face of communist insurgencies such as aid to France in Vietnam, to the Netherlands in Indonesia, and to Britain in Malaysia (Go 2011: 140).

IMPLEMENTING AND DEEPENING REDEMPTION

True to its goals, the GATT did indeed facilitate the reduction of tariffs in the post-Second World War era. This was especially true for trade among the major industrial economies that established GATT and dominated its membership in its early decades. It should be added that the GATT had a running start. The lessons of Smoot-Hawley had already been learned before the Bretton Woods conference and before the start of GATT; Congress reversed Smoot-Hawley's protectionism with the Reciprocal Trade Agreements Act of 1934, which authorized the president to lower tariffs with other countries through bilateral agreements, so long as there was reciprocity. The United States entered into thirty-two such agreements between 1934 and 1947, when the GATT began, bringing down the tariff on dutiable items by about half (Carbaugh 2015: 185).

But to be sure, the GATT itself lowered tariff rates substantially and this was an achievement. Trade barriers became lower than at any time in history. The GATT made trade far more rules-based, theoretically minimizing the role power—especially economic power—would play in trade relations more than in any previous trade governance (leaving plenty of room for powerful countries to dominate weaker ones as previous trade governance was scant, essentially allowing the codification of colonialism, for instance). The GATT sought to reduce the role of power through its core principles of reciprocity (all countries will lower barriers toward one another) and non-discrimination, which includes national treatment and the granting of most favored nation (MFN) status (Baldwin 2016b: 97). National treatment means governments will not distinguish between foreign and domestic production once the foreign product has been imported. For instance, a law on fuel formulations that falls negatively on imported fuel but not domestic fuel would violate this principle.[9] MFN means that all GATT members, and now all WTO members, will grant other members the lowest tariff rate they grant to any other member (with some exceptions).[10] Thus, if a member lowers its tariffs toward one member country it does so for all members, allowing liberalization to ripple across the organization's membership. Another GATT principle is that members are given a degree of flexibility in granting themselves a safety valve to delay the impact of greater liberalization. Importantly, the GATT's safety valve mechanisms are rules-based and can be challenged by other members if perceived as being abused. This rules-based flexibility gives countries greater confidence to agree to liberalization about which they would otherwise be more hesitant.[11]

While all of this, on the face of it, diminished the role of power in the trade regime, it also facilitated the end of colonial trade preferences for metropole powers. It thus expanded US access to the former colonies of other western colonial powers, despite the US injection of capital into metropole economies that otherwise sustained colonialization (Go 2011: 139–40).

REDEMPTION'S IMPERFECTIONS: WE ARE ALL SINNERS

The story of GATT's success at lowering tariffs is often told with a celebratory tone and includes moral approbation against trade protectionism. But the openness the GATT facilitated must be tempered by the unevenness of trade liberalization. The largest reduction in tariff barriers was in economic sectors that industrialized powers dominated: manufactured goods, while those industries that were opposed to greater trade liberalization and powerful enough to stop it, especially in the United States, successfully ensured that their economic sectors were left out of GATT altogether. As the United States (especially) and other industrialized powers were preaching the gospel of free trade, they were also not-so-secretly echoing Augustine's famous prayer, "Give me chastity and continency, but do not give it yet" ([1631] 1912: 441). Textiles and apparel and agriculture were specifically excluded from GATT and these are the most important economic sectors for developing nations. Textiles and apparel are among the most labor-intensive sectors in the world, thus low-wage developing nations have a competitive advantage. That low wages and poor working conditions are a competitive advantage also means that developing countries have little incentive to regulate labor conditions in these economic sectors. Exploitation is common in the industry: low pay, long hours, and unsafe conditions. Western companies, sadly, also profit from these conditions. Simply put, apparel production moves to Bangladesh, for example, precisely for its low wages and lackadaisical regulation.

Agriculture is the largest employer in many developing countries and accounts for a high percentage of developing country exports. In fact, an important group of agriculture exporters that are promoting greater liberalization in agricultural trade in ongoing negotiations is the so-called Cairns Group. It consists primarily of former western colonies; over half of the 19 Cairns members are former colonies in South and central America: Argentina, Bolivia, Brazil, Chile, Colombia, Costa Rica, Guatemala, Paraguay, Peru, and Uruguay. Former western colonies in Asia make up most of the rest of the group's membership: Indonesia, Malaysia, Pakistan, the Philippines, and Vietnam (Cairns Group, n.d.).

The exclusion of textiles and apparel and agriculture from GATT was simply to protect those industries in developed countries. Had they been included in GATT, there would have been no GATT. This demonstrates clearly the degree to which the GATT was primarily a US creation (and secondarily of other western powers) and that globalization in the post-Second World War years would be shaped to benefit it. Simply put, any agreement that threatened US agriculture could not make it through the US Senate and, given US economic dominance during GATT's creation, there would be no GATT. It remains the case today that any new WTO agreement would also have to get through the US Senate where agricultural states are extremely overrepresented: the top four per capita agriculture producers have just over two percent of the national population, but have eight percent of the Senate's representation. This is equal to the Senate representation of the four most populous states, despite the fact that they account for 33 percent of the population (US Census Bureau 2016; USDA Economic Research Service 2016).[12] Agreements that US agriculture broadly dislikes will not make it through the US Senate. Similarly, textile and apparel producers were under enormous threat from imports and were also among the most powerful lobbies in Washington for much of the Cold War era. Dynamics such as this played out in some other industrial countries, but with the US as the economic giant of the immediate postwar period, the United States' domestic political concerns were enough to ensure agriculture and textiles and apparel's exclusion.

As the United States and the other leading industrial countries excluded agriculture and textiles and apparel from the GATT, they preached free trade. In the early GATT negotiating rounds, developing nations were not typically involved at all. But the exclusion of these significant economic sectors, and the preaching about the merits of free trade, continued well after developing countries were more involved in GATT negotiations. The hypocrisy was definitely noticed by developing countries and the sectors' exclusion led developing countries to further distrust the dominant industrial powers. The distrust continues today and hinders the WTO's ability to successfully bring the Doha Development Agenda (DDA) negotiations, launched in 2001, to a conclusion.

This distrust was made worse because many of the proposals that were initially discussed at Bretton Woods came from developing countries and posed alternatives to orthodox liberal capitalism and were ultimately rejected by developed countries. The most influential developing country voice was that of Raúl Prebish, an Argentine economist with the UN's Economic Commission for Latin America (ECLA), but there were many others that called for the Bretton Woods institutions to focus more on development, not just the stability of the overall system. US interest in pro-development changes to international economic governance on the road to and at the Bretton Woods Conference was higher than it has typically been portrayed in the scholarship on the subject, in part because that interest diminished as the Cold War became a larger concern (Helleiner 2014: 16–22). The ill-fated ITO, a product of the Bretton Woods Conference that could not get US Congressional approval, was certainly more pro-development than either the GATT or the WTO. For instance, the ITO included calls for focusing on full employment and had provisions that considered trade more expansively, including labor standards (Drache 2000: 7). The ITO's developmental bent and more expansive view of trade were anathema to the new Republican majority in the US Congress in 1950 and thus President Truman, who had backed the ITO, stopped seeking its Congressional approval to avoid a significant and public legislative loss. This also underscores the degree to which the GATT was an instrument of the United States. To economic liberals, this was simply the political reality, the level of free trade the GATT created was better than without the GATT. To former colonies, and other developing countries, it underscored that their lack of influence over international economic governance before GATT would continue in the GATT itself.

Developing countries would have to wait nearly fifty years for agriculture and textiles and apparel to be included in the GATT as it evolved into the WTO. Even then it required developing countries' insistence and was a reward for accepting many new provisions they were otherwise unenthusiastic about, but that developed countries strongly sought, such as intellectual property rights (IPRs). To developing countries' ears, greater protection of copyrights and patents and other IPRs sound like royalties going to the industrialized "North" from the less developed "South" and the South's governmental resources being drained from the greater administrative costs that enforcing IPRs would entail. Even with the inclusion of agriculture and textiles into the WTO, liberalizing provisions were phased in slowly and the sectors remain among the most protected sectors covered by the WTO.

REDEMPTION GETS COMPLICATED

As the GATT became more successful at lowering industrial tariffs, countries began to rely on non-tariff barriers such as quotas or safety standards to maintain protectionism that was no longer being provided by tariffs. The GATT negotiations therefore turned their attention to lowering non-tariff barriers (NTBs). In fact, much of the GATT/TWO's development since the 1970s has been focused on reducing or harmonizing non-tariff barriers. This has brought the WTO closer and closer to activities once considered the purview of domestic governments such as environmental or health and safety laws and regulations. This has been controversial and certainly has made achieving consensus on major trade agreements difficult. Also making consensus more difficult is the growing and diversifying membership. When the GATT was established in 1947, there were only twenty-three signatories. As the GATT lowered tariffs in successive negotiating rounds, it also gained members and began taking on additional trade-related issues. By the Kennedy Round of negotiations in the

1960s, there were sixty-two members and the agenda was expanding beyond that of previous rounds. By the Tokyo Round in the 1970s, there were over one hundred members and the agenda expanded significantly again with a particular focus on NTBs. By the time the Uruguay Agreement was signed in 1994, there were 123 members (OECD 2009: 81). The Uruguay Round negotiations lasted approximately seven and a half years and covered far more issues than past rounds: the establishment of the WTO, a more institutionalized (i.e., quasi-legal) and rigorous dispute resolution mechanism, trade in services, agriculture, textiles and apparel, trade-related aspects of investment, and intellectual property rights (IPRs), among other issues. The Uruguay Round's legal text, called the final agreement or final act, was 550 pages long, excluding the other WTO ministerial declarations necessary to clarify it (WTO, n.d.). The next round of WTO negotiations was (and continues to be) more complicated. It took years of failed attempts, that included riots by protestors in Geneva and Seattle outside WTO meetings and quieter but more consequential disagreements within the conference halls, before WTO members were ready to launch the next round of talks in 2001. The developing world, though very diverse, was in agreement that the next round of talks would not start without a greater focus on their needs.

Developed countries wished to expand the WTO's agenda further and typically wanted greater access to developing countries' manufacturing markets, yet were not willing to open their own agricultural markets substantially. Developing countries were not eager to expand the agenda further, and instead wanted greater openness in developed countries' agriculture markets. This included lower tariffs for developing country agriculture exports, of course, but also a decrease in rich-country agricultural subsidies. These subsidies would turn out to be a major hurdle to starting and completing an agreement. Developing countries also resisted further opening of their own manufacturing markets and, in fact, sought to weaken some other elements of the Uruguay Round.

One such call for change arose as part of a global social movement relating to the HIV/AIDS pandemic. Africa was by far the region most devastated by HIV/AIDS and the area with the fewest resources to adequately respond. As HIV/AIDS-related medications became available, they were well outside the financial reach of most Africans afflicted by the disease and the disease went, essentially, untreated. As protests mounted, lowering drug costs became a major focus of the movement and calls went out to weaken the WTO's IPR provisions in order get more medicine to African patients. In order to begin the next round of trade negotiations, developed countries did concede that for medical emergencies, countries could produce medicines that would otherwise be a violation of the WTO's IPR rules.[13] Thus, the Doha Development Agenda (DDA), or the Doha Round, was finally launched in 2001, but at the end of 2016 there was still no final agreement in sight (although there have been some less significant spin-off agreements). The Doha Round now includes the WTO's 164 members, with radically different levels of development and thus different trade-related interests. Many of the divides that made the Doha Round difficult to start have made it difficult to complete. It now appears unlikely that the Doha Round will successfully create substantial continued liberalization. Besides the obvious problem of disagreement between trade negotiators, there has been growing disenchantment on the part of the public in many developed countries. Since they continue to account for the bulk of world trade, economic liberalization's future—and therefore the role of trade in former colonies' development models—appears to be in jeopardy.

MUCH ADO ABOUT SOMETHING

Proponents of free trade often speak in soaring evangelical rhetoric, giving free trade credit for spreading opportunity, prosperity, and freedom. Critics deride trade as a killer of jobs in rich countries and an enabler of exploitation in poor countries. Such critics blame trade for all manner of economic ills that beset an economy. Trade is clearly important to jobs, investment, national productivity, and more, but some additional perspective is warranted. Trade flows are substantial, but they are dwarfed by financial flows. Global merchandise and services trade was valued at $20.7 trillion in *all* of 2015. Foreign exchange markets averaged over $5 trillion dollars per *day* in 2016. Every four days the value of money moving through foreign exchange markets is equivalent to an entire year's value of all trade (Bank for International Settlements 2016: 4; WTO 2016: 18).

In fact, it may be that trade flows are the result of, not the cause of, financial flows. Foreign demand for US treasuries, for instance—widely seen as the safest investment in the world—plays a substantial role enabling or, put more strongly, creating US trade deficits. How so? Foreign purchases of US treasuries strengthen the US dollar relative to other currencies, making imports cheaper for US consumers and making US exports more expensive for foreign consumers. If financial flows can substantially influence the trade flows of the world's largest economy, imagine their impact on former colonies and other developing countries.

Similarly, trade is vilified as causing a great deal more job loss than economists believe is warranted and, in fact, on balance creates jobs, as economists overwhelmingly agree. Some specific jobs are lost to trade, but the scale of the job loss is small compared with job churn from other sources. Trade-related job loss often packs a greater psychological and political punch than trade-related job gains and far more than trade-related non-employment gains such as greater variety and cheaper consumption. Trade-related job loss is often concentrated—an entire plant may be moved to another country where wages are lower—and the pain is real, immediate, and obvious. The gains to the broader economy—cheaper consumption, for instance—are diffused. No one votes or joins an interest group or protests to save, say, $500 on consumer products, but they will to save their $50,000 per year job. The $500 savings per person, over an entire economy may outweigh the economic cost of the jobs at the plant. Further, jobs gained from trade are less visible than those lost from trade. Job gains from trade are often more diffused than trade-related job losses—companies already producing may expand due to greater exports, but this is typically marginal for any one producer. Less visible still are the jobs that come from cheaper inputs for domestic final product manufacturers that can source from around the world.

Trade is indeed important, but it is less so than is commonly perceived. To give a sense of how much job loss does not come from trade, during much of the 1990s as China was soaking up manufacturing investment from around the world and new manufacturing facilities were being built at a dizzying pace in coastal China, the country actually lost industrial jobs. It closed some of its famously inefficient state-owned enterprises, some of which employed hundreds of thousands of workers. If more efficient production created job loss in China as it expanded industrial capacity so quickly, imagine what is happening in other countries that are not gaining Chinese levels of inward foreign investment. Trade, industrialization, and globalization in an era of growing automation may not be as beneficial to development to former colonies as it was for their metropole powers during their industrial expansion.

LIBERALIZATION—SUCH THAT IT IS—HOLDS

The Great Recession posed a challenge to former colonies and other developed countries on two fronts. First, there was a precipitous drop in demand for their exports, be they primary products or industrial goods. This economic pain would reverse itself upon the recession's end. Second, the global economic pain in the developed countries and in the largest developing countries posed a threat to trade liberalization. Would there be a Smoot-Hawley-like response in the large markets?

The Great Recession was notable for the degree to which it did not roll back liberalization (although given the backlash noted earlier in industrialized countries, perhaps it still will). One reason liberalization was not diminished is that it has been increasingly institutionalized in the WTO itself, and through the growing number of bilateral and multilateral free trade agreements, referred collectively as regional trade agreements. They are not new, but what is new about them from the 1990s onward, is the degree to which they include provisions for deeper integration than previous generations of Regional Trade Agreements (RTAs). Many of these "modern" RTAs, for better or worse depending upon one's perspective, include provisions that offer WTO-plus levels of access. They are more apt to include coverage of investment, services, and intellectual property rights than previous generations of RTAs. As with free trade more generally, RTAs have been controversial. If this was not already clear, the 2016 Brexit vote—the British referendum to "exit" the EU—and the popularity of President Donald Trump's criticism of NAFTA have clarified the point. But the EU, NAFTA, and other RTAs have powerful constituencies and any country that abandons an RTA will not solve the problems posed by globalization. In other words, liberalism is likely to hold, however uncomfortably, for the foreseeable future.

NEW AND OLD GLOBALIZATION

One reason that liberalization may be holding is simply because protectionism no longer has the same impact it once did given changed production patterns. Raising barriers on those products made wholly outside a given country by a foreign company (or a domestic company with foreign operations) using foreign inputs is how production is portrayed. Thus, protectionism would raise barriers on specific foreign production, helping wholly domestic producers. But trade and globalization have not worked this way for some time and are rapidly moving away from this image. Sourcing and production are increasingly regional or global in scope. Comparative advantage may still drive production, but what drives comparative advantage is less understood, more complicated and volatile. Trade theory has multiple explanations for comparative advantage—relative factor endowments (e.g., relative abundance in labor or a type of labor), research and development capacity, process innovation, product innovation and product life cycles, high-quality infrastructure, properly functioning government, and so on. A leading trade economist argues that comparative advantage shifts so much, so rapidly, and for so many reasons, it is best understood as "kaleidoscopic comparative advantage" (Bhagwati 2005). Raising a tariff barrier or engaging in some other form of protectionism may have implications that are difficult to understand in this environment. Manufacturing that does take place in a given country is likely to have components from around the world—not just foreign raw materials—but manufactured components. Components are likely to have crossed multiple borders already in their own production before they are sent across more borders still for final assembly. This type of production has spread so rapidly that trade regulations and our thinking have not kept pace.

Richard Baldwin points out the major shift toward new globalization came in roughly 1990. That is when the G7 countries, long the richest and largest industrialized economies in the world (the United States, Japan, France, Germany, Great Britain, Italy, and Canada—all colonial powers, except Canada) began losing income shares to rapidly industrializing countries (especially China, South Korea, India, Poland, Indonesia, and Thailand) exceptionally fast. From 1820 to the mid-1980s, the G7's gross domestic product rose from about 20 percent to roughly two-thirds of the world total, often called the Great Divergence. Then, from approximately 1990, the G7's share of world income dropped to just over 40 percent in about twenty years, a level last seen in 1914. This "shocking share shift," as Baldwin calls it, is reversing the Great Divergence (Baldwin 2016a: 1–3). He argues a Great Convergence is under way and it is driven by the spread of information and communication technology (ICT) that allowed ideas to flow across borders through production networks. Technology designed to help facilitate joint production between low- and high-wage areas has in fact done so beyond what has been predicted and that is fundamentally different than joint production that preceded this era. Technological and managerial ideas have flowed from high-wage countries to lower-wage countries as part of this joint production. The impact of globalization may thus be speeding up, both in high-wage industrial countries and those developing countries that can successfully take advantage of the ideas flowing through production networks. This has enormous consequences for trade and trade regulation. Putting up barriers to trade in developed countries is more like putting up a wall in the middle of a factory (Baldwin 2016c). Hindering production networks' ability to work in a given country is very unlikely to increase jobs and production in that country.

While the forces leading production to newly industrializing countries is on balance good for these countries, questions remain about its environmental sustainability and even about the degree to which industrialization will deliver the much-needed jobs as had been the case for previous industrializers, predominantly the metropole countries. Dani Rodrik has found industrialization is peaking earlier in the industrialization process than was once the case (2015: 15). This premature deindustrialization suggests the trajectory of early industrializers that so many countries have sought to reproduce may not deliver the same development punch it once did. This is all the more worrying because productivity gains in manufacturing have been higher than in other economic sectors and thus help countries sustain economic growth once manufacturing takes hold. He suggests other growth models may be needed, such as services-led growth. This, he notes, requires higher skill labor when many developing countries need employment for large numbers of lower skilled workers (2015: 23–4). Industrialization, long seen as a development panacea may not be what it once was. The rungs of the ladder that worked for the metropole powers when they industrialized may not hold as former colonies climb them in their attempt to develop.

The controversies associated with trade will continue due to its centrality to development and because it is a hook onto which many issues can be placed. What is less clear is what story will be told about trade in the era of new globalization. Will former colonial countries escape the long shadows of their industrialized former metropoles?

CHAPTER THREE

Natural Worlds

ROBERT ROUPHAIL

INTRODUCTION

As Cyclone Nargis' storm surge overwhelmed Myanmar's Irrawaddy Delta in 2008, as the catastrophic 2011 Japan tsunami unfurled itself across the Fukushima prefecture countryside in full view of the entire world, and as looming fears of antibiotic resistance begin to percolate through public consciousness, one of the most sacrosanct conceits of the twentieth century—of human mastery of the natural world—reveals itself again and again to be fiction. It is, however, a powerful fiction, one that has informed the ways in which states have constructed bureaucracies and social policies, and how nations and their citizens narrate collective pasts. Throughout the twentieth century, it was an imperial fiction, and one this chapter argues was critical to producing cultural registers of difference as a foundation of colonial rule in Asia, the Americas, and in particular in Africa, a geographic space long considered outside the dynamics of historical change and technological development. Indeed, the history of colonial projects to extend state power over the natural world in the twentieth century reveals that questions of political, social, and cultural relations to nature developed in relation to, and quite often in the service of, the expansion of imperial power.

What marks the temporal moment of when the twentieth century as distinct from earlier eras saw the ascendance of revolutionary forms of technological power that sparked unprecedented changes in understanding, changing, and moving through the natural world? As John McNeill has suggested, the twentieth century saw the "screeching acceleration of so many processes that brought ecological change" (McNeill 2000: 2). In the colonial world, this "great acceleration" of the human ability to shape the natural world was a product of new technological advancements wielded in the service of imperial high modernism, when French, British, Portuguese, and American imperial powers sought to bring the natural world and their subjects under the auspices of the state and under those of globalized capital more broadly. The harmonizing of technology and centralized forms of colonial governance have allowed for societies to intervene in the natural world on an unprecedented geographical and temporal scale; from the thinning of the ozone layer to the melting of polar ice, changes whose effects are dramatic and durable. This has led historians to develop an arsenal of methodological and conceptual tools to interpret these changes, from the much-celebrated climate proxy sources like tree rings and ice core samples, to the historical/geological category of the "Anthropocene."

The integration of technologies of governance with technologies of control over the natural world is historically significant not just in the history of the development of modern statecraft in relation to the environment, however, but also in understanding the cultural assumptions of difference that both emerged out of, and informed, these processes. The cultural history of twentieth-century Western empires and the natural world reveals that the development of technological power, the kind that sparked McNeill's "great acceleration," was a conceptual site for the production of cultural difference between colonizer and colonized, European and native, modern and primitive (McNeill and Engelke 2016). This chapter thus positions the synthesis of methods of governance and modes of rationalizing, categorizing, and ultimately "mastering" nature and people as exemplary of how the "natural world" was conceived, mobilized, and acted upon in the twentieth century.

This history is not, however, a linear story of western mastery over nature. To be sure, the development of technological refinement, the folding of technology into state power, and the wielding of that power against the natural world and imperial subjects is critical to understanding the history of the last century. But it is also important to interrogate the extent to which narratives that privilege the acceleration of scientific and technological expertise offer a built-in structure that reproduces the very logics of state power which historians are meant critically to bring to light. In other words, the smooth story of the ascent of technological expertise and colonial efforts at rendering the natural world legible to human institutions can, without careful attention, merely reflect the ideological commitments of those very states. These Whiggish histories can obscure just how contested that knowledge could be and how its development reflected not a triumphant colonial power, but rather an embattled one, one reckoning with multiple forms of threat. The first two sections of this chapter, then—which focus on settler societies and imperial logics of development—conceptualize the intersection of state, nature, and culture as a site of disruption for Western empires in Africa and Asia in particular.

This argument synthesizes two fields of scholarly literature that emphasize the instability and historicity of technological change, empire, and the environment. First, the positioning of the natural world as a thorn in the side of empire rather than as a space purely on which empire acted draws from recent work by Antoinette Burton, who positions ever-present sites of "dissent and disruption" within British imperial spaces as catalyzing forces in the historical development of empire. For Burton, dissenting and disrupting were the logics that undergirded the work of the British Empire around the globe. In this model, British imperialism was never natural or stable, but an assemblage of multiple and locally driven projects constantly in flux, ones in constant negotiation between the metanarratives of the global with the vicissitudes of the local. Burton offers this argument as a corrective to the pervasive "rise and fall" narratives, which take imperialism as a given and a constant, moving across time and space with unifying moral and political agendas articulated by its administrative and political elites. "What's needed, in short," Burton argues, are "wide-ranging accounts of the limits and possibilities of empire's method on the ground, whenever and wherever it met local responses and was compelled to deal with them" (Burton 2015: 8). An initial reading of source material that illuminates these imperial "methods" of dominance in relation to the natural world would suggest that colonial states were interested in the "improvement" of the environment, the stewardship of indigenous peoples that inhabited it, and that technological power was a tool to accomplish these projects. But often these sources mask a different reality: that questions of natural improvement and technological power were often reactionary efforts that sought to cement political power or settle capital in the face of threat, and that European powers often did so by relying on assumptions of cultural difference *vis-à-vis* the natural world, assumptions that would appear to vitiate the violence inherent in those processes.

And just as empire has proven to be a category often naturalized in scholarly literature, so has technology and technological change. Beginning in the late 1980s, scholars began applying a similar analytical approach to technology that Burton has done in the 2000s. George Basalla's *The Evolution of Technology* (1989) initially broke conceptual ground, for example, by arguing that cultural, social, and political forces drive the evolution of technology. This argument flew against the "hard-determinist" paradigm, which offered a vision of technological change as an internally evolving field, one driven by its own periodization and methodological parameters. Emphasizing externality and contextually offered a new model for understanding technological change, one defined by the tensions between interior logics of technological refinement and the external forces that gave those refinements meaning. In an imperial framework, Basalla's work has been debated and refined. In particular, his characterization of "colonial science" has been subject to critique because of its insistence on "dependency" of expertise between colonial and metropolitan scientists (Adas 1989, 2009; Arnold 2000). The more recent work of Clapperton Mavhunga, moreover, has shown that the notion of technology was not the sole prerogative of colonial powers, but also that of colonial populations by exploring the "technologies of everyday innovation" that subject populations wielded (Mavhunga 2014). For Mahvunga, the question of emphasizing everyday African innovations offers a corrective to Eurocentric assumptions of Africa, and in particular the rural borderlands of Zimbabwe, as sites of technological stasis.

This chapter is comprised of three sections. The first two on settler colonies and the rise of "development" colonialism, respectively, foreground the two arguments outlined earlier: that twentieth-century technologies of state control were sites for the production of difference, and that these technologies were often wielded defensively to affirm European cultural and political power in the face of significant threats to that power. This generally follows a categorization first advanced by Michael Adas, who identifies two schools of imperial thought that shaped how European powers deployed technological knowledge in the colonial world: a "racist" school, which affirmed a fundamental inability of non-Europeans to be able either to use technology or conceptualize its achievements in any form and "the improvers," referring to a cadre of colonial officials who saw the ever-widening technological gap between Europeans and non-Europeans as the result of environmental conditions, a lack of education, and despotic governance. This school saw its ideological adherents push for greater investment in colonial development projects and a more specific focus on the education of colonial subjects in scientific disciplines. This "developmentalist" ideal most firmly took hold after the Second World War, when British and French imperial planners sought to turn African subjects into economically and socially disciplined and urban-dwelling wage workers through the development of industry and the building of European-modeled urban centers.

The final section, which looks at the lives of two postcolonial environmental activists, Wangari Maathai and Ken Saro-Wiwa, evaluates their political activism in light of the institutional echoes of colonialism that they addressed, specifically the production of "native" forms of knowing the natural world and how environmental catastrophe sheds light on global and local political economies. Both Maathai and Saro-Wiwa are exemplary of a contemporary concern over environmental justice and environmental racism, and in particular how the natural world, resources, and ecological epistemologies of the "Global South" become folded into neoliberal networks of capital and political power.

SETTLING LAND, MAKING DIFFERENCE

Histories of settler colonialism show just how central cultural constructions of foreign landscapes have been to articulations of European power and of settler belonging. For the purposes of this chapter, the interstices of technology, landscape, and settler culture in Algeria and Kenya, the sites of perhaps the two most dramatic anticolonial uprisings of the twentieth century, offer productive conceptual spaces to examine the extent to which methods of producing difference relied on tying cultural difference to the "natural world."

Within the field of settler colonial studies, the question of human relationships with nature has been foundational in articulating political community, material power, and cultural belonging in settler societies. Alfred Crosby's argument for the production of "neo-Europes" in the Americas suggested that European settlers did not arrive only with an ideological commitment to property rights and value, produced via labor in nature, but also with a "grunting, lowing, neighing, crowing, chirping, snarling, buzzing, self-replicating and world-altering avalanche" (Crosby 1986: 194). In other words, contemporary settler colonialism was a process catalyzed by multiple invasions: of people, of biomaterial, and of ideas. The most foundational of these ideas was to denude the landscape of its original people and of meaning. In earlier settler colonies like the United States, Canada, and Australia, the discursive emptying of the landscape was matched by a physical, genocidal violence. This destruction or replacement of indigenous bodies with European ones would ultimately render the landscape devoid of indigenous meaning, allowing for European peoples and ideas to flood in and claim mastery over it (Griffiths and Robin 1997). And more specifically, beyond the political violence that has become well documented in Kenya and Algeria, both colonies saw settlers rely on technologies of mobility as particularly potent tools that affirmed the idiom of cultural difference in relation to nature in an effort to make claims to landscapes.

On February 12, 1923, French aviator and businessman Georges Estienne—the founder of the Companie General de Transport Transsaharienne, the first private company to peruse a trans-Saharan road and air route—and a group of French travelers arrived at Fort Kidal, a French colonial outpost in the Adrar region, now part of modern-day Algeria, on specially rigged jeeps that could cross sand dunes. He was there to meet with a man named Baba Oueld Abidine, the son of a family of Touareg nobility who was imprisoned at the fort and who would, an acquaintance assured Estienne, provide critical information needed for Estienne and his team to fulfill their plan of establishing an official overland route from the Algerian coastline to the Sahel.

Crossing the Sahara by car or plane was no simple task. Twentieth-century French Africa was an amalgamation of multiple political entities and ecological zones, from the Moroccan protectorate ruled nominally by a representative indigenous monarchy, to the settler state of Algeria, to the geographically massive administrative units of French West Africa and French Equatorial Africa. The landscapes ranged from Mediterranean maritime spaces on the northern rim, to the high peaks of the Atlas, to the steppes and dunes of the

Sahara. For Estienne, however, the lure of the Sahara was too great not to try to cross it. The romance for the desert, a deeply Orientalist trope inherited from generations of French travelers and writers in Algeria, was a source of inspiration.

Thankfully for Estienne, Abidine did not disappoint him. Piece by piece, Abidine sketched a route from Adrar to the Niger River, informing him of the safest routes used by camel caravans, where the indigenous Touareg knew of fresh water sources, and where Estienne's tires would not sink in the sand. Estienne waxed poetic over the knowledge he had received: he was learning the roots of the "old caravan drivers, whose routes were not known by anyone outside of the Sahara" (Estienne-Mondet 2005: 21). But he also noted that although he believed to be following in the footsteps of the indigenous interlocutors he enlisted to aid his plans, his methods were decidedly different and would yield different results. "New and modern forms of locomotion," he observed, "would make new routes," inspired as they were by the "spirit" that guided earlier attempts to cross the Sahara. As the meeting progressed, Estienne posed a few solitary questions as Abidine "divulged his memories . . . of the infinite plains that only he knew," a land marked by fine, hard sand and the occasional puddle of muddy water (Estienne-Mondet 2005: 21).

At around the same time as French adventurers and Algerian *pieds-noirs* had taken up the Saharan challenge with enthusiasm, white settlers in Kenya were also taking to the skies. On June 27, 1927, *Flight* magazine, an aviation-focused periodical published in the United Kingdom, ran a short piece on the growing enthusiasm for flying among white settlers in East Africa. The article, entitled "Private Flying in Africa," celebrated the arrival of the airplane in East Africa and noted the strong enthusiasm that this form of technology engendered among settlers in the region. The author observed, "The country [Kenya], too, is more enthusiastic by far about aviation matters than the mother country. I know of no other country in the world where the goings of the Air Line [*sic*] are given leaders on the front page of the local papers . . . every word . . . said about aviation was printed, quoted and reprinted dozens of times" (Elliot-Lynn 1927: 354). That same year, Kenyan newspapers covered the gradual growth of aviation in the colony, with a particular focus on the evolution of Imperial Airway's route that would connect Cairo to Cape Town through Kenya at Kisumu, a port city on Lake Victoria. The *East African Standard* kept its readership updated on the details of the construction of runways and hangers at Kisumu, and reported that when the imperial government finished the planning of an air-mail route to Kenya, the Nairobi post office became overrun with enthusiastic patrons hoping to get their first letters out by plane. Excitement over this new form of technology had gripped Kenya's white settler population.

Flying emerged as a technology of Kenyan settler mobility through what was perceived to be a once impenetrable natural world. A series of letters between

Margery Perham and Elspeth Huxley, two European writers intimately familiar with Kenya, engaged the politically fraught topic of land settlement, usage, and civilizational difference in colonial Kenya by alluding to the ways in which European mastery over technology and nature produced a specific cultural register unique to white Europeans in Kenya. Perham suggested:

> Imagine that you are in an airplane over Kenya accompanied by a stranger of common sense and a feeling for justice who is completely ignorant of the Kenya situation . . . Your stranger, leaning over, observes the crowded little farmsteads of the Kikuyu and remarks [on] the dense population . . . [next] your plane sails over the boundary of the European highlands. The stranger makes an exclamation of astonishment . . . At last he says 'who lives in these large farmhouses and wide estates?' [You answer] 'They are Europeans, a different sort of people, and—if you don't understand its rather difficult to explain' (Perham 1944: 43).

Literary scholars have been at the forefront of interrogating this relationship. In the Kenyan case, for example, Tirop Simatei observes that, "What a colonizing topography . . . maps out as untamed, depopulated, [and] wilderness is acknowledged by the indigenous perspective as a scenic landscape of valleys, ridges, and hills that constitute 'the heart and soul' of [indigenous] land" (Simatei 2005: 89). Simatei has also argued, "colonial representation of land and its inhabitants becomes a form of epistemic violence to the extent that it involves immeasurable disruption and erasure of local cultural systems . . . [a] colonial representation aimed at the suppressions of the difference of the 'other'" (Simatei 2005: 85).

As scholars of French imperialism in North Africa have shown, French settlers also filled the Algerian landscape with historical and cultural meaning (Heffernan 1991; Lorcin 1995; Ford 2008; Zarobell 2010). From the beginnings of the occupation of the country after the Ottomans, the French constructed the northern rim of the territory as a decidedly Roman one (Lorcin 2002). The landscape ceased to be a patchwork of Ottoman-administered units of Arab or Berber political identities but one with a direct link to a classical past. Even more specifically, it was referred to as the granary of the Roman empire, linking it inextricably in the French cultural imaginary to European landscapes (Davis 2007). The Sahara was different, unsurprisingly. Describing the artistic work of painters such as Gustave Guillaume and Eugene Fromentin, Michael Heffernnan, for example, suggests the desert emerges as a place not just of adventure but also of expiration. This notion of expiration, of uncertain European death, while first articulated in the nineteenth century, is central to understanding how twentieth-century explorers, moving through the desert in cars and planes, imbued their relationship to the landscape with meaning. And, as Benjamin Claude Brower (2011) has shown, efforts at expanding imperial statecraft to the reaches of the Sahara most distant from Algiers were ultimately piecemeal, as the material power of the colonial state being was unevenly distributed in regions distant from the loci of the French colonial state in the more populous northern reaches of the colony. Growing frustrations with the inability to manage the peoples and ecologies of the desert saw the French embrace systematic violence as the predominant register of a perpetually enervated colonial state. Ultimately it was the indigenous people of the desert—the "noble" Tuareg of the French imaginary—who truly understood the desert (Figure 3.1).

It was for this reason that the Sahara endured in the French imagination as a place only understood by indigenous peoples, making Estienne's meeting with Abidine significant at the time. It also demonstrated the limits of the French colonial state. Close to eighty years after taking control of the North African territory, the Sahara was still a massive natural obstacle to contiguous unchallenged French rule. Estienne's appropriation of Tuareg ecological and commercial knowledge of the desert landscape—where the safest and most efficient routes lay—speaks to the cultural cleavages the French imagined that the Sahara produced. In lieu of becoming peoples of the desert, however, technological power would ultimately grant them access to that knowledge; the

FIGURE 3.1: French Foreign Legion postcard, 1952. Credit: Art Media/Print Collector/Getty Images.

wing and the tire would eventually eliminate whatever knowledge gap there was between European and African.

In East Africa, the question of European belonging in the central highland landscape was a defensive strategy aimed at two distinct communities: displaced Gikuyu peoples whose homesteads had been wrestled away by newly arrived Europeans, and an immigrant South Asian community that sought land holdings in the highlands after the establishment of a politically powerful settler community. The supplanting of European farms in place of Gikuyu ones and the turning of the Gikuyu into agricultural "squatters" on their own land was a critical component of turning the highlands into a European landscape, a history that would rear its head most saliently in the Mau Mau uprising of the mid-twentieth century. But in the aftermath of the First World War, the question of Indian political integration into the East African polities of Kenya and Tanganyika emerged as an explosive political question, and one in which the white settlers in Kenya sought to intervene to preserve the racial order of the colony.

The white settler response to the perceived threat of Indian settlement in the highlands was articulated through ecological idiom. They drew on a growing body of pseudo-science throughout Africa and Asia that linked race to environment (Kennedy 1987). Throughout the continent, opinions varied as to what was the most hygienic distance above sea level that would sustain European life. Original estimates ranged from a mere ten to fifteen feet of elevation to as high as many thousands of feet. Perhaps the most extreme example was in central Africa. Explorer MacGregor Laird believed that safety from malarial mosquitoes could only be found above five thousand feet, a conclusion that would influence the Germans to build their colonial capital, Buea, on the slopes of Mount Cameroon. Prominent Kenyan pro-settler paper, *The East African Standard*, frequently ran advertisements for "The Equatorial Hotel" in Entebbe, Uganda that boasted a property that stood "on high ground with two views of the lake" and that it was "high and airy" throughout the 1920s and 1930s. But ultimately this separation was not only a putative question of racial biology, as the multiracial cities of Nairobi and Entebbe are many thousands of feet above sea level. Rather, as Phillip Curtin noted, the "avoidance of disease was not the only motive for moving administrators to higher places. It also satisfied the need to segregate the governors from the governed . . ." (Curtin 1992: 236). The central highlands of Kenya fit this bill, then: the landscape was cool and breezy, reminiscent of England, in stark opposition to the hot and humid coast, and wildlife filled the savannas that dotted East Africa. Its temperate climate mirrored what white settlers saw as temperate cultural and political predilections of Europeans. What technological mastery of the natural world would offer, then, was a strategy to empty that landscape of the native peoples therein, and any others who sought to gain access to it.

In the eyes of European settlers, this temperance of climate and of culture was threatened by the specter of Indian landownership. Not only was it a threat to white political hegemony, but it was also a natural transgression. Indians, as the ghettos of Nairobi and Mombasa had shown in their opinion, lived in perpetual states of squalor and disease, a condition they naturally embraced. The breezy green spaces of the highlands would either ultimately not suit Indian cultural norms it was thought, or the space would be corrupted; it would be better for the Indians to stay in the prophylactic urban spaces of Nairobi or in the tropical lowlands of the coast. And it was from the airplane ultimately that these differences could be properly understood, as Perham suggested in her letter.

What both the Kenyan "Indian Question" and the perpetual inability of the French to establish political control in the Sahara reveal is that the natural world was a site of political and cultural contestation, not merely a grid across which European power naturally unfolded. It was for the multiple reasons outlined earlier that these spaces disrupted European aspirations, and that technological feats of mobility exemplified in the automobile and airplane fit into a broader strategy of the political displacement of indigenous peoples and the marginalization of upwardly mobile Indian communities. Separate from the multiple land acts and racialized urban planning schemes that sought to physically separate by race, the enthusiasm for flying added cultural grist to this political machine by defining how Europeans saw themselves in relation to the natural world. Arjun Appadurai's work has, for example, attempted to theorize questions of race, indigeneity, mobility, and ecological space by suggesting that the European efforts to systemize the social life of indigenous people created the category of the "native" as persons "who are from certain places . . . belong to those [and] are *incarcerated*, or confined, in those places . . ." (Appadurai 1988: 37). This corresponds with an assumption of physical immobility as well as intellectual immobility. Natives are confined, in Europeans' minds, to the "ecological niches" they occupy and "modes of thought" that inform their relationships to those niches. The native thus emerges not only as animalistic—confined to its ecological niche—but also cognitively incapable of intellectualizing this predicament; modern technology is rendered superfluous to the immediate needs of the native. The intellectual consequences of this mode of thought are made clear in how Europeans represent Africans through the framework of aviation.

But ultimately, the argot of ecological difference that technology like the automobile and airplane allowed in colonial spaces offered a teleology of European mastery over both time and space, a methodological critique first identified in George Basalla's work. This sentiment of historical change was perhaps most succinctly articulated in writer Léon Sougnenet's observations on his travels through the Algerian M'zab, entitled "The Last Camel, the First Tire, the First Wing" (1918), which evinced the naturalness of both technological development and imperial power suggesting that European technology of mobility had replaced "traditional" ones, a replacement that harkened a new cultural and political rule by Europe. A closer look at the Kenyan and Algerian moments shows that the nearly contemporaneous examples of Algerian adventurers and Kenyan settlers embracing new forms of technology and mobility and wielding those developments in relation to the natural world do not only speak to a methodical and inevitable movement of European mastery of the environment. Rather, they show just how contested a cultural terrain these respective landscapes—the White Highlands and the Sahara—had become to affirming European imperial power.

ENVIRONMENTAL TECHNOCRACY AND CULTURES OF DEVELOPMENT

Of course, white settlers did not constitute a significant proportion of the population in most spaces under imperial colonial rule in the twentieth century. And while this demographic difference meant substantive alterations in the cultural history of these colonial spaces, the foundational twentieth-century assumption that linked European power to technological mastery over the natural world endured. This belief took new and significant meaning in the post-Second World War era of British, French, and Portuguese colonial rule, where older models of resource-extractive industries and "indirect rule" political structures were supplanted by a discursively more genteel form of colonial rule, which emphasized the building of European-style governmental institutions and the explicit construction of an urban, wage-earning proletariat.

In the years following the end of the Second World War, imperial powers embraced an agenda broadly considered as "development colonialism" that sought to "stabilize" what were perceived as unruly and culturally incompatible colonial subjects. The shift in governing philosophy to "development" by colonial states, produced efforts to rationalize both indigenous populations and landscapes to make them legible to colonial states. This legibility, as James Scott first argued, sought to simplify state efforts at collecting taxes, at conscription, and at suppressing rebellion (Scott 1998: 2). In the African context, Frederick Cooper has shown the extent to which development colonialism shaped the historical development of the continent, most notably around questions of citizenship and civic participation in ascendant forms of colonial statecraft. Africans became colonial citizens, labor organizers, schoolteachers, and civil servants, positions that integrated indigenous peoples into the structures of state government in then unprecedented ways (Cooper 2002: 38–132).

An important corollary to the production of new colonial bureaucracies and subject populations was the wielding of new technologies against the natural world. These efforts took place most spectacularly around the building of massive infrastructure projects as well as efforts to build governmental institutions that would ostensibly protect colonial subjects and the state more broadly against threats that the natural world would play, from disease to natural disaster. Throughout Africa and Asia, colonial states of the British, French, and Portuguese built dams, canalized rivers, spread pesticides, constructed new homes, and sought to eradicate endemic diseases. This happened, of course, at the same time as these technologies also devastated the natural world in places such as French Indochina and British Malaya through the extraction of rubber, among other things.

Collectively, efforts at intervening in the natural world through new methods of technological expertise both relied upon and produced new cultural logics that reflected, in part, a significant departure from settler societies. The moral prerogatives of development that sparked state technological intervention in the natural world required a cultural construction of indigenous peoples as incapable of fully understanding the ecological spaces they occupied. On one hand, this affirmed earlier assumptions of indigenous entrapment in ecological niches, while it also suggested that this positionality was ultimately transgressive, a drag on the teleology of state development, the refinement of technologies of natural management, and the unifying of that ability with new technologies of governance. This shift resulted in an uneven folding of native peoples into new systems of "rational" environmental stewardship in the service of state-building.

The (un)production for indigenous "rationality" was, and indeed continues to be, most often argued in the realm of human–environment relations. As African economic historians have shown, for example, early European explorers assumed that African land usage patterns belied certain cultural assumptions that "embedded" decision-making in social relations, not rational, profit-seeking decision-making abilities. Africa was, after all, relatively land rich and under-populated in the eyes of Europeans, rendering most of its territory vacant and underexploited in their estimation. This was, of course, both a willing misrepresentation by some and misunderstanding by others on the part of newly arrived colonial agents. The power of this supposed epistemological (and indeed civilizational) cleavage was subsequently folded into questions of economic development through the work of Karl Polanyi. Polanyi's hugely influential 1944 study, *The Great Transformation*, argued that the production of markets in Great Britain allowed it to develop at an exponential rate compared with the rest of the world (Hopkins 1973; Austin 2005). These markets presupposed that actors within them adopted a logic of maximum efficiency and profit-seeking in an environment of scarcity. It was thus argued that native peoples throughout the colonial world made decisions not through rational, profit-maximizing choice but rather by cultural compulsion, for reasons that responded to their societal and cultural commitments. This argument drew from and affirmed colonial-era ethnographic descriptions of African societies operating outside of the parameters of rational choice.

The idea that the natural world could be rationally improved upon was, of course, not a new belief solely possessed by mid-twentieth-century imperial powers. As many scholars have shown, the notion of the "Anthropocene" extends back centuries (McNeill and Engelke 2016; Mikhail 2016). But in imperial spaces in the twentieth century, the acceleration of human intervention brought by technology allowed for colonial planners to articulate notions of state-centered developmentalist paternalism while also emphasizing the cultural cleavages between Europeans and non-Europeans. The postwar construction of massive infrastructure projects and the initiation of disease eradication efforts exemplified, in the eyes of colonial planners, an indelible marker of difference between European, African, and Asian forms of collective governance and the cultural priorities therein against the foil of the natural world. But like the settler cultures of before, these projects should also be viewed as broader state strategies of self-preservation and protection.

The Second World War and immediate postwar environmental history of Mauritius, for example, shows just that. The 1943 Japanese occupation of Burma and the Bengal cyclone of the same year shattered the food economy of the Indian Ocean World.[1] The dramatic collapse of the oceanic rice markets, for example, led to a profound reorientation in the comestible regimes of the island, spearheaded by hand-wringing colonial officials who, remembering riots in 1937 that were sparked, in part, by a chronic lack of food, saw the reconstruction of domestic nutrition systems as critical not only to the economic longevity of the island but also to its political stability. These new efforts saw women become the objects of state plans to build families around sustainably produced and highly nutritious food. This shift was informed by detailed studies of the anatomical and molecular structures of poor Mauritians, whose skin, spleens, and blood served as the raw data around which resources to build a sustainable society were mobilized. In one example, the colonial state argued for a move away from the south Asian staple of *daal* to meat, in order to increase protein in the poor's diet: a shift that pleased some Indo-Mauritian leaders, horrified others, and thus emerged as a focal point for mid-century articulations of belonging for Indo-Mauritians.

Two assumptions were at the heart of the actions of these colonial officials: the first being that the politics of cultivating local food production was a prudent defensive strategy against potential political unrest, the kind which had gripped the colony less than a decade earlier when peasants effectively temporarily upended the colonial sugar economy. The second was the contention that development in Mauritius had to be centered around a set of cultural prerequisites that Indo-Mauritians possessed. The Labor Department, which oversaw the massive development schemes of the mid-century, was under the direction of a handful of colonial officials who believed deeply in the cultural incommensurability between African and Indian peoples and Europeans that revolved around distinct relationships to the natural world. So, while much of continental African economic development was directed toward the construction of an urban proletariat, "development" in Mauritius was conducted under the auspices of an imperial commitment to inculcate a south Asian work-ethic, one leaning more heavily toward agricultural work than wage earning. "The Indo-Mauritian Laborer", the commissioner of labor in the colony observed, "did not want to be industrialized" (Wilkinson 1939).

This assumption, that Indo-Mauritians were fundamentally anti-industrialization, is revelatory of the broader political and social questions that informed how colonial states exerted material power over their subjects and over the natural world more broadly. Throughout the colony, efforts at improving the landscape—making it more amenable for the production of the island's monocrop, sugar—reproduced assumptions of cultural difference. Anxious about allowing Indians to migrate to the steadily expanding urban centers of the islands, colonial officials within the labor and public welfare departments of the colony, the two state institutions tasked with managing the social and political development of the colony, drafted their development plans along two critical and closely linked beliefs about Mauritius. The first was that Mauritius was a "hyperendemic" space, one where disease, and in particular malaria, was indigenous and perpetually a threat. This was, it should be said, a stark departure from centuries of colonial thought regarding the environment of the island, which was long thought to be a tropical paradise. The second was the cultural incommensurability of Indian laborers with urban life. Indians, one public welfare official observed, reproduced "like flies" when housed in the burgeoning peri-urban centers around Port Louis and throughout Plaines Wilhems, the most populous of the island's districts (Wilkinson 1939: 2–3). At the same time, however, the erstwhile governor of the island in the postwar era, Sir Bede Clifford, embarked on a mission to produce massive irrigation works that would source fresh water from the island's reservoirs to the estates and small Indo-Mauritian landowners. These irrigation works would also seek to eliminate pools of stagnated water throughout the island, a breeding ground for *Anopheles* mosquitoes, the vectors of malaria (Figure 3.2).

Taken together, then, efforts to make the colony food-independent and disease-free were informed by broader cultural assumptions that envisioned an island worked by agriculturally oriented peasants while overseen by a techno-state responsible for irrigation, disease eradication, and the management of a nutritionally healthy population. As the history of this corner of the Indian Ocean shows, the middle of the twentieth century was also a moment of the harmonizing of state strategies of management in regards to both natural and social threat. Indeed, the concurrent ascendance of the figure of the social

FIGURE 3.2: Irrigation channels for sugar cane crops, Mauritius. Credit: Kate Hopper.

scientist, natural scientist, and bureaucrat at mid-century points to what Timothy Mitchell has called the "rule of experts" (2002), when technocratic expertise harmonized with state technologies of control over its subjects and its landscapes.

RECKONING WITH POSTCOLONIAL ECOLOGICAL LEGACIES

Postcolonial theorists have sought to understand how colonial forms of knowledge and state governance that produced gender, racial, and class subjectivities in the colonial era, have endured beyond the formal end of empire. With regards to the environmental history of the twentieth century, scholars of environment and technology initially folded questions of the exercise of state power in nature into already established paradigms of economic asymmetry such as dependency theory (Portuondo 2009). More recently, however, scholars working across geographies and temporalities have asserted that while the history of violent resource extraction from naturally rich Africa and Asia is critical to understanding the ways in which late colonial and postcolonial nations were folded into neoliberal global commodity and financial markets, environmental historians writing on the cultural history of empires and the natural world have embraced the interventions first made by postcolonial theorists by focusing on how questions of racial and gendered difference first articulated around moments of colonial intervention in the natural world have endured (Nixon 2013).

Pursuant of these critiques of culture and empire, the examples of two world-renown African environmental activists in the postcolonial era—Kenyan Wangari Maathai and Nigerian Ken Saro-Wiwa—shed light on the ways in which the echoes of colonial statecraft and subject-making have shaped the post-independence history of their respective nations. Maathai's work to re-center indigenous forms of land management and women's relationship to the ecological spaces they inhabit was in direct response to colonial era institutional norms that emphasized the cordoned-off political and cultural space of British expertise. Saro-Wiwa's work, similarly centered on the question of ethnic belonging in a multi-ethnic petrol-state, where the narrow channels of political power and international capital first cemented in the waning days of empire systematically damaged the ecological spaces that Niger Delta communities called home.

In 1972, faced with a growing scientific consensus on climate change and the need to build systems of ecological, social, and political resilience to respond to this crisis, the United Nations Environmental Program (UNEP) was founded, establishing its first office in Nairobi, Kenya. One of the first members of the Nairobi office was the late Wangari Maathai, the renowned Kenyan biologist, veterinarian, and environmental activist. Born in 1940, Maathai was educated in both East Africa and the United States, as a member of the Kennedy airlift program, where she studied biology at the University of Pittsburgh. Her work for the United Nations was a logical outcome of her previous work and life experience. She observed that, "[m]y background as a biological scientist and daughter of a peasant farmer provided the seed for growth and long-term commitment to the environment" (Maathai 2004: 9). In the decades following this introduction into environmental activism, Maathai would go on to found the world-renowned Greenbelt Movement (GBM) in Kenya, an initiative to combat growing concerns over deforestation throughout that country.

Greenbelt was a revolutionary movement, and one for which Maathai would ultimately win the Nobel Peace Prize. Its mission was to replace deforested areas throughout Kenya with new trees, an effort that was spearheaded by Kenyan women, a decision which Maathai noted had allowed many Kenyan women to become amateur forestry experts in their own right (2004: 26). Greenbelt democratized professional forestry knowledge by bringing non-experts into countrywide efforts to halt deforestation. This was not without its challenges. Maathai noted that the expansion of forestry as an amateur art irritated professionals. Claims that forestry had become "adulterated" was a common complaint she noted, but one ultimately that did little to stymie the movement. "After all," Maathai noted, "they had for a long time successfully cultivated various crops on their own farms. What was so difficult to applying this knowledge to tree planning?" (2004: 27). The observation that technical know-how was not solely proprietary to the realm of the expert was a theme she observed in her own autobiographical sketches. Maathai saw herself as an inheritor, as were many Kenyan women, of an intellectual and social tradition of ecological stewardship. Equally important, Maathai situated her work within a deeper historical context that extended beyond her personal life, one that accounted for Kenya's fraught colonial history. As she notes in her recounting of the Greenbelt Movement, the political will to organize women in Kenya was not merely a fashionable accouterment of development language, but rather a corrective to a long history of gendered violence and political exclusion in colonial Kenya. She traced the genesis of the Greenbelt Movement to the national Council of Women in Kenya (NCWK), an organization founded in 1964, the year after Kenya's independence. The NCWK itself, she noted, was an outgrowth of the Maendeleo ya Wanawake Organization (MYWO), an organization "established, packaged, and managed by wives of British administrators during the Mau Mau struggle" (2004: 31). That the genesis of a major women's organization in Kenya was to be found in the governmental struggle against Mau Mau is significant, as it was structured around institutional powers and the political prerogatives of the state; the group was seen as a palliative for women eager to participate or at least support Mau Mau in the central highlands.

Greenbelt, however, was not only a women's organization that sought to heal political and ethnic fault lines opened during colonial rule, but also one invested in environmental stewardship and building regional and national identity around the question of environmental care. The initial goal was, Maathai noted, "to raise the consciousness of community members to a level that would drive them to what was right for the environment because their hearts had been touch and their minds convinced." This took place most saliently around the tree-planting campaign initiated by the GBM. The goals were multiple: to help community members establish a sustainable source of wood fuel, to generate income for rural women, to promote environmental consciousness among the youth, to empower people at the grass roots, to demonstrate the capacity of women in development, to curb soil erosion, and to disseminate information on environmental conservation (Maathai 2004: 33–40).

On the other side of the continent, and about three decades after Maathai had begun her work, Ken Saro-Wiwa was organizing a disruptive political machine against a postcolonial Nigerian state increasingly reliant on a political and economic structure that privileged the extraction and marketing of crude oil in the Niger Delta. An ethnic Ogoni intellectual and environmental activist, Saro-Wiwa hailed from the Ogoni region of what is now known as the Rivers State, in the country's south-east. The Ogoni people, together with the other ethnic groups of Rivers State, have been at the epicenter of the ecological degeneration of their lands, lands on which in the late 1950s Shell Oil discovered massive amounts of subterranean crude oil. Crude extraction in Rivers State began in earnest in 1958 and almost immediately thereafter the colonial government granted concessions to Shell Oil to commence drilling, who argued that only they could provide the technical know-how to extract, refine, and bring to market the newly discovered crude. And although there were efforts to "indigenize" the oil economy in the early postcolonial decade, particularly through the establishment of the Nigerian National Petroleum Organization, the industry remained a "enclave industry," one where "technology, management, and profits are mostly controlled by transnational corporations" (Adamson *et al.* 2012: 233).

For the Ogoni people in particular, the discovery of oil was catastrophic (Figure 3.3). One of many ethnic groups in a plural colonial and postcolonial Nigerian state, they were particularly vulnerable to Shell malpractice: spills, leaks, and political corruption saw their lands both violently expropriated and heavily polluted. It was out of these conditions that Ogoni political action against Shell and the complicit Nigerian state emerged in the 1980s and 1990s. Officially, the movement is believed to have begun with the drafting of the Ogoni Bill of Rights in 1990, a document that Saro-Wiwa himself is believed to have authored. The document outlined not only the grievances of the Ogoni related to the injustices of Shell's work in the region, but also emphasized the

FIGURE 3.3: Nigeria. Bomu, Kpor, Ogoni Area—ecological destruction due to petroleum. Credit: Markus Matzel/ullstein bild via Getty Images.

historical and cultural specificity of the Ogoni. This document laid the intellectual groundwork for what would become the Movement for the Survival of the Ogoni People (MOSOP), a political action group of which Saro-Wiwa was the head.

The question of Ogoni history and cultural specificity was a critical component to articulating their ecological grievances. In a 1993 speech before three thousand Ogoni at the city of Bori, Saro-Wiwa made sure to couch his critiques of the petro-capitalism of Nigeria in the language of indigeneity and the significance of the landscape. While celebrating the achievements of indigenous peoples of Asia, Australia, and the Americas in raising their political profile, African indigenous peoples received only "scant attention" from international organizations (Tal 2006: 186). The Ogoni were no different he argued than the Maori of New Zealand and the Indians of the Americas. But what bound them together more tightly within the category of indigeneity was "their common history . . . of the usurpation of their land and their resources, the destruction of their culture, and the eventual decimation of their people" (Tal 2006: 186). He went on: "For a multinational oil company, Shell, to take over thirty billion dollars from the small, defenseless Ogoni people and putting back nothing but degradation and death is a betrayal of all humanity" (Tal 2006: 187). Saro-Wiwa thus saw his activism as situated within a global conversation on belonging and environmental justice. And by linking the struggle of the Ogoni to broader political questions of nation, ethnicity, and ecology, he sought to internationalize the questions of ecological justice as a counterpart to the global movement of capital that enabled the destruction of Ogoniland. Ultimately, the state sought to silence Saro-Wiwa's activism, after being arrested on trumped-up charges pursued by the Abacha regime that accused him of participating, along with eight other activists, in the execution of four Ogoni chiefs. He was hanged in 1995 in the Rivers District capital city of Port Harcourt.[2]

The histories of environmental activists like Wangari Maathai and Ken Saro-Wiwa offer two distinct perspectives on the nature of postcolonial ecological politics and culture. The first, exemplified through the sketch of Maathai, was the reappropriation of technological and environmental know-how previously coopted by the techno-state of late colonial rule that affirmed presuppositions of backward colonial subjects. Secondly, Ken Saro-Wiwa's life shows, among other things, that the echoes of what Frederick Cooper has identified as the "the gatekeeper state" model of political economy in continental Africa had profound cultural resonances in the second half of the twentieth century.

As the previous section outlined, the rise of the techno-state was a process initiated by colonial powers in the aftermath of the Second World War as part of a shift toward "development colonialism." With political independence, however, a cadre of urban, educated elites took control of the state bureaucracies that had once been occupied by Europeans. The image of the backward "native" would, in many cases, endures as a caricature of the rural citizen of the postcolonial state. Peasants from Egypt, Tanzania, India, and Indochina emerged as both the symbolic cultural heart of the postcolonial state, while also as potential threats to its economic and cultural advancement. As such, the political inheritors of the colonial state directed their reformist efforts at these rural subjects. As Dipesh Chakrabarty has noted, there existed a "pedagogical style of developmental politics" in the "Third World:" anticolonial and postcolonial leaders emphasized the need to "catch up with" western powers by devoting resources to scientific knowledge production and cultural modernization (Chakrabarty 2010: 54).

In Egypt, for example, Timothy Mitchell points out that one of the clearest examples of this kind of postcolonial developmentalist ideology was made manifest in the construction of the Aswan high dam in the south of Egypt. The high dam was spearheaded by the revolutionary nationalist government of Gamal Abdel Nasser, but was ultimately an extension of the broader project of Aswan low dam, a British colonial endeavor meant to facilitate agricultural development through the management of flooding and irrigation techniques on the Nile. Nasser's high dam wielded the political and ecological power that came with the dam's construction for the political advancement of the postcolonial Egyptian regime, arguing that its construction in the 1960s was necessary to develop a postcolonial Egyptian state. In Nasser's estimation, it would both allow the country to produce its own energy independence, and demonstrate its technical acumen. The state would "bring the expertise of modern engineering, technology, and social science to improve the defects of nature, to transform peasant agriculture, to repair the ills of society, and to fix the economy" (Mitchell 2002: 15).[3]

Wangari Maathai's insistence on equipping rural women with forestry skills, though, was never in the service of the political prerogatives of the Kenyan state.[4] Maathai saw her work as enacting democratic change by pulling ecological expertise out of the realm of the institutionally sanctioned expert, and by foregrounding previously ignored methods of understanding, rationalizing, and existing with nature. Similarly, Saro-Wiwa's struggle against the environmental damage and economic plundering of Nigeria affirms Frederick Cooper's contention that postcolonial African nations were "successor" states in that they operated as an assemblage of inherited institutions and that they unflinchingly embraced the state project of development from their colonial pasts (Cooper 2002: 155–6). Development, of course, in south-eastern Nigeria meant the wholesale exploitation of crude oil. Nigeria emerged in the postcolonial world, and in particular in relation to the production of crude oil, as exemplary of the "gatekeeper state," where national governments acted as overseers and collectors of profit that these states could bring from the export of raw materials. In large part, then, questions of environmental stewardship were thus sidelined under this model of postcolonial statecraft to the prerogatives of globalizing capital through the facilitation and development of export-oriented markets.

Indeed, Saro-Wiwa's political organizing illuminates the ways in which local political economies of oil exploitation not only lay the foundations for domestic political repression, but also how they undergird networks of production and exchange that supply the world with oil. This critique speaks poignantly to the contemporary political and ecological moment, as the relationship between oil production and postcolonial statecraft is front and center of American political and economic interests in the Persian Gulf and in growing concerns over the sustainability of carbon-driven economies. As Timothy Mitchell has shown, however, methods of crude oil extraction, refinement, and movement across space also shape the very political, social, and economic structures of the sites of production and consumption, as well as at intermediary sites. More specifically, oil defines debates over governance, citizenship, and belonging, a power that Mitchell (2001) calls "carbon democracy." The reliance on carbon-based fuels in the United States, moreover, is not merely a material reality but also a cultural one: the cultural significance of, say, the gas-powered automobile lays front and center of American cultural touchstones of expansion, mobility, and domesticity. So just as oil defines systems of governance and modes of articulating citizenship in places like Kuwait and Iraq, so does it in the United States.

That these connections between carbon and governance in the United States render it a "petro-state" like those in the Middle East for whom the title is usually reserved, speaks to intimate and enduring ties between ecological exploitation and global imperial power. Indeed, while the legacies of French, Portuguese, and British imperial power shaped the political and cultural histories of postcolonial nations, the ascendancy in the twentieth century of the United States as a global imperial force also contributed to the environmental histories of once colonized places. Indeed, as the Cold War ran hot throughout much of Latin America, Africa, and Asia, the United States became the inheritor of a global political and economic order defined by European control over peoples, places, and resources. And while the United States, itself a settler state, had extended its formal political control over territories in the Pacific and Caribbean in the nineteenth and early twentieth centuries, American global expansion also shaped "natural worlds" of former European colonies in later years, including ones that do not produce crude oil.

South-east Asia is a particularly illustrative example where American power was articulated, in part, in relation to the natural world in the decades following the end of empire. The Vietnam War, for example, proved to be an intractable conflict for the Americans not only because of the military strategy pursued by North Vietnamese forces, but also because of the difficulty of fighting a war in tropical rainforests. Throughout the 1960s, American forces initiated operation

FIGURE 3.4: A Fairchild C-123 Provider cargo plane sprays Agent Orange over a forest in North Vietnam. Credit: Bettmann/Contributor.

"Ranch Hand," which was the spraying of twenty million gallons of herbicide that defoliated millions of trees, allowing for American pilots more easily to identify targets that had once been obscured. Agent Orange, as the herbicide is now widely known, would scar not only the landscape of Vietnam, but also the Vietnamese and Americans fighting in the war (Figure 3.4). Agent Orange was later identified as a cause of multiple forms of cancer and bodily disfigurement (Haberman 2014). The embedding of toxicity into the Vietnamese landscape, a task also advanced by the wanton use of napalm against Vietnamese civilians by the Americans, was mirrored in the bodies of those who fought there. As Leslie Regan as showed, not only had physical disfigurements emerged among those initially exposed to the herbicide, but also in the children of American soldiers, effectively inscribing the violence against the natural world into the genetic material of those who first inhabited it (Reagan 2016).

CONCLUSION

If the global environmental history of the twentieth century is, in part, a story of how technological change expanded the temporal and spatial scales of human intervention in the natural world, a culturally focused history of how Western empires wielded that change reveals multiple stories on how colonial states and their postcolonial progeny produced difference through the register of human–environment relations. Synchronizing argumentative frameworks that emphasize the contingency of categories like empire and technology shows that imperial myth-making relied heavily on the assumed inability of non-European peoples to escape the ecological prisons Europeans presumed they inhabited. Technological advancements in the twentieth century not only appeared to affirm this assumption, but also stood as evidence of an ever-evolving European cultural inheritance.

But these technological feats—the crossing of the desert by car or surveying the landscape by plane—often belied political instability. Technological change was not merely a tale of raw innovation, but rather a reaction to threat. The inability of the French to "pacify" the Sahara and the fears of racial invasion in the Kenyan highlands pushed both settler communities to invest technological change with moral and cultural values that would mark them as different from the colonial subjects they shared space with. The legacies of these colonial cultures were ultimately inherited by postcolonial states. To this end, the lives of activists like Wangari Maathai and Ken Saro Wiwa show just how colonial-era projects aimed at managing and exploiting the natural world ultimately molded questions of citizenship, gender, and ethnicity in the postcolonial world.

CHAPTER FOUR

Labor

DANIEL BENDER

In 1934, George Orwell published *Burmese Days*, an alcohol-soaked depiction of life in an outpost of the teak-producing colony in the waning days of British rule in Burma. Orwell, most obviously, focused on the degradation of British colonists, trapped by their longing for a metropolitan home they had barely seen and by the grim reality of life in the humid colony. The novel is also a startling labor history. Its plot revolves around the evil plan of an indigenous government official to destroy his enemies, in particular a well-meaning native doctor seeking entry into the colonial club. The few white colonists nearby gather at the club for desultory conversation and many drinks. A refuge for white men and women surrounded by natives they hire, fear, and despise, the club is emblematic of a weary, bankrupt empire. Even ice has become a rare treat in the threadbare club, built, like the empire itself, on a foundation of racial exclusion and white supremacy. At the story's climax, an angry native mob surrounds the club, a microcosm—again—of an empire besieged by colonial peoples increasingly reluctant to accede to an imperial racial division of labor.

In Orwell's interpretation (so well versed in the experience of the European labor and socialist movements), the uprising is not a radical rebellion or a labor struggle. Instead, he describes it as a spontaneous, if easily dispersed, mob intent on venting their rage on an obvious symbol of colonial rule. Looking out from the windows of the club, Orwell scorned the justification of empire as civilizing and modernizing. His native characters are a sad bunch: a devious low-level official who has (literally) fattened himself through his corruption; a doctor pathetically supportive of an empire that insulted him; a woman cynically selling sex to a white man; a disapproving, if loyal, servant; and a faceless crowd of workers hired to cut teak in Burma's jungles. The white men and women, meanwhile, are middling sorts forced by the pressures of inheritance to seek their fortunes in the colonies.

From teak cutters to sex workers to servants, each of his characters reveals the vast mobilizations of labor of the British empire. The bitterness they all express provides an important insight into the labor and cultural history of the twilight years of imperialism. It highlights how notions of racial superiority had hardened over the nineteenth century and into the post-First World War years. Management regimes based on notions of race hierarchy struggled to contain the liberationist impulses of the millions mobilized to meet the labor needs of empire. Yet, like so many other European critics of empire, Orwell had little faith in the ability of Burmese teak workers to transform the empire. They were rioters, not revolutionaries.

Notions of racial difference profoundly shaped the multifarious experiences of those workers who made empires work. Yet that same racial logic that underpinned colonial capitalism faltered under the stresses of economic collapse, Fascism and Nazism, and Cold War. Organized workers also collectively challenged empire and the capitalism it forged. Yet Orwell's dismissal of the resistance of ordinary people is telling. Both leaders of independence movements and imperial officials (and, too often, latter-day historians) treated "solidarity" as little more than a slogan. It deserves closer analysis, set against the long and comparative histories of empire. At the end of the imperial age and into the era of decolonization, how did shared cultures enable workers to stand together? What impact did solidarity have upon independence movements? How did working-class solidarities challenge the racialized systems of labor mobilization that shaped modern, global capitalism?

REPRESENTING THE COLONIZED WORKING CLASS BETWEEN THE WARS

In March 1924, the journalist Donald Maxwell enjoyed a pre-opening tour of the British Empire exhibition in the London suburb of Wembley. The buildings and grounds were finished, but awaited their crowds. With the British Empire still reeling from the staggering costs—both human and financial—of the First World War, the British Empire Exhibition highlighted the commercial possibilities of empire. If Orwell's *Burmese Days* presented a bleak picture of the whole empire embodied in the drama of a small colonial outpost, this world's fair optimistically showcased progress and industry. First, Maxwell marveled at the soaring arches of the great halls advertising the mechanical genius of British industry and the many products exported to the metropole from the colonies.

Then, he found what he was truly looking for: the African Village. He boasted about the creativity of British carpenters, trade unionists who had so mastered their scientific skill that they could faithfully reproduce humble African houses with all their cracked, uneven corners. This was the Africa he—and visitors after him—longed to see: a preserve of the primitive, not an industrialized outpost of global capitalism (Britton 2010). Here in the African Village, the exhibition contrasted African picturesque savagery with British industry, a passage from savagery to civilization.

This was a common cultural trope, born in prewar world's fairs and continued apace after the Armistice. In 1937, the Exposition Internationale des Arts et Techniques dans la Vie Moderne opened in Paris. The long shadow of the Eiffel Tour tied the fair to prewar expositions that also showcased the many industrial triumphs of European empires. Yet the imposing Soviet and Nazi buildings faced each other in a somber warning of future conflict and of the ideological currents of the new era. World's fairs on both sides of the Atlantic persisted in their representation of colonial subjects, less as workers intensely engaged in the wage labor world of colonial capitalism, than as primitive curiosities (Greenhalgh 1988; Barton 1994). World's fairs, of course, were not alone in picturing Africa and Asia as remaining pockets of savagery in a modern world. Growing cinematic cultures, for example, including blockbuster films like "King Kong" or "Tarzan," still caste Africans as tribal peoples caught in savage jungles, not proletarians coerced into wage labor by the structures of imperial rule.

Yet world's fairs were not free from working-class and union protest. Fairs were, as historians have only recently recognized, big workplaces and just as world's fair were meant to represent the colonized world both in miniature and in ideal, so, too, did they represent a microcosm of a global working class fractured and divided along racial lines. At Wembley, for example, workers protested the "sweated" conditions of exposition workers and again in New York in 1939, unions actively organized those workers who built the buildings or performed music—except those imported from the tropics as evidence of savagery. Workers' union wage, hours, and conditions demands extended only to white workers. Promoters were granted dispensations from "closed shop" enforcement only when they employed dancing girls from Bali or Malayan hunters (Bender 2016).

Interwar world's fairs in London, Paris, Chicago, and New York deliberately enforced the gap between the imperial representation of colonized peoples as primitives and their proletarian lived experiences in places like Zambia (formerly the colony of Northern Rhodesia), at the heart of the British southern African empire, or in rural Angola, one of the last vestiges of the Portuguese empire. In both cases, wage labor, instead of subsistence farming, was the norm rather than exception. Especially during and after the First World War, British colonial officials sought to develop Zambia, the colony they once regarded as a labor reserve for South African mines. Even before the war, residents north of the

Zambezi River had migrated in large numbers to mine mineral deposits in Zimbabwe (formerly the colony of Southern Rhodesia). Postwar, with the construction of new railroads and the development of Zambian copper mines, most native Zambian men had experienced wage labor of some kind and duration. Coercive labor recruitment drew native men into wage economies. Local recruiters often threatened native men with jail for their inability to pay taxes in cash-poor economies unless they signed labor contracts (Henderson 1974).

If in Zambia the exploitation of cash-poor farmers induced wage labor, forced labor was the official policy of the Portuguese in nearby Angola. Local officials collaborated with local police and native guards to enforce the labor tax (*taxa braçal*) (Keese 2013). Some worked in coffee and cotton plantations; others who remained small-scale farmers were forced to plant products (especially cotton) critical for the colony's export and extractive economy. The recruitment, transport, and disciplining of workers in the abusive conditions of European-owned plantation or state projects, became the leading priority of the Portuguese colonial state even into the post-Second World War era (Martin 2012).

The lean times of the interwar years had both economic and cultural effects. The First World War had generated vast new demands for colonial labor (a pattern that would be repeated in the next war), and its effects on Euro-American empires were profound. In the face of new strains placed on Western empires, the era of self-determination in Europe was accompanied by a hardening of the racial logic of colonial capitalism throughout the tropics. Imperial advocates employed a racial logic to defend the insatiable demands of Europe and America for teak, rubber, tropical fruit, cotton, coffee, tea, peanuts, and oils. As the German empire lost its colonies in the postwar treaties, the realization that "self-determination" was an ideal for Europeans alone was not lost on colonial workers in Asia and Africa and the Caribbean.

In the era of high imperialism before the war, colonial boosters had defended empire against critics like John Hobson by arguing that empire was actually a selfless project that led colonized peoples from savagery to civilization. Yet set against the backdrop of the Western Front, claims to civilizing were hard to defend. Instead, increasingly, colonial governments advanced models of empire as partnership, modernizing more than civilizing (Adas 2004). Vast amounts of labor had been mobilized before the war for the grand projects of high imperialism like the Panama Canal (Greene 2009). Such projects, like plantations, docks, and mines, still needed managing.

Thus in 1939, when the artist Georgia O'Keeffe arrived in Hawai'i at the invitation of the Dole Pineapple Company, she encountered both tropical lushness and roiling labor ferment. Just the year before, police had attacked an unarmed and multiethnic union demonstration. A 1922 strike that had engaged thousands of Chinese, Philippine, and Japanese sugar workers was also still fresh in the memory of islanders (Jung 2006). As O'Keeffe visited Hawai'i's sprawling pineapple plantations, she witnessed the human side of a vast Pacific mobilization of Philippine, Japanese, Chinese, and Portuguese workers to cut cane and pineapples (Okihiro 2009: 148–9; Khor 2014: 102–27). O'Keeffe, though, had been brought to the island to produce advertising copy and, soon, her colorful picture of a pineapple bud graced Dole ads.

When they diverted attention to lushness and away from the reality of the industrialized work of colonial economies, O'Keeffe's illustrations met metropolitan consumers' expectations of tropical abundance. The gap between the actuality of imperial economies and representations of the colonized tropics produced its own forms of cultural labor. Even alongside the labor conflict that gripped Hawai'i, the islands were experiencing a boom in tourists arriving by ship and, soon, plane. Upon arrival, lei sellers greeted them. For tourists, it was ample proof that they had stepped into a friendly paradise; for sellers, lei-making was hard work. The leis' flowers "went a long way towards recasting imperialism into a fragile relationship characterized by a longed-for welcome and benevolent friendship," notes Vernadette Vicuña Gonzalez (2015: 161–84). New tourism industry helped Americans make peace with the reality of an empire characterized by economic power, military presence, and geographic expansion.

Lei makers, like those working hard in world's fair villages, were laborers whose very livelihood depended on performing the roles demanded by Euro-American visitors. Yet they were also defending longstanding cultural practices, like the giving of leis, against the intrusion of outsiders. Their labor, rather than complicit or collaborationist, was part of the way the mobilization of labor needed by empire depended on notions of racial hierarchy that were at once firmly defended and filled with contradictions.

RACE, RULE, AND CULTURES OF RACIAL MANAGEMENT BETWEEN THE WARS

In 1921, the South African mining industry was suffering in a postwar slump. As gold prices fell, mining companies sought to save money by opening a few slight doors for the promotion of black miners, a cost-cutting move, not a baby-step toward racial equality. In an industry defined by the color line, black workers still did the most perilous work at the worst pay. Yet in a troubled postwar world, as the imperatives of capital sometimes conflicted with the cultural demands of white supremacy, white mineworkers went on a strike.

Strike became rebellion. In the Rand Revolt, armed white mineworkers and their supporters—including the new Communist Party of South Africa—occupied a handful of cities and Johannesburg suburbs. "Workers of the world unite and fight for a white South Africa," read the slogan. South African Prime Minister Jan Smuts called upon 20,000 troops to quell the insurrection

FIGURE 4.1: Mounted Police patrol the South African mine region during the Rand Revolt. Credit: Bettmann/Contributor.

(Figure 4.1). The strike suppressed, the revolt still drew the battle lines for almost a century's fight against white minority rule in South Africa as it passed from imperial dominion status to independent republic. By 1924, the National Party came to power and introduced a swathe of legislation enshrining the principle of racial segregation and laying the groundwork for Apartheid. The updated Mines and Work Act (1924) updated for a new era the racialized systems of mobilizing workers for the empire (Krikler 2005; Béliard 2016).

Rather than an aberration of history, South Africa's Apartheid should be recognized as part of the long legacy of racial logic in the managing of colonial capitalism—a culture of racial management. In Brazil, Henry Ford (who also brought production to South Africa) also connected fantasies of modernization to a racial logic (Adas 2006). In 1928, Ford turned to the Amazonian rainforest to produce the rubber he needed to outfit his new Model A car. Like a world's fair visitor, he contrasted the vigor and vision of American colonies with the timeless savagery of the rainforest. He believed that he—and his managers—could tame the jungle with American know-how and, in the process, free his company from a dependence on British companies and their Malayan rubber plantations. As large as many colonies, Fordlandia, as Ford boldly named his vast plantation, perfectly embodied the merging of extractive capitalism and the vision of post-First World War imperialism as a strategy for modernization (Grandin 2009; Roediger and Esch 2012: 122). Fordlandia with its model towns complete with city squares, golf courses, and flush toilets, was bound for failure. Managers knew little about how to grow rubber and the saplings died of leaf blight. Local workers rejected coercive labor rules. Even canned goods and American burgers led to open revolt in 1930 when raging workers (real-life versions of those besieging Orwell's Burmese club) destroyed trucks, tractors, and time clocks. By 1945, Henry Ford II quietly sold the area back to the Brazilian government at a significant loss.

Why did Fordlandia fail so miserably? Its ruins, today partly reclaimed by the rainforest, have different stories to tell. On one hand, they reveal the insistence that American technology and industrial knowledge were the only roads to modernization. Deaf to local knowledge and understandings of climate, health, and environment, Ford's engineers planted rubber trees that would inevitably shrivel and die. Ford sought to mobilize workers upon the same cultural terms trading social control for higher wages that he used in his Detroit factories. Ultimately, Ford turned to the same methods of coercion and military power used in other imperial circumstances.

Ford planned Fordlandia based on his own moral strictures, banning prostitution, alcohol, and even tobacco. Yet the new labor colony actually became a ribald city. Recent scholarship in the history of empire has focused on the intimate encounters that it created. Only rarely, though, have historians recognized that the intimacies of colonial encounters were also laboring encounters of cooking, cleaning, nursing, and raising children (Choy 2003; Stoler 2006; Ballantyne and Burton 2009). Like so many colonial capitalists before him, Ford longed to regulate the intimate and sexual encounters between colonizers and colonized, but the formal demand for primarily male workers in Fordlandia or other mining camps, plantations, docks, railroads, and military bases also mobilized sexual labor in more informal ways. Stretching back to the nineteenth century, the British Empire regulated and licensed brothels through the medical examination of sex workers. If the interwar years witnessed such a renewed concern about "white slavery" that the League of Nations released a report in 1927, its worries were restricted only to white female sex workers (White 1980; Höhn and Moon 2010).

During the Second World War and the postcolonial wars that followed, displaced, mobile male sailors and soldiers had ready cash to pay sexual laborers. The experiences of female workers in colonial Lagos are illustrative of the sexual, intimate, and laboring encounters catalyzed by military mobilization. A port city with a large migrant population, Lagos was a strategic British outpost, visited by both sailors patrolling the equatorial Atlantic and by soldiers protecting British African possessions. If wartime British authorities tacitly acknowledged the sex trade by introducing the familiar practice of medical examination, the mobilization of sex workers was informal, depending on acquaintances or even family friends (George 2014).

Military bases, as Cynthia Enloe has importantly written, represented critical outposts of empire, especially with the increasing power of the United States (2014). By the end of the Second World War and into the Cold War, the United States maintained military bases stretching across the Pacific and into the Caribbean, as well as in Europe. American forces occupied vast military bases in Korea after the Second World War and during the Korean War, as well as in the former colonies of Vietnam and the Philippines. If, as Seungsook Moon notes, postwar Koreans regarded Americans as liberators, soldiers understood their occupation in different and imperial ways. They expected sexual rewards for their fighting and like the British colonial officials before them, American administrators began regular examination of Korean prostitutes. As postwar became Cold War and Vietnam War, Okinawa and Korea even created special zones on the edges of sprawling American bases where prostitution was regulated and permitted.

SOLIDARITY AND CULTURES OF RESISTANCE

Lagos, Okinawa, and Fordlandia all represent different efforts at imperial labor mobilization. Lagos was a colonial city. Okinawa was, first, an occupied territory and later the site for a massive American military base. Fordlandia was a vast plantation and company town (Dinius and Vergara 2011). In such divergent forms of imperial labor mobilization, could workers succeed in blunting the power of colonialism and capitalism, especially at a time when colonial officials were seeking greater output and accelerated extraction of resources all the while decreasing expenditures (van der Linden 2008: 173–286)?

A return to Angola provides some insights. Local peoples challenged in subtle ways the labor mobilizations upon which the colony depended. In what should be interpreted as an astute understanding of intercolonial politics, residents took advantage of the under-policed borders between empires and colonies by hiding out on the other side of the border when labor recruiters neared. Similarly, their patterns of migration, sometimes from rural areas to cities and even their insistence upon day labor as opposed to long-term labor contracts, represent examples of working people subtly challenging the terms of colonial capitalism (Scott 1990).

This focus on the informal and cultural roots of resistance against colonial capitalism itself raises several questions about solidarity as a cultural practice of resistance. First, was the resistance of colonized workers grounded in a preindustrial culture and community or was it the collective and individual resistance of a proletarianized working class? Second, when and how did their resistance against the conditions and terms of their lives in employment merge with opposition to empire itself? Dipesh Chakrabarty has argued for the persistence of "illiberal" and "pre-bourgeois" traditions at the heart of colonial capitalism. In his study of Calcutta's jute mills, Chakrabarty identified forms of managerial control, methods of labor mobilization, and worker solidarity within the "undemocratic cultural codes of Indian society" (1989: 229). Rather than assuming that colonial workers were inevitably incorporated into a "third world" proletariat, Chakrabarty urged historians to examine the cultural roots of both colonial resistance and capitalism.

Still, the kinds of resistance historians have typically associated with metropolitan workers, notably unions and strikes, were hardly exotic organizations for colonial laborers. Rather, whether in India or Angola, local collective movements—including trade unions—were firmly rooted in indigenous forms of group affiliation and communities (Basu 2004). Cultural practices and traditions, far from immutable, could and did change as workers formed new collective identities alongside those of caste and religion. Working-class movements throughout the colonized world emerged and constructed forms of solidarity in the interwar years, not because of metropolitan models, but often in the face of real resistance from established metropolitan unions (Chandavarkar 1994; Simeon 1995; Joshi 2003; Curless 2016: 1–19). Indeed, as the experience of Ho Chi Minh, the Vietnamese anticolonial leader suggests, forms of anticolonial and anticapitalist politics, such as Communism, could merge organically with locally cultivated forms of resistance.

COLONIAL SOLIDARITY IN THE GREAT DEPRESSION

Ho Chi-Minh, before he challenged French colonialism and American militarism, was one of the millions mobilized for work in the colonial capitalist global economy. Ho was drawn to the imperial metropole where he labored, ironically enough, making *faux* Chinese "antiques" in Paris. After the Bolshevik revolution, he was drawn, instinctively, to Lenin, not because he had yet studied Marx or his Russian followers, but because he regarded Lenin as a patriotic liberator. Ho, like many working-class leaders across the colonies, combined nationalism and patriotism with a growing belief in Marxism-Leninism as responses to imperialism. While late imperial policy tended to fear, imprison, and ultimately negotiate with comparatively well-off and educated anticolonial figures, working-class collective movements played a critical role in destabilizing colonial regimes as early as the Great Depression (Chi-Minh 1970: 156–8).

Working-class resistance challenged colonial regimes from Jamaica to French West Africa to India, not necessarily because they were deliberately anticolonial in focus, but because they defied the racial underpinnings of the colonial system. In 1938, for example, strikes in Jamaica were the climax of a general labor uprising throughout the Caribbean (Figure 4.2). The export of sugar, bananas,

FIGURE 4.2: Alexander Bustamante leads a march of striking dock workers and other laborers in Kingston, Jamaica, 1938. Credit: Bettmann/Getty Images.

oil, and bauxite remained the cornerstone of local economies, but prices and demand had dropped in the lean Depression years, impoverishing already precarious populations. As Jamaican labor leader, Alexander Bustamante reported in a letter to the *Manchester Guardian*: "hundreds of ragged men, women, and children marched to the doors of the prison in Kingston pleading for admittance so that they might get food" (Palmer 2014: 31).

Meanwhile, for the island's few white residents, a life of racialized privilege combined intimacy with female black servants with strict racial segregation. As Jamaica approached the centenary of the abolition of slavery, white planters still owned the most fertile land and the colonial labor system depended on the representation of a sunny island of happy, picturesque natives, eager to serve. As one white resident boasted: "women bow when white people pass; greet you as 'master' or 'mistress'" (Palmer 2014: 72–3). The Caribbean labor revolt challenged this poisonous image of Jamaican workers as loyal subjects. The strike wave began in 1934, hitting sugar fields, banana plantations, docks, and oilfields in Trinidad, Saint Kitts, Saint Vincent, Saint Lucia, Barbados, the Bahamas, British Honduras, Guiana, and Antigua. In Jamaica, the strikes started on Kingston's docks before spreading to the sugar plantations.

The legacy of the strikes can be read in several ways. First, they contested the racial hierarchy of a colonial society that was the legacy of unfree labor. Strikers advanced immediate economic demands for increased wages, for example on the docks, as well as for upward mobility into the kinds of jobs long reserved for white residents. Second, the strikes as a cultural challenge laid bare the notion of the happy colonial workers of color. Appointed in the immediate aftermath of the strikes, a commission led by Lord Moyne described an economic crisis rooted in a plantation system that monopolized power, choice jobs, and land for a white elite (James and Whittall 2016: 166–84). The report was significant enough and so damning that the British Colonial Office decided to release only its recommendations, not its detailed findings. Moreover, the report rejected one of the basic tenants of the imperial system: the notion that colonies must pay for themselves. Now Lord Moyne recommended sending monetary and social aid to the West Indies, if only nominal amounts.

The Moyne Report contained a tacit recognition that the strikes in Jamaica (and elsewhere) were grounded in local conditions, but revealed larger fault-lines in the British imperial system. Catalyzed by the penury of life in the Great Depression, the strikes opened up for Jamaicans new potentials for mobility, threatened the racial order, and bequeathed a party system that after the Second World War would lead Jamaica toward independence. Bustamonte founded the Jamaica Labour Party in 1943, after breaking with his cousin Norman Manley, the elite lawyer who had helped mediate the strike, and his People's National Party.

General strikes in Jamaica and Trinidad like those in Dakar (1946), Nigeria (1945), Mombasa (1939 and 1947), and Malaya (1948) were flashpoints in a period when the contradictions within cultures of racial management revealed the hollowness of justifications for imperial rule as modernization and development. In Mombasa, strikes that (like those in Jamaica) began on the docks, forced colonial officials to reorder the way they recruited, paid, and managed African labor. Once such officials had encouraged casual employment as a cheap way of mobilizing African workers. After the strikes, these same officials worried openly that mobile, migrant workers had become a dangerous class that challenged the very stability of the colonial regime. They were concerned that the daily hiring of workers handed far too much power to work gangs and their leaders. The very ways that workers adapted to the labor demands of the colonial state had become the focus of suspicion on the part of employers and colonial officials. In his landmark study of Mombasa workers (1987), Frederick Cooper encouraged greater attention to the cultural accommodations of workers to colonial capitalism. Unions and collective action were not the obvious and universal response of proletarianized colonial subjects, he argues, but specific cultural responses that drew upon a range of community and group affinities, including local Beni dance societies.

If, as Cooper demonstrates, the origins of working-class collective movements could be found in localized cultural responses, so, too, could and did working colonial subjects engage with larger transnational political forms, in particular Communism and Marxism, that challenged both capital and colonialism. That was certainly the case in Malaya where a racial logic guided the mobilization and then management of the vast amounts of labor needed for its commodity export industries. Like employers in Mombasa, Malayan planters and mine-owners turned to indigenous labor recruiters (in the Malayan case, in India and China) who capitalized on local affinities of caste, religion, and family to find the laborers needed in tin mines and rubber estates. Cultural ties did not disappear in colonial Malaya even as migration dramatically reshaped the Malay Peninsula into a multi-ethnic society embedded in imperial production and trade. Chinese workers, by 1920, were virtually all members of ethnic societies and Chinese trade guilds.

Trade unions emerged in Malaya after the 1911 Chinese revolution. Bolshevik influence arrived soon after and, by 1927, the General Labour Union confederation, affiliated with the Profintern (the communist international union organization) included 42 unions with 5,000 members. The Great Depression hit Malayan industry hard, as global rubber prices plummeted. By 1936, Malaya was paralyzed by strikes in the coal and tin mines and in pineapple plantations. The British colonial regime led by the few white planters and overseers who governed Malaya's vast industries were worried. Some quickly blamed communist influence. It was, according to the Inspector General of Police, "the trial of strength between the Communist Party and the Government" (Stenson 1970: 15; Loh Kok Wah 1988: 57–101).

That announcement spoke especially to colonial administrators' sense of vulnerability. A deeper analysis points to the kinds of cultural ties that Malayan workers relied upon to organize in the face of vast ethnic and linguistic divides and the deliberate effort of the colonial regime to maintain a division of labor and hierarchy of pay based on ethnicity. Communism, international in its organization and, even, leadership, still gained local meanings, grafted onto other kinds of affinities. In Malaya, communist organizing drew from the strength of Chinese secret societies and schools. Later, it flourished among Chinese migrant workers as a form of anti-Japanese nationalism. Resistance to Japanese aggression in China influenced radical labor organizing among Chinese labor migrants in British colonial Malaya. There were, nonetheless, a few notable examples of cross-ethnic strikes that engaged Malay, Chinese, and Tamil workers. In particular, the multi-racial Traction Company Employees' Association led a 1927 strike of transport workers in Singapore.

The strikes that roiled interwar Malaya suggests that the growing organizing of working people and their labor movements stressed and weakened colonial regimes, not necessarily because they were vocally anticolonial, but because they took the developmentalist rhetoric of interwar colonialism at face value and demanded the benefit of legal labor rights. They sought to win for their rank-

and-file the promises already made to metropolitan workers, but did this make growing labor movements complicit? Rather, colonial workers' demands for the benefits accorded metropolitan workers complicate historians' understandings of the anticolonial movement, less as the actions of heroic individuals who led their nations, against all odds, to independence, than as broad-based social movements that undermined the colonial system—just as it was badly needed to win another world war.

MILITARY LABORS IN WORLD WAR AND COLD WAR

As Allied troops neared Paris in 1944, the leader of the Free French forces, General Charles De Gaulle hastily reshuffled his order of battle. For the triumphal march into the capital, he replaced black African soldiers with white resistance fighters, a *blanchissement* (as it was termed) that tacitly recognized that the war had irrevocably transformed the viability of empire. The removal of African soldiers from the parading French ranks, much like the segregation of the American military, raised uncomfortable comparisons between Nazi racial theories and colonial practice (Parsons 2015: 3–23).

If Nazism tarnished imperial racial hierarchies, De Gaulle's *blanchissement* rewrote a history of the war effort to insist that the fight against Nazism and to free France had nothing to do with empire. He sought to obscure the reality that Africans had worked hard and fought bitterly for war efforts (Figure 4.3). The stripped bare metropole could offer nothing in return. African (and Asian) workers were essential to the Allied war effort. From the cocoa grown in West Africa and consumed by sailors scanning for submarines in the North Atlantic to uranium mined in the Congo and used to build the atomic bombs, African production increased dramatically during the war years. British and Free French governments all mobilized workers to produce vital war materials and to replace supplies no longer available from Japanese-occupied Asia. As well, African and Asian men served in enormous numbers in British, Free French and even Vichy French, Italian, and Nationalist Spanish forces. As many as 350,000 African soldiers served for both Vichy and Free France (Brown 2015: 43–70).

That military mobilization of colonial workers did not end in 1945. Rather, the ascendant American empire in the postwar world was characterized not only by corporate expansion but also by the far reach of its military. Military bases and navel fleets were (and remain) vast workplaces, dependent on military and civilian as well as formal and informal labor. Yet bases, governed by military law, remained apart from the social promises of development that sought to justify imperial rule. Nowhere was (and is) this more obvious and more ominous than in the Cuban city Guantánamo and the nearby American naval base.

The United States retained its Guantánamo base after 1898 as the linchpin of American Caribbean naval power. Bases require military labor to man the

FIGURE 4.3: African soldiers take part in the Battle of France, 1940. Credit: Galerie Bilderwelt/Getty Images.

guns as well as civilian labor to clean, cook, and construct. Others worked, notably as sex workers, to meet the leisure demands of American soldiers and sailors. Thousands of Cubans worked at the Guantánamo base; others came from around the Caribbean, including Jamaicans and Puerto Ricans. During the Cuban revolution, base workers were caught between the laboring demands of the US military and the liberationist dreams of revolution. Many used their liminal position to support the revolution, smuggling arms and material off the base to rebels of the M-26-7 movement, camped in the hills around Guantánamo (Lipman 2009). Yet soon the new Cuban government, aware of American subversion campaigns, doubted the loyalty of base workers. Ironically, the American military also treated with suspicion Cuban workers, who now crossed a highly militarized border every day as they commuted to work. Soon, military managers replaced Cubans with Jamaicans and other contract workers from across the empire.

The history of Guantánamo and its workers is emblematic of the larger experience of workers—from soldiers and sailors to migrant workers to sex workers—mobilized to meet the labor demands of a military empire. From the domestic draft to labor contracts, the American "military-industrial complex" displaced and managed millions of workers in Korea, Vietnam, the Philippines, western Europe, the Middle East, and the Pacific (Flores 2015: 813–35). A conscripted American soldier serving in Vietnam and seeking the comfort of a sex worker while on leave in Okinawa might have felt little solidarity with former French colonized subjects. Still in the midst of war and revolution in the Post-World War II era, anti-imperialism could forge global solidarities. Black revolutionaries in Oakland, California, for example, could find common cause with Vietnamese soldiers (Bloom and Martin 2012).

LABOR SOLIDARITY AND LIBERATION

Revolutionary movements might forge solidarity across differences of race and region, but it was often harder for working-class labor movements who struggled to build alliances with nationalist and anticolonial leaders. At the end of the Second World War, the Martinique activist Aimé Césaire was living in Paris and serving as a legislator. Césaire was a Communist Party member and an anticolonial politician who reached out hopefully toward colonial workers. His *Discourse on Colonialism* (1950) was part of a flurry of postwar writing on imperialism in English and French by activists like W.E.B Dubois, C.L.R. James, and Frantz Fanon (Césaire [1950] 2000).

Their writing was set against the backdrop of war, revolution, and organizing. Dubois, in particular, was a towering figure of authority at the Fifth Pan-African Congress convened in Manchester in 1945. This postwar Pan-African Congress differed markedly from its predecessor meetings in its support of trade unions and calls for strikes. As the Congress saluted the independence of the Philippines and India as well as recognized uprisings in Kenya, Vietnam, and Algeria, the Congress' new engagement with workers and student movements acknowledged that working people and their collective organizations represented powerful forces for independence. Working-class movements and their leaders did not always overtly call for the end of colonial rule but they threatened the justifications for and feasibility of the racialized system of imperial capitalism.

Césaire reflected this engagement with working-class movements. In his writing, Césaire flipped colonial discourse on its head. Rather than Europe civilizing the savages, empire had brutalized Europe, he argued. Fascism wasn't an aberration but the natural outgrowth of colonialism. He acknowledged the long history of ruptured solidarity that divided metropolitan and colonial workers, but showed little faith in European trade unions, even if he concluded his essay with call for socialist revolution. In an essay inflected with excitement about Negritude movements and surrealism, the gestures toward the Soviet Union at first appeared formulaic, an expectation for someone still a member of the Communist Party (he later would publicly resign). More deeply, though, it also reflected an understanding of the double burden of imperialism and capitalism.

Nationalist politicians and historians still often describe the slow road to colonial independence as about open rebellion (such as the Mau Mau revolt in Kenya); fraught negotiation led by charismatic independence leaders (such as Kwame Nkrumah in Ghana; Sukarno in Indonesia; and Jawaharlal Nehru in India); or anticolonial wars (such as those in Vietnam, Malaya, or Algeria). The impacts of labor movements and strikes on the re-imposition of colonialism after the war are only beginning to be measured. The history of postwar African strikes, for example, re-centers the role of working-class movements in helping blow the winds of change, all the while revealing the tensions between anticolonial leaders and wage workers. Railroads, of course, were one of the grand projects of the British and French colonial states in Africa. They linked local economies into a larger colonial capitalism by allowing for easier extraction and export of agricultural and mineral products (Jones 2002). From 1947 to 1948 in French West Africa, crippling strikes engaged 20,000 workers. About a decade later, railroad workers led strikes in Kenya and Tanganyika in British East Africa.

Such strikes challenged the very economic foundations of empire itself, but how did striking workers—whether in Senegal, the Ivory Coast, Kenya or Tanganyika—link anticolonial politics to workplace demands? In West Africa, railway strikes began as the French (as in Vietnam, the Dutch in Indonesia, or the British in Malaya) sought to reestablish metropolitan rule. In French West Africa, the loss of colonial legitimacy was particularly acute especially because of the wartime legacy of forced labor by the collaborationist Vichy government, which coerced tens of thousands of workers from the Ivory Coast to Guinea into war work (Cooper *et al.* 2000: 135–6). African politicians and wage workers pressed both the Free French and then the post-liberation government in France to renounce forced labor systems. This was a cultural and political as well as economic demand for recognition as citizens entitled to the protections of metropolitan industrial labor relations.

The spark was a strike in Dakar in December 1945 led by market hawkers and indigenous civil servants. This diverse alliance called for wage increases and the legal recognition of unions. Their demands complicated distinctions between metropolitan wage workers (protected by systems of collective bargaining) and colonial workers (long the subjects of forced labor). As Césaire joined the Côte d'Ivoirian Félix Houphouët-Boigny in introducing a law forbidding forced labor in "overseas territories," politics from below continued to roil. By 1947, foment for strikes spread from Dakar to the racially segregated railways. A small number of white Europeans were at the top of the wage hierarchy. Below them were thousands of Africans. The Fédération des Travailleurs Africains demanded the elimination of the racial wage system. Condemning the "colonist sprit of the Europeans," union officials organized for a strike up and down the railway lines. By October 1947, the walkout began with the almost unanimous support of African workers.

The railways workers' solidarity shocked colonial and railway officials who had expected only a short strike. The strike proved far more enduring than railway and colonial officials alike predicted. Cooper describes a "complex web of affiliation within the communities in which they lived" (1996a: 94). The union, with few funds, depended not only on the solidarity of railway workers but also on money, food, and transportation from local merchants and communities. Local women supported the strike through market-selling that helped augment the meager strike support the union could offer. Solidarity crossed the boundaries of colony as well as ethnicity and religion, engaging black and Islamic Africans in common cause.

Yet if the strike was a popular movement, did politicians recognize it as a blow against empire? Railway solidarity expanded from railway yards into the community, but anticolonial politicians like Houphouët-Boigny and Leopold Senghor responded with ambivalence. Beyond the scenes, Houphouët-Boigny worked quietly to resolve the strike in the Côte d'Ivoire and in Senegal, Senghor was only marginally more supportive. Trade unions with their claims to labor rights as citizens challenged the racial systems of colonial capitalism, but the political parties of anticolonial leaders remained largely distant. The cause of labor was not necessarily the cause of anticolonialism.

French African railway strikes came at a time when workers were still incorporated within the evolving French imperial state. Railway strikes in British East Africa, by contrast, occurred during the transition to independence in 1960, after the British brutally quelled the Mau Mau "emergency." Railroads were of particular importance, especially in protecting the fragile position of white ranchers in the interior who needed to transport their products to the coast for export. The strikes on the railroads came at a time when not only was the government seeking to protect the position of white ranchers but also recognizing the effect of a racially stratified official wage system that placed African workers at the very bottom below European and Asian workers. African wages, calculated as "bachelor" wages, aimed to encourage the migration of single, African men from rural hinterlands to urban centers. By early 1960, strikes were spreading across Kenya, Uganda, and Tanganyika. During the following year, a million working days were lost to strikes in Kenya alone as tribal and community affinities bolstered workers' solidarity across national lines.

Yet even as politicized workers came to see their strikes as a transnational campaign, the emerging labor departments of newly independent states confined their unions. Independence movements were also wary, emphasizing moderation among trade unions. Independence, for moderate trade unionists like Tom Mboye, was a political problem; trade unions, he argued, should represent working-class needs in new nations, not subvert colonial cultures (Hyde 2015: 147–69; Hyde 2016: 71–91). Such nationalism, divorced from working-class movements, promised a change of government, but not necessarily an economic change. As independence activists became postcolonial leaders, they rapidly distanced themselves from indigenous labor leaders and the impetus for development was shorn of demands for fair and equitable working conditions. In Senegal, Senghor was forced to acknowledge the bitter irony when, as president, he ordered the imprisonment of the very labor leaders he had once defended against the French regime. Senghor's orders highlighted the ruptures that too often separated postcolonial leaders from indigenous labor movements, thus leaving the descendants of colonial workers still prey to the exploitation of growing international corporations and distanced from metropolitan workers.

WORKING PEOPLE IN NEOLIBERALISM

Near the end of the Second World War, Americans began singing about bananas. The United Fruit Company created a new advertising campaign featuring the cartoon character Chiquita Banana. Singing her catchy jingle hundreds of times daily on radio stations, she eased the transition of United Fruit, that most imperial of companies, into the postcolonial era of globalized capital. Most immediately, Chiquita Banana protected the company's domination of the American consumer market and insulated it from a domestic critique of its brutal management practices and exploitation of low-paid women workers.

Chiquita Banana represented both continuity and rupture with older imperial representations of imperial labor and economy. On one hand, it retained the popular representation of tropical places as idylls ripe for development and of its peoples as eager to serve. But if world's fairs put real peoples on display, Chiquita Banana was a cartoon character (half woman, half banana) and even if she was meant to recall the popular star Carmen Miranda, she helped remove tropical workers from the view of temperate consumers. In this way, she helped inaugurate the model of the postcolonial, but still imperial extractive economy. Goods, whether agricultural, mineral, or (as the new century approached) increasingly manufactured, arrived in (former) colonial metropoles. Yet labor conditions and conflict were carefully obscured.

United Fruit Company had well deserved its sobriquet "el polpo," a sprawling octopus of a company whose tentacles squeezed Latin American countries. Coined in 1935, the term "banana republic" highlighted the practice of United Fruit that demanded the subservience—and, if needed, military force—of notionally independent governments. Chiquita Banana put a softer face to naked power and, not surprisingly, the much-maligned United Fruit has since changed its name to Chiquita Brands. Largely out of the view of domestic consumers, postwar labor relations in the banana industry have remained tense, challenging not only dire working conditions but also political repression (Colby 2011; Enloe 2014: 211–49; Coleman 2016).

If, by the 1950s, banana workers' unions had won some victories, solidarity was hard to build. This was especially the case when metropolitan unions were often complicit with Cold War efforts to undermine left politics. Too often hostile to local issues or the cultural contexts of organizing, union federations like the American AFL-CIO joined campaigns to subvert left leadership, for example, in Columbia's banana fields owned by the United Fruit Company (Chomsky 2008). By the 1980s, women workers, calling themselves *bananeras*, advanced new models of international solidarity by placing calls for gender equity at the center of campaigns for union democracy and leadership.

The activism of the *bananeras*, challenging the happy image of Chiquita Banana, has highlighted new ways of bringing the laboring conditions to a global consciousness (Frank 2005). Yet, too often, goods, whether French beans from West Africa or sneakers from Vietnam, are produced in appalling conditions in the postcolonial world—the Global South, as it was increasingly termed. Rupturing transnational solidarity and shielding Northern consumers from postcolonial economies became essential for corporations. Nike, a prototypical example of the globalized corporation, offers advertisements of its celebrity athlete endorsers, but obscures its production practices through complex webs of contracting and sub-contracting. When the exploitative conditions of labor in shoe, clothing, or electronics factories in places as diverse as Bangladesh or Vietnam come to global attention through journalistic exposés or horrific industrial accidents and fires, companies rush to disavow connections to contract businesses (Figure 4.4).

By the 1980s and 1990s, a postcolonial "rush to the bottom" in wages and conditions had come to replace the insistence that empire was a project of civilization and modernization. French beans, for example, are grown in the former French colonies of West Africa. Picked in African soil, they sit on the shelves of Paris or London supermarkets within hours. Somewhere along the way those beans become "French" and their African origins reduced to small print (if at all) on the plastic packaging. They are prime examples of an updated extractive economy (Freidberg 2004). If the exhibits and world's fairs with which this essay opened celebrated colonial production, companies edging toward the new century obscured their overseas business. Eager for consumers in the Global North, the business of empire was best left behind closed doors.

In many ways, the story of French beans reflects the way in which postcolonial workers are rendered invisible by the many consumer demands of the global economy. The advent of neoliberal trade policies and treaties (from the Caribbean Basin Initiative that transferred garment work out of the United States to NAFTA) shifted production of consumer goods, like sneakers and clothing, out of metropolitan industrial centers to former colonies. Behind triumphant "globalization," companies from Nike to Gap have "outsourced"—a phrase that entered global discourse toward the century's end—production to

FIGURE 4.4: Demonstrators protest Nike's sweatshop production. Credit: Alan Dejecacion/Getty Images.

multiple layers of contractors. Building solidarity, often by decrying "sweatshop" production, tried to create alliances between workers in the Global South and consumers in the Global North. To be sure, although horror stories of sweatshops could (and still do) provoke the ire of consumers, such campaigns typically struggled to advance systemic critiques of global inequalities (Bender and Greenwald 2003).

If the sweatshop emerged by the end of the twentieth century as one obvious incarnation of a new imperium entwined with globalized capital, resorts are another. The contemporary resort, far more plush and polished than Orwell's tawdry Burmese club, links the contemporary to the older and colonial. The colonial club with its flowing drinks and racial segregation also persists. Behind guarded walls, proliferating resorts, the built environment of the rapidly growing tourist empire, provide vacationers from former colonial metropoles the chance to enjoy the kinds of service once expected by colonial residents, yet remain sheltered from the realities of everyday and postcolonial life. They indulge in an imperial nostalgia that deliberately recalls a bygone colonial era, yet evading difficult questions about racialized global divisions of labor. Resorts, sweatshops, plantations, export processing zones (EPZs), and military bases all lay claim to prime lands in the heart of independent former colonies. As a new imperial infrastructure, they poignantly demonstrate the way the new imperium can be built on the foundations of older Euro-American empires.

CHAPTER FIVE

Mobility

JESSICA NAMAKKAL

> You disembark from your plane. You go through customs. Since you are a tourist, a North American or a European—to be frank, white—and not an Antiguan black returning to Antigua from Europe or North America with cardboard boxes of much needed cheap clothes and food for relatives, you move through customs swiftly, you move through customs with ease. Your bags are not searched. You emerge from customs into the hot, clean air: immediately you feel cleansed, immediately you feel blessed (which is to say special); you feel free.
>
> Jamaica Kincaid, A Small Place (1988: 4–5)

People move about the world for many different reasons. Those with the economic and social means travel for cultural enrichment, while those who lack money and the right passport are often viewed as being rich in culture, but poor in every other way. In her 1988 long-form essay *A Small Place*, Jamaica Kincaid, the Antiguan-American writer, reflected on her experiences growing up on a decolonizing island that had once been a site of the Atlantic slave trade.[1] Kincaid's essay traces the uneven and intersecting networks of mobility, and immobility, that cross the cultures and geographies of her island home, making visible the deep divides between those who travel because they can and those who travel because they must. The academic literature on mobility has only occasionally considered these two groups together: as Stephen Greenblatt (2010: 250–3) has noted, "certain forms of movement—migration, labor-market border-crossing, smuggling, and the like—are marked as 'serious' while others, such as tourism, theater festivals, and (until recently) study abroad, are rendered virtually invisible." Yet, as Kincaid tells us, the interaction between people who travel with ease and those who travel with great difficulty happens not only at the many border controls installed at airports and land crossings throughout the world, but also on the streets of cosmopolitan megacities like London, Paris, and New York, and in former colonies that today depend on the tourist industry as a major source of income.

It is easy to show how common transnational mobility is in the twenty-first century. According to the United Nations' 2015 International Migration Report, the number of people living in a country other than where they were born has reached 244 million, including 20 million refugees. More than half of all these refugees (53 percent) originate from Afghanistan, Somalia, and the Syrian Arab Republic. All three of these countries are in the throes of brutal civil wars rooted in struggles incited by imperial proxy wars and fractured colonial geographies (Gregory 2004). Meanwhile, the United Nations' World Tourism Organization (UNWTO) estimated that in the first nine months of 2016, almost a billion tourists traveled to global sites, up four percent from 2015. Amidst prolonged and vicious wars, what one could call the afterlives of Western empires, tourism is booming.

Cultures of mobility—whether through the guise of tourism, forced or voluntary colonial and postcolonial migrations, the expansion of "global education," population displacement as a result of war and state-making, or the ubiquity of transnational military service—marked the twentieth century in ways that built on the "contact zones" established by earlier imperial networks. The idea of the "contact zone," theorized by Mary Louise Pratt as "social spaces where disparate cultures meet, clash, and grapple with each other, often in highly asymmetrical relations of domination and subordination" (1992: 4), helps us to understand the uneven terrain of mobility. Mobility is in many ways a cultural expectation and marker: a person's ability to move through a multitude of spaces signifies class status, educational level, and race, sexuality, and gender privileges. While many of these inequalities were codified in colonial jurisprudence, this chapter shows that they continue to regulate contemporary networks through cultural practices.

The greatest change in the history of mobility since 1920 has been the systematic rise of racial, ethnic, and religious nationalisms, which have become primary cultural markers of deciding who has the right to free movement and who does not. The participation of colonized peoples in the two world wars and their increased movements from colony to metropole and between colonies, the partitions and changing borders of the postwar period and the subsequent displacement and migrations of people, and the transition from networks of formal empire to a regime of informal empire, often understood as neoliberal globalization, define the contemporary cultural history of mobility in relation to Western empires.

TECHNOLOGIES OF (IM)MOBILITY

Technological culture, from innovations in transportation to the widespread emergence of the Internet and social media, are often given primacy in understanding how people, materials, and ideas move in the contemporary era (Castells 2009). Transportation and communication technologies that made empire both possible and successful have often been interpreted as cultural signifiers of modernity as well as tools of inclusivity and exclusion. For example, according to the historians Marjory Harper and Stephen Constantine (2011: 342), in the nineteenth century "railways and steamships reduced the risks to life but also limited the interruptions to income flows" for potential migrants weighing the benefits of moving throughout empires in search of economic opportunities. While Harper and Constantine argue that these technologies "helped turn potential migrants into travelers" (2011: 342), this experience was uneven, determined by the racialized travel routes forged by imperial networks. Though it might have been the case for white settlers hoping to set down roots in Australia, New Zealand, Canada, Algeria or parts of West Africa or Indochina, colonized, and almost always non-white, migrants were rarely "turned into travelers" but were more accurately turned into slaves, aliens, immigrants, refugees, rogues, outlaws, and criminals when they strayed or were forced from their perceived homes.

While the explosion of the transportation industry, especially the expansion of the commercial flight industry in the 1950s, made the tools of mobility more accessible to a growing middle class in the West (Lyth and Dierikx 1994), global anticolonial movements threatened the stability of imperial borders, leading to increased border security and the intensified policing of movement within and between states. A culture of supporting technological innovation in the interest of strong empires and states encouraged the development of new forms of governmentality. Since the widespread movements of decolonization in the 1960s, states have systematically implemented regimes of security that regulate who can cross national borders and how long they can stay: tourists, students, laborers, and refugees all need to be tracked, surveilled, and, depending on their economic status, nationality, sexual identity, gender, race, and/or religion, welcomed, tolerated, or deported.

Take, for example, the Schengen Agreement in Europe, signed in 1985 and implemented in 1995, that eliminated border controls between participating European states. As of 2017, there are twenty-six Schengen countries, twenty-two in the European Union and four that are not (Iceland, Norway, Switzerland, and Lichtenstein).[2] Schengen made mobility within Europe much easier for many Europeans and western tourists, encouraging a culture of inter-European travel and exchange: according to the European Commission webpage (2017), "the border free Schengen Area guarantees free movement to more than 400 million EU citizens, as well as many EU-nationals, businessmen, tourists or other persons legally present on the EU territory." Yet, as Schengen eased travel for those "legally present," the "external border" of Europe saw a steady increase in security and policing, making it much more difficult for migrants from Africa and the Middle East, people often fleeing civil wars, political persecution, and economic and climate insecurity, to enter Europe (Balibar 2004). Schengen States can reinstate the border when they deem it necessary, an action used with increasing frequency in 2015–16 as significant numbers of Syrian refugees sought asylum in Europe. The Schengen States are required to "cooperate with law enforcement agencies in other Schengen States in order to maintain a high level of security" (Schengen Area), which has meant the construction of detention centers for migrants and asylum seekers on European borders in Greece, Hungary, and throughout the Balkans.

Allowing free movement within borders while strengthening the external border is a process Etienne Balibar (2004: 39) has deemed "immigration recolonized," as migrants originating from former colonies are blocked from following the paths of labor migration formed during the period of formal colonialism. Similarly, in the United States, President Donald J. Trump's 2016 campaign promise to build a wall between Mexico and the US operates on a faulty colonial logic that border walls prevent mobility. The building of the wall on the US–Mexico border intensifies the already blocked labor migration patterns established by the United States and Mexico during the *bracero* program, which brought an estimated 4.5 million Mexican contract laborers to the United States between 1942 and 1964 (Henderson 2011) (see Figure 5.1).

FIGURE 5.1: Mexican men being registered to work as braceros in 1951. Credit: PhotoQuest/Getty Images.

The contradiction inherent in a system that allows states to decide who can cross specific borders within a world that frames the freedom to move as a human rights issue is often clear to the people trapped in airport immigration and customs cells and being held in container detention facilities along the borders of Europe. In reality, the right to mobility is highly contested by growing popular conservative cultural movements that see the right to mobility as belonging only to the wealthy, the white, and the Western educated. Anti-immigrant political organizing and the election of xenophobic politicians throughout the West since the early 2010s has reproduced regimes of border control that largely mirror the national divisions of Western empire, despite the supposed freedoms brought about by Schengen and liberal immigration policies in the United States.

PASSPORTS, OR, THE FREEDOM TO MOVE

The passport is a modern tool that came into widespread usage in the early twentieth century as transportation technology became more advanced and imperial nation-states faced a steady increase in colonial people looking to labor and settle outside the colonies. The growing ease of global movement by the early twentieth century made Western empires and states nervous for a variety of reasons. Without the ability to exclude certain people from crossing national borders, borders become irrelevant, thus creating a need for a system of counting and controlling the movement of citizens and non-citizens alike. The reasons for exclusion were numerous, but tended to emphasize a need to keep the population within the fixed borders safe from a variety of "foreign" threats: who exactly was viewed as a threat ebbed and flowed, but was based primarily on religious, racial, and economic factors. Sociologist John Torpey has argued that the development of a system of passport controls is the state's "monopolization of human mobility" as "states must develop the capacity to 'embrace' their own citizens in order to extract from them the resources they need to reproduce themselves over time" (2000: 2). Creating documents—passports, identity cards, and papers—that specify who belongs to which state is the only way for the state to ensure who is a national and who is a non-national, despite deeply held cultural beliefs of the time based on racial science suggesting an organic relationship between race and nation.

The two main strains of thought in the development of European citizenship regulations are of *jus soli* (right by territory), which states that a person born in a particular country should be granted citizenship to that particular territory, and *jus sanguinis* (right by blood or descent), which determines the citizenship of an individual based on race and/or origin of the birth parents (Brubaker 1998). While western states, including those in western Europe, as well as the United States, Canada, and South Africa, have a history of choosing to abide by one or the other principle, or sometimes a combination of the two, the complications brought out in the colonies by subjects having parents of different races and/or origins led to colonial courts making legal distinctions between race and nationality. As Christopher Lee (2011: 509) has shown, in British Africa during the interwar period, both categories of *jus sanguinis* and *jus soli* were at work in determining how colonized peoples were subject to state laws. A subject born, for example, in Nyasaland (present-day Malawi) to one African and one Indian parent was deemed by the courts in 1929 to be "non-native," a "half-caste Indian," thus not subject to the laws governing native peoples, yet still a British subject. All persons born on territory that was under British rule were British subjects, but their "race" or "origin" was a separate matter for a different set of regulations (Lee 2011: 511). And although France was a *jus soli* state that promoted assimilationist policies in the colonies, most *indigènes* in the colonies were barred from French citizenship because of a changing mixture of perceived racial origin, religious affiliation, language skills, and education level. While a small number of colonized peoples managed to become French citizens, even they were subject to regimes of racialist ideology meant to protect the whiteness of the French Republic.

Imperial systems meant to advance the interests of racial capitalism required the massive movement of populations far from their homes to labor as slaves on plantations, as indentured servants in factories and homes, and as middle managers to oversee colonized workers. The forced removal of people from their homes was a cornerstone of colonial conquest in the eighteenth and nineteenth centuries; however, this began to change by the early twentieth century, when colonized peoples began to explore the possibilities of migrating outside of their imperial networks and were often shut down by the creation of new passport regulations (Mongia 1999). The difference between movement throughout empires and between nation-states is important here. Radhika Viyas Mongia has argued that from the early twentieth century to today, mobility has been dictated by the increased belief by states that race is inherently linked to national territory. The passport, as a tool of mobility, speaks to the unequal dimensions of contemporary access to transnational movement, what Mongia has described as a global system of "raced-migration," "the specifically modern imbrication of the state, the nation, and race" (1999: 528). The development of the global passport regime increased in use as primarily non-white colonial subjects became increasingly mobile because of the two world wars and movements for anticolonial liberation, leading to a new cultural standard of identification linking personal identity directly to the passport one possesses and the details it provides (Kumar 2000).

MOBILITY, EMPIRE, AND THE WORLD WARS

The first waves of mass migration from the colonies to the metropole happened during and following the First World War. Colonial subjects had served in both the British and French militaries prior to 1914, though their service was almost entirely geographically limited to the colonies and at sea. England followed a set of racial policies that prohibited black (mostly African and Caribbean) soldiers from fighting alongside white soldiers, based on the understanding that interaction between the races, particularly the policing of whites by blacks, would lessen the authority of white rule (C. Hall 2002). However, the massive loss of life during the First World War led to British officials calling on their colonial subjects: over one million Indians served in the British military during the First World War, as well as 100,000 Egyptians and over 80,000 black South Africans, though the latter two groups were mostly limited to serving outside of Europe. France was less reluctant than England to bring non-white soldiers and workers into France. In France, over 600,000 "citizen-soldiers" came from West Africa, North Africa, Indochina, Madagascar, and even French India. In addition to soldiers, France recruited over 220,000 overseas peoples as workers, including Algerians, Indochinese, Chinese, Moroccans, Tunisians, and Malagasy (Stovall 1998: 741). During this time, there were also thousands of workers from southern Europe who arrived to work in western Europe, but it was the arrival of peoples from the colonies during the period that led to a racialization of the workforce (Tabili 1994).

The arrival of colonized peoples in the metropole (primarily in France and England) during and after the war caused new debates on two main issues that reveal underlying anxieties about the preservation of the boundaries of race, sex, and class within the rapidly changing demographics of western Europe.[3] First, there was the issue of mixed-race couplings, and second, the question of the make-up of the working class and whether or not this traditionally white political community should or would accept non-white workers in their ranks. By the end of the war, France lost 1.4 million and England 700,000 men, while many more in both countries were severely disabled as a result of war injuries. In the aftermath of war, people worried about reproducing the lost population, but were also fearful because of the appearance of colonial workers. Fears of miscegenation and the degeneration of whiteness were catalysts for the race riots that swept across Britain in 1919 (Webb 2017), while in France "pronatalists, industrialists, work scientists, and eugenicists argued for '*méstissage* among whites'" (Camiscioli 2009: 130) to discourage white French women marrying non-white men. People ranging from feminists to politicians across a broad spectrum described relationships between "French women and non-white man as racially unsound and potentially dangerous" (2009: 131).

The direct threat of colonial subjects being accepted as part of the national body led to many in England and France redefining the nationalist subject, which was increasingly marked by race, religion, and language. The war not only brought massive destruction and fatalities into the homes of western Europeans, it also served as an opening for the colonized to move into the metropole in a way that forced working-class and middle-class Europeans to confront empire directly, in the form of new neighbors, workmates, and members of the community. Following the end of the war, many of the colonial laborers and soldiers remained in Europe. French authorities, in response, continued to segregate the non-European workers, including those from the French colonies and territories as well as a substantial population of Chinese workers, through housing schemes and special labor contracts. The contracts that colonial laborers signed often stipulated that they could not change jobs and had no leverage to negotiate higher wages or better working conditions. Tyler Stovall (1998: 745) has argued that "the contrasting lack of mobility among colonial workers soon made them the poorest paid laborers in France." In addition to limiting the colonial workers' ability to move between jobs, the arrival of significant numbers of non-white workers led to the French state creating institutions and technologies to track those perceived as threats. During the interwar years, the French police "developed systematic means to enforce distinctions between citizens, nationals, and foreigners," applying technologies developed to surveil criminals to a population of immigrants who "had done nothing wrong" (Rosenberg 2006: 5). A culture of surveillance became the norm and was installed in hospitals and health clinics, at schools and through social welfare agencies, often based on the argument that non-western cultures were anti-assimilationist and thus non-western subjects refused to become proper national subjects (Foucault 1977).

Britain had recruited fewer colonial workers to work in factories at home, thus following the end of the First World War, the populations of colonial subjects in England remained relatively minor.[4] Still, there was a significant and growing presence of both Asian and black folks originating from the Caribbean and West Africa who found ways to settle, especially in port cities like Liverpool (Jenkinson 2012). Many Afro-Caribbean people who came were merchant marines, hired in colonial ports in Africa, Asia, the Middle East, and the Caribbean, and were viewed with great suspicion by both the state and local populations who saw them as a threat to both the purity of white women and the local economy (Tabili 1994). Anxieties over the economy and sexual purity manifested into laws such as the Alien Seaman Order of 1925, which required non-white sailors to register as "aliens" with the state. The order "was an episode in an ongoing process that reconstructed colonial racial categories in the mother country," a move not toward the dissolution of empire but instead toward bringing the benefits of white supremacy into the metropole from the colonies (Tabili 1994: 63). Neither France nor England could stop the influx of non-white people during the interwar years, but they were able to put into place systems of surveillance and segregation that continued to determine who was a legitimate member of the state. Although colonial subjects arrived in Europe during a time when they were almost always legally members of the imperial state, as subjects or citizens, the seeds of seeing the colonized as fundamentally different, based on race, ethnicity, race, religion, and culture, were planted during these early waves of migration through the cultural transmission of the white, Christian, heteronormative family as the legitimate successor of Western Empire.

GLOBAL REVOLUTIONS AND THE ANTICOLONIAL DIASPORA

The interwar period was a time of exile and circulation for many colonized peoples active in liberation struggles. While mobility was necessary for the expansion of empire, it was also a threat to the imperial order, as anticolonial agitators traveled to Europe, Russia, Japan, Cuba, and Mexico to learn bomb-making skills and revolutionary theory. The ability of colonized peoples to mobilize, especially through imperial travel routes, was a cornerstone of the success of anticolonial organizing. Despite increased surveillance and attempts by imperial states to limit immigration and demobilize the troops who had come to Europe, the cosmopolitan contact zones of Paris, London, Lisbon, and Berlin, as well as cities in the United States including New York and San Francisco, became important centers of global anticolonial agitation in the 1920s and 1930s. A great number of anticolonial thinkers and leaders were educated in the heart of Western empire, including Mohandas K. Gandhi, Muhammad Ali Jinnah, Jawaharlal Nehru, and Aurobindo Ghosh in England; Ho Chi Minh, Zhou Enlai, Frantz Fanon, Aimé and Suzanne Césaire, Léopold Sédar Senghor, and Messali Hadj in France; Amílcar Cabral and Eduardo Mondlane in Portugal; and Kwame Nkrumah and B.R. Ambedkar in the United States.

Anticolonial nationalist movements were a key cultural element of the anticolonial diaspora throughout the twentieth century: movements were often formed in diasporic meetings and funded by colonial migrants who came together to share resources as well as agitate for political change (Goebel 2016). Thousands of anticolonial pamphlets were printed in the United States, France, Germany, Belgium, and other European countries and smuggled abroad, to circulate among the global colonial diaspora. The south Asian anticolonial Ghadar Party, which was instrumental in advocating for Indian independence, was almost entirely organized in the United States and Canada (Ramnath 2011). Kwame Nkrumah, the anti-imperialist leader and first prime minister of Ghana, established a political group of West Africans against the British Empire while he was a student in London in the 1940s (Rooney 1988). Many future leaders of various African liberation movements against Portuguese rule, including Amilcar Cabral, Agostinho Neto, Mario de Andrade, Lucio Lara, Eduardo Mondlane, and Marcellino dos Santos, met while studying in Lisbon and living together at the *Casa dos Estudantes de Império*, a government-funded dorm for

Portuguese-African colonial students (Benewick and Green 1992: 36). The future leaders of the MPLA (People's Movement for the Liberation of Angola) and FRELIMO (the Mozambique Liberation Front) met while studying in Lisbon. Imperial networks were of key importance in bringing together the future leaders of anticolonial movements, decades before the same leaders would meet again at international gatherings in Bandung, Cairo, Tehran, Belgrade, Buenos Aires, and Havana (Prashad 2008).

Owing in part to nationalist protest as well as external factors brought on by the war, anticolonial agitation became louder and stronger in the interwar period, especially in the colonies that were sending significant numbers of soldiers and laborers into the heart of imperial spaces. Movements for independence mobilized hundreds of thousands of people calling for the end of colonialism and often for national liberation, leading to a widespread culture of work stoppages, boycotts, and armed insurrection. In response, imperial powers began to restrict mobility in new ways. England, France, Portugal, and Belgium all sanctioned and carried out military suppression of anticolonial uprisings, but the attempts to quell the masses were largely unsuccessful at stopping the movements, despite mass casualties. As a result, anticolonial agitators were often put into prison, making *immobility* through incarceration a primary tactic of counterinsurgency.

Incarcerating and immobilizing anticolonialists was not limited to one imperial power, but was widespread throughout the colonies during the decades of anticolonial struggle. The British Raj imprisoned, at various times, many Indian National Congress leaders, including Jawaharlal Nehru and M.K. Gandhi. In British-controlled Gold Coast, Kwame Nkrumah was arrested and imprisoned in 1950. In the French protectorate of Tunisia, Habib Bourguiba, the leader of the Tunisian nationalist Neo-Destour Party was held in detention throughout the early 1950s, and in the Belgian Congo the freedom fighter Patrice Lumumba was imprisoned after an anticolonial uprising in Stanleyville in 1959. Of course, major figures were not the only anticolonial resistors to be imprisoned: police and military throughout the colonized world arrested and imprisoned students, workers, those deemed sexually deviant, communists, and other opponents of empire, including significant numbers of women and youth.

Often the political writings and speeches of those imprisoned, in addition to the act of imprisonment, mobilized more support for the anticolonial cause as large numbers of people organized protests to free political prisoners. When Mohammed V, the Sultan of Morocco, and his two sons were forced by the French into exile on Corsica in 1953, he was transformed into a nationalist hero (Thomas *et al.* 2015: 189). The Dutch exiled several nationalist leaders from the Dutch East Indies in the early 1940s, including Tjipto Mangoenkoesoemo, Mohammed Hatta, and the future Indonesian president, Sukarno. Agostinho Neto, leader of the MPLA and eventually the first president of Angola, was arrested in 1960 and quickly exiled to Cape Verde, at least partially because his imprisonment in Angola led to massive protests by his supporters. He was sent to jail in Lisbon, then placed under house arrest following international protests. Despite imprisonment and exile, many of the prisoners could call on their supporters to carry on the anticolonial mission, giving mobility to ideas and actions when physical bodies had been rendered immobile.

POSTWAR DISPLACEMENTS AND GLOBAL GOVERNANCE

The end of the Second World War, which came in May 1945, initiated a refugee crisis in Europe itself that would come to greatly affect population demographics in many parts of the world. In addition to the over 11 million people who were exterminated during the Nazi genocide and the more than 25 million military causalities, millions of civilians had fled their homes, either in search of safety or because the Nazis had forced them into some sort of service. After the war, approximately 11 million people in Europe, 4.5 million of whom were in Soviet-controlled areas in Poland, Austria, and Germany, were not only far from home, but were not sure that they still had homes (Hitchcock 2009). The Allies, working with NGOs and the United Nations Relief and Rehabilitation Administration (UNRRA), repatriated around 10 million of the "displaced persons" between March and September 1945, but around 1.5 million displaced persons remained in refugee camps (often the same concentration camps they had been imprisoned within) until the early 1960s.

The postwar refugee crisis was one of the first major tasks that the newly created United Nations (1945) faced. The majority of displaced persons were victims of Nazi campaigns, and although the Allied nations did accept some of the displaced people, their doors would only open so far. This issue was on the minds of the creators of the one of the first major documents the UN produced, the Universal Declaration of Human Rights (UDHR) (1948). The UDHR deals explicitly with the right to movement. Article 13 reads: "(1) Everyone has the right to freedom of movement and residence within borders of each state. (2) Everyone has the right to leave any country, including his own, and to return to his country." It is important to note that the association with a person's right to movement is explicitly tied to his or her national belonging, a resolution consistent with the widespread implementation of passport controls during and after the wars. The UN, while committing to the rights of all people to the freedom of movement, also became deeply embedded in the system of state controls as they created a network of institutions that track and monitor refugees.

Even though colonial conquest had been the direct cause of the displacement of millions of colonized subjects for centuries prior, the United Nations High Commissioner on Refugees, the governing body that wrote the contemporary definition of refugee, was founded to address the crisis Europe faced at the end of its own war, not to deal with issues of colonial displacement. Despite the flourishing of the Non-Aligned Movement that brought together anticolonial leaders in a series of international meetings, as well as the participation of recently liberated countries to the UN, it was not until 1960 that the UN produced a document that addressed the problem of colonialism. The "Declaration on the Granting of Independence to Colonial Countries and People" came about after great pressure was put onto the UN from the bloc of formerly colonized nation-states, and sought global anticolonial liberation. This attention to the displaced people of Europe, and a lack of interest or concern for the colonized people who had faced centuries of brutal resettlement was not lost on the colonized. As the Martinican poet-intellectual Aimé Césaire ([1950] 2000) wrote in his essay *Discours sur le colonialisme* (Discourse on Colonialism),

> It would be worthwhile to study clinically, in detail, the steps taken by Hitler and Hitlerism and to reveal to the very distinguished, very humanistic Christian bourgeois of the twentieth century that without his being aware of it, he has Hitler inside him, that Hitler *inhabits* him, that Hitler is his *demon*, that if he rails against him, he is being inconsistent and that, at bottom, what he cannot forgive Hitler for is not *the crime* in itself, *the crime against man*, it is not the *humiliation of man as such*, it is the crime against the white man, the humiliation of the white man, and the fact that he applied to Europe colonialist procedures which until then had been reserved exclusively for the Arabs of Algeria, the "coolies" of India, and the "niggers" of Africa ([1950] 2000: 36, original emphasis).

Displacement was a cornerstone of western imperial expansion, from settler colonialism which decimated indigenous populations in the United States, Canada, Central and Latin America, Australia, and New Zealand, to the racially segregated regimes in South Africa and Algeria, to the massive forced migrations initiated by the Atlantic slave trade. Césaire, in this postwar moment, gave voice to the deep contradiction in the European panic over the "refugee crisis" attributed to the inherent evil of Hitler, when in fact the West had turned a blind eye (when not actively involved) to centuries of violence and genocide in the European colonies. That the largest and most violent movements of people in the twentieth century occurred in the wake of imperial collapse should thus come as no surprise.

THE PARTITIONS AND MIGRATIONS OF 1947–8 AND THEIR AFTERLIVES

The beginning of the end of the British Empire was ushered in on a wave of partitions that spoke to the importance of cultural nationalism in the postwar period. The partition of India into India and Pakistan on August 15, 1947 and the end of the British Mandate and the creation of the state of Israel on May 15, 1948 caused two of the most important mass displacements and migrations of the twentieth century. The partition of India came at the same time as its independence, leading to both celebrations and atrocity for the millions of people who were displaced, exterminated, or made into refugees in their own newly liberated countries (Pandey 2006). Likewise, using the marker of "the creation of Israel" to frame the events in Palestine in 1947–8 celebrates the new state while eclipsing the displacement of the Palestinian people, the destruction of the Palestinian state, and the loss of Palestinian homes and livelihoods. As Ilan Pappé (2006) notes, while the 1948 war was the "war of independence" for Israelis, it is better known as *al-Nakba*, or "the catastrophe," to Palestinians and others in the Arab world. Both partitions were accompanied by massive violence, including forced removals, systematic rape, and murder. In south Asia as well as Palestine, entire villages were destroyed. South Asian women— Hindu, Muslim, and Sikh—were forced, often by way of sexual assault, into religious conversion and joining new families, changing their ancestral names, and erasing their previous lives. In Palestine, families were forced into refugee camps in neighboring states as their homes were occupied or destroyed. Many of these families and their descendants continue to live in exile today.

The establishment of Israel in 1948 was the result of colonial interest in the region combined with the desire of the Jewish diaspora for the establishment of a homeland, speaking to the importance of belonging to a state in the contemporary world system wherein people are recognized primarily through their state belonging. Zionism, a form of Jewish nationalism, is a political movement founded in the late nineteenth century intent on the reestablishment of a Jewish homeland in Palestine, believed to be the ancient homeland of the Jewish people. Theodor Herzl, an Austro-Hungarian Jew who grew up facing rampant anti-Semitism in Austria, Germany, and France, founded the movement in 1897.[5] Zionist migration into Palestine before the creation of Israel occurred throughout five waves, heavily tied to anti-Semitic movements in Europe and Russia, including the Dreyfus Affair in France and anti-Semitic pogroms in Russia. Herzl desired the establishment of a Jewish state recognized by international law, an idea he discussed with both the Ottoman Sultan Abdülhamid II and the German Kaiser Wilhelm, and while they both turned him down, Zionists thought for a time about accepting the British offer to establish a Jewish homeland in Uganda.

While these discussions about the future of the Jewish people took place, Zionist migrants began to settle in Palestine. Between 1882 and 1903, 25,000 Zionist migrants, mostly from eastern Europe arrived; 40,000 between 1904 and 1914; 35,000 between 1919 and 1923; 67,000, originating primarily from Poland, between 1924 and 1928; over 250,000 in the lead up to the Second

Word War between 1929 and 1939; and finally, during the war between 1940 and 1945, another 60,000-people arrived (Khalidi 2006: 571–9). The percentage of the Jewish population in Palestine grew from six percent in 1880 to over 31 percent by 1945. In contrast, by the end of the war fought to create the state of Israel, "more than half of Palestine's native population, close to 800,000 people, had been uprooted, 531 villages had been destroyed, and eleven urban neighborhoods emptied of their inhabitants" (Pappé 2006: xiii). Fifty-four percent of the total Palestinian population at the time were made into refugees (Khalidi 2006: xxxiii).

The drawing of the border between India and the newly created Pakistan, which was geographically split into two, East and West Pakistan, with India in the middle, and the association with these new borders as a religious border meant to segregate the Muslims from the Hindus, Sikhs, Buddhists, Jains, Zoroastrians, Christians, and Jews led to the targeted rapes and killings of millions of people. Estimates of the dead vary from 200,000 to two million (Butalia 1998). As historian Yasmin Khan (2008: 157) writes, most people, especially in the highly contested area of the Punjab, fled their ancestral homes without notice, leaving behind the majority of their belongings and whatever amount of wealth they possessed, many not knowing where they were going or what would be there if and when they arrived. Refugee camps sprung up around India, a temporary measure that created "refugees" out of supposed national subjects. Tensions between India and Pakistan (and Bangladesh, the area that was West Pakistan until 1971) remain high today. It is still impossible for many people who were displaced in 1947 or during partition to return to their ancestral homes, and the governments of India and Pakistan are reluctant to issue visas to each other, keeping families who were separated far apart (Butalia 1998).

Unlike India and Pakistan, which were partitioned as a final act of colonial rule, the establishment of the state of Israel and the colonization of the Palestinian homeland "evolved in the post-heyday of the classical European colonization of Asian and African countries and in the wake of the espousal by the Western democracies of the principle of self-determination" (Khalidi 2006: xxxi). The Balfour Declaration, issued by British foreign secretary Lord Arthur James Balfour in 1917, declared British support for the creation of a Jewish "national homeland" in Palestine. While the British were in conversation with various Arab leaders about mutual interests in the region, the move for Jewish settlement in Palestine increased with this support from England.

Normalizing occupation has become an essential part of the Israeli state's campaign against Palestine, as Israel has become a western space situated within the Middle East. Displacement of populations often occurred simultaneously with the growth of the tourist industry: the "opening" of spaces from the control of "undesirable" populations also opens the doors to tourism (Cohen-Hattab and Katz 2001). The tension at the center of this contradiction is the gap between those who choose to travel for leisure, pleasure, or economic opportunity, and those who are compelled, coerced, or forced to move for a wide variety of reasons, including but not limited to war, economic depression, targeted state violence, and changing state borders. Western tourism—from Jewish birthright trips and other types of religious nationalist tourism to the marketing of beach vacations—allows non-Palestinians to have access to ancestral Palestinian lands that Palestinians are no longer allowed to access. Anthropologist Rebecca Stein (2008: 647) has shown how, after 1967, a "tourist event of massive proportions" took place as Israelis surged to sites that had been off limits to Israeli passport holders since the creation of Israel in 1948. Narratives of tourism that circulated in Israeli media gave cultural expression to the recent Israeli military victory, and tourism "was a crucial means by which many Jewish Israeli civilians came to know or reacquaint themselves with the newly occupied territories and confront their newfound status as occupiers" (Stein 2008: 648) (see Figure 5.2). Kashmir, a territory between India and Pakistan that remains contested territory, is also involved in a delicate balancing act of military occupation and a thriving tourist industry: while Kashmiris are placed under curfew and made subject to military and police control, tourists from the West and throughout India move freely about the territory to ski, sightsee, and camp. The culture of tourism, popularized through narratives of circulation and consumption, makes military occupation a quotidian issue.

FIGURE 5.2: Western tourists take pictures of destroyed military vehicles in the Golan Heights, 1967. Credit: Morse Collection/Gado/Getty Images.

POSTCOLONIAL MIGRATIONS

The two world wars caused a population shortage in Europe while simultaneously creating new labor needs. The postwar creation of social welfare institutions such as the British National Health Service (1948) required an influx of new types of labor. A major change in the postwar migrations from the colonies into Europe was that women were actively recruited from the colonies, especially for jobs in health care and as domestic laborers, and entire families began to migrate instead of only single men (Olwig 2015). Though western states, including the United States, which carried out mass deportations of Mexican workers in the 1930s (Henderson 2011), hoped that once their labor needs had been met, "guest workers" would return to their home countries, it was also the case that for a great majority of these workers, shifting conceptions of national territory and empire made identification with a state complicated.

For colonial subjects recruited to England, the "white Dominions" (Canada, Australia, New Zealand), France, and the United States, the position of being a subject of empire while simultaneously considered a foreign or guest worker was difficult to navigate. Algeria, for example, was formally a department of France, and while many Algerians faced barriers to French citizenship during the colonial period, due to their adherence to Islam, they were technically born on French land and were thus "native subjects" (Shepard 2006). During the years of the Algerian War of Independence, metropolitan France issued curfews that targeted North Africans, allowing police to arrest people based on their physical appearance, even though the Constitution of the Fifth Republic, put into place in 1958, extended French citizenship to all Algerian men and women, whether or not they were Muslim (Shepard 2006: 46). Todd Shepard (2006) argues that this last-ditch attempt to extend full citizenship rights to Algerians was an attempt to keep Algeria French, a move that was at least in part due to the intense lobbying of the French Algerian settlers, the *pieds-noirs*, whose lives in Algeria were threatened by decolonization.[6]

The possibility of having to provide substantial resources for the repatriation of colonial subjects—some of whom were settlers, others mixed race, or simply pro-French, English, Dutch, or Portuguese—is sometimes stated as a reason for the prolongation of empire. Whether this was the case, populations in the metropole regularly reacted negatively to the arrival of colonial populations in the metropole. For example, an estimated 250,000 Dutch and pro-Dutch Indonesians, many who had never been to the Netherlands before, arrived in Dutch cities after 1945 (Thomas *et al.* 2015: 278). Racism and xenophobia that targeted these groups quickly escalated after their arrival. While the French state knew that the independence of Algeria would mean some amount of repatriation, they were completely unprepared for virtually all *pieds-noirs* to enter France at the end of the war in 1962. When the Evian Accords were signed on March 18, 1962, Algerians became Algerian citizens, and there was a mass exodus of around one million people, 85 percent of the overall *pieds-noirs* population, from Algeria to France. As Claire Eldridge (2013) has shown, while the *pieds-noirs* largely considered themselves French and thus were fully expecting to be welcomed with open arms in metropolitan France, many soon found on arrival that they were viewed as unwanted foreigners, associated with the violence in Algeria and disruptors of French national identity.

Migration also occurred as a result of unrest in newly formed postcolonial states, sometimes based on the perceived injustices of colonial rule. In an exceptional case, south Asians who had been settled for generations in the former British colony of Uganda were expelled in 1972 by the new Ugandan President Idi Amin, and many were forced to relocate, placed in London in urban refugee camps (see Figure 5.3). Amin believed that the continued presence of Asians in Uganda was a form of cultural imperialism that needed to be cut off to restore the state to (black) Ugandans. In 1973, Ugandan writer and scholar Mahmood Mamdani found himself living in a refugee transit camp on Kensington Church Street in London (Mamdani [1973] 2011). Over 4,000 Asians had arrived in London from Uganda, most with no money because Amin had forbidden them from taking currency out of the country, and thus relied on family and friends, and to some extent the British state, to help them settle.

FIGURE 5.3: Ugandan Asians arrive at Stansted Airport on a charter flight after being expelled from Uganda, September 18, 1972. Credit: Keystone/Getty Images.

Those expelled were essentially stateless: writing in 1973, Mamdani noted that "bitter experience has taught us that in both Uganda and Britain, it has mattered little what passport we held. Our fate was determined by political and not legal factors" ([1973] 2011: 9).

The end of formal empire led many to reconsider what "home" meant to them, especially among the resurgence of ethnic, racial, and religious nationalisms. Although south Asian Ugandans were eventually allowed to return to Uganda, they had been rendered foreigners in their absence, Ugandan nationalism taking on a distinct racial character. Mamdani, writing on what it was like to return to Uganda in 1980, following almost a decade of exile in London, the United States, and Tanzania, remembers that since the expulsions in 1972, no one in Uganda seemed to remember the Ugandan Asians, transforming him *muzungu* (a white person) upon his return. In the new 2011 preface to his now classic 1973 book *From Citizen to Refugee*, Mamdani writes, "Even though I had come home, in the eyes of those who did not know me, I would be a foreigner. I knew I would never be able to take 'home' for granted" ([1973] 2011: 7).

By the late 1960s and early 1970s, anti-immigrant sentiments grew in England, France, and the Netherlands as former colonial subjects became more active in local politics and communities, making space for themselves through political organizing and cultural expression. Stuart Hall (1997), the Jamaican-born intellectual and cultural theorist, has argued that British national identity was built on the existence of its global cultural empire, and the threat the colonized posed to this identity caused a deeper commitment to a culture of whiteness among British nationalists. The backlash against the growing diversity of the metropole in the 1960s to today has been met with a proliferation of xenophobic political ideologies. While these political parties throughout Europe and the United States ebb and flow in popularity, the foundational idea that Europe, including the United Kingdom and by extension the United States, is threatened by immigrants persists. On April 20, 1968, Enoch Powell, a Conservative Member of Parliament gave the now infamous "Rivers of Blood" speech in Birmingham, England in which he responded to continued reform of Commonwealth immigration policies and antiracist legislation by invoking the fear that "decent Englishmen" had expressed to him that "in 15 or 20 years' time the black man will have the whip hand over the white man." This formulation of the "decent Englishman" is of course of a white, English, Christian man, a worker who was threatened by the deep otherness of "Commonwealth immigrants" who were arriving *en masse*, with all their children, to infiltrate proper British society. He called out the Sikhs, many of whom had arrived in England following the massive violence of partition in the Punjab, for practicing religious customs that are "inappropriate" to "native-born" Englishmen. While this type of fear-mongering will not be surprising to anyone in the post–9/11 era, this speech, and other ones like it, mark an important moment when the politics of mobility became explicitly linked to states, race, nationalism, and the "end of empire."

THE NEW IMPERIAL BORDERS: TOURISM AND MIGRATION

> In contemporary travel accounts, the monarch-of-all-I-survey scene gets repeated only now from the balconies of hotels in big third-world cities.
>
> Mary Louise Pratt, Imperial Eyes (1992: 216)

To speak of mobility is also to speak of its impossibility. That some people, typically white Europeans or North Americans, were free to "explore uncharted territory" while brown and black people from non-western areas were seen as threats, especially when mobile, is a colonial construction that remains in circulation today. While adventure narratives that portray white European and North American explorers such as Henry Morton Stanley and David Livingstone, T.E. Lawrence (better known as "Lawrence of Arabia"), Gertrude Bell, and the fictional anthropologist Professor Indiana Jones, remain contemporary hallmarks of popular culture, colonized and formerly colonized subjects often struggle to gain access to imperial spaces beyond their "native lands." As the historian Matthew Stanard (2014) has shown, in the case of the Belgian Congo, Belgium was extremely conscious of making sure that colony and metropole were kept divided. Well into the late 1950s, and through decolonization in 1960, Belgium actively denied access to white Belgian spaces to Congolese people, even those brought to the metropole as cultural performers for the benefit of the Belgian public. This is an example of what Stanard calls the "immobility" of the colonized, a theorization that is important in understanding contemporary regimes of border securitization (2014: 89). While Belgium may be a unique case in which mobility was more restricted than in the larger British and French empires, it is also indicative of the spectrum of approaches by which imperial nation-states regulated the flows of colonial subjects.

Imperial expansion—from the arrival of western "explorers" and militaries to the movement of colonial settlers and the forced migrations of subjugated peoples from land desired by the West—depended on the relationships and ideas forged in the contact zones to succeed. In contemporary society, we are seeing contact zones emerge as a confluence of tourists and refugees and/or migrants in the same space but often for very different reasons. Take, for example, the situation in Greece during the summer of 2015. Amidst an economic depression that was reaching its sixth year—a depression that had caused many members of the Greek middle class to lose their jobs, their life savings, their pensions, and their homes—Syrian refugees, fleeing violence at home, began arriving in great numbers on Greek shores. Over the summer, major western media publications, including *The Guardian*, *New York Times*, and *Wall Street Journal* ran pictures of mostly white western tourists in Greece watching as brown and black refugees, primarily from Syria but also Iraq, Libya, Eritrea, and elsewhere on the African continent, arrived on the shores of their beach holidays. While most Greeks were too economically depressed to vacation, English, French, Dutch, American, and German tourists arrived at this scenic border on the beach. Journalists wrote of tourists unwittingly rescuing migrants lost at sea while out on their own leisure tours, and of tourist establishments that sometimes became temporary "welcome centers" for recent arrivals who needed food, water, and shelter.

The combination of the Greek economic crisis, the tourist season, and the dramatic increase of refugees seeking entry to Europe resulted in a contact zone that revealed the ways in which tourism and migration are at fundamental odds with each other. That most of the EU countries currently involved in this system of fortification did not have colonial empires shows how pervasive and powerful the culture of maintaining and rebuilding colonial systems and tools of control continue to be. Contemporary debates around mobility are concentrated on the threat that refugees, primarily from Afghanistan, Syria, Iraq, and parts of Central and West Africa, pose to "fortress Europe," the former seats of empire. While far-right nationalist parties that espouse xenophobic platforms that are anti-Muslim and anti-immigrant, such as the National Front (FN) in France, Golden Dawn in Greece, and the Alternative for Germany (AfD), continue to gain popularity, the numbers of migrants risking their lives to cross the Mediterranean and reach Europe has also increased, exceeding 300,000 people in 2015 (Fleming 2015).

Many of the security regimes in place today began as tools of colonial governance. As Ann Laura Stoler (2016: 4) writes, "colonial counterinsurgency policies rest undiluted in current security measures." For example, the counterinsurgency tactics the French military developed during the Algerian War of Independence were exported to the United States (Macmaster 2004) and have been used in US military campaigns abroad and domestically, including, recently, the #NODAPL (No Dakota Access Pipeline) protests, a movement led by Indigenous peoples against the building of the Dakota Pipeline. The military tactics employed by federal and local police agencies at Standing Rock in North Dakota, including police and military agents clearing camps that protestors built to prevent the physical construction of the pipeline, made it clear that the United States continues to view Indigenous peoples as threats to the US rather than as legitimate citizens, a clear sign of continued settler colonialism. While pipeline workers, contractors, and police and military are free to move throughout the United States, #NODAPL protestors, allies, and even journalists covering the conflict, including *Democracy Now!*'s Amy Goodman, have been subject to surveillance, arrest, prosecution, and incarceration, all counterinsurgency tactics that limit movement.[7]

Though empire officially "ended" with the liberation of the former colonies, mobility continues to be regulated by hierarchical institutions of race and nation rooted in colonial systems of control, which comes as no surprise to the currently and formerly colonized. Despite the hopes that increased access to transportation technology, a global regime of free trade, and network connectivity would, as neoliberal pundit and *New York Times* columnist Thomas Friedman (2005) has suggested, make the "world flat," it has become obvious that globalization has not meant detachment from nationalism or the weakening of borders. The borders are only getting stronger, yet narratives and practices of tourism and consumption continue unabated, signaling to the wealthy that if you have enough capital, you can simultaneously travel abroad and build up your borders at home to keep those without wealth out (Jones 2016).

Despite the cultural and political resurgence of xenophobia in western countries, there has also been the proliferation of social movements, including No Borders and No One is Illegal, that bring together activists, migrants, and refugees to protect anyone seeking shelter and safety. Independent of state institutions, NGOs, and the United Nations, these movements operate at the local level without central leadership, and undertake autonomous actions such as squatting in an Airbnb in Berlin and claiming it for refugees, working to stop

FIGURE 5.4: Protestors at Raleigh-Durham International Airport protesting the Muslim travel ban, January 29, 2017. Credit: Leo Ching.

individual deportations by mobilizing call-ins and protests, and the mass mobilization of protestors and lawyers who worked to halt President Donald J. Trump's Executive Order 13769 (issued January 27, 2017) that suspended the US Refugee Admissions Program and banned entry of persons from Iran, Iraq, Libya, Somalia, Sudan, Syria, and Yemen (see Figure 5.4). As the activist-scholar Harsha Walia (2013) argued, it is the mission of these solidarity and mutual-aid networks to name and "undo" the borders created by empire and to establish a world in which no person is illegal. Security regimes are becoming more sophisticated, but they have not prevented the movement of people who continue to find ways to work together to resist the continuation of systems of empire that persist through the protection of national borders.

CHAPTER SIX

Sexuality

ANNA CLARK AND ELIZABETH WILLIAMS

Sexuality is always an issue in imperialism because it is the most intimate site for the clash of cultures and power relations. The term "sexuality" encompasses a broad range of practices, identities, and relationships. Often, it refers to physical acts that challenge the boundaries between bodies. For instance, interracial sex and reproduction created offspring and relationships that undermined racial boundaries. Sexual practices that were deemed "repugnant" to colonial norms, or (perhaps more to the point) a threat to colonial rule, could become targets of regulation.

Sexuality can also refer to the discourses which use sex (real or imagined) as a framework to discuss larger anxieties about power and control. For instance, as more white women settled in the colonies, a discourse which highlighted the threat of "black peril," the supposed rape of white women by black men, symbolized the perceived threat to white male power. Furthermore, by the 1920s, sexuality had been created as an object of study not only in the discipline of sexology, but in medicine, psychology, anthropology, and sociology as well, all disciplines important in the project of colonial management of populations. Imperialism had always been key to these studies, since differences in sexual cultures were used in racist thinking. In a language of evolutionary hierarchy, parallels were made between colonized peoples, the European working class, and children: all supposedly characterized by a primitive sexuality that was excessive and unrestrained. Yet as twentieth-century sexologists strove to define and even invent what was "natural" in terms of sex and to create sexuality as identity, some sexologists also claimed that so-called primitive people had a purer and more natural sexuality, unencumbered by civilization.

Finally, sexuality served as a potent tool for the management of colonized populations. Imperialists sought to regulate sexuality not only by disciplining individuals, but also at a biopolitical level: the imperative to measure and manage populations, especially through reproduction. In the twentieth century, modernity brought new elements to these clashes with a greater focus on development and bureaucratic management (Stoler 1995: 4; Burton 1999: 1). In the interwar period, imperial powers increasingly justified their actions as "trusteeship" to manage populations for greater health and efficiency. European imperialists sought to develop their colonies for greater economic success, and even claimed to prepare colonized people for self-rule in the distant future. This management was especially important in efforts to maintain reproduction and health, key for the maintenance of a labor force.

No single approach to the production, management, and disciplining of sexuality held true at all times and places; rather, great variation existed among the various European empires. Even within a single colony, opinions about sexuality varied greatly among different colonial actors. For instance, while missionaries often sought to "reform" indigenous sexual practices, efforts to modernize and assimilate could clash with philosophies of British indirect rule and French accommodation, the notion that it was easier to rule through local authorities who would respect indigenous customs (Hobsbawm and Ranger 1992; Mamdani 1996; Conklin 1997: 165). Colonial planters cared most about maintaining control over land and labor—they therefore tended to be most interested in biopolitical agendas. Attempts to "reform" sexual practices could also become rallying points for cultural nationalists, who argued that such "reforms" represented an assault on the values and identity of indigenous groups. Such contested approaches to the management of sexuality are by no means incidental. Rather, sexuality proved a potent imperial discourse precisely because it was malleable enough to serve multiple agendas. Whether colonized people were seen as primitive and barbaric or pure and natural, sexuality was an excuse to control their lives.

EUGENICS 1918–39

Eugenics became an important aspect of modernist racial thinking on both the left and right. Eugenics can be defined as the pseudo-scientific management of human breeding, and it was particularly concerned with race and class in the effort to define the "abnormal" and "unfit." Eugenics sought to discourage the reproduction of the "unfit," and conversely to encourage the reproduction of those in valued categories. Eugenics, of course, reached its murderous apogee in the Holocaust, but it also played a key role in imperialist endeavors. The genocide of the Herero people in German South-West Africa between 1904 and 1907 is a particularly salient example; in fact, several scholars have argued that the genocidal techniques of Nazi Germany had been developed in this colonial genocide (Hull 2005; Madley 2005; Zimmerer and Zeller 2008).

Imperialist eugenics was also about managing populations to preserve racial boundaries in more subtle—and more insidious—ways. For instance, Chloe Campbell has shown that eugenicists in colonial Kenya used arguments of "the inherent biological limitations of the native population" to suggest "the futility of native development" (Campbell 2007: 32). Settlers thus ensured a population of laborers on their farms by suggesting that Africans were genetically unfit for any other work.

As the earlier example indicates, in colonies where settlers relied on indigenous labor, management of marriage and childbirth became important issues. During the interwar period, several African colonies saw declines in population as a result of famine, disease, and war, endangering efforts to develop colonial economies. Colonial regimes thus attempted to "reform" indigenous practices surrounding reproduction in order to ensure a healthy labor supply. In the Belgian Congo, for instance, settler women attempted to increase birth rates and reduce infant mortality by "educating" African women in hygiene and "mothercraft" (Hunt 1988).

Colonial officials sometimes claimed to be protecting women from practices such as child marriage, but as Martin Thomas writes of French territories in Muslim North Africa, "legal regulation enforced French control over the Muslim population rather than affording women greater freedom" (Thomas 2005: 160). Conversely, African elites were sometimes able to exploit these biopolitical anxieties to their own advantage. In interwar colonial Asante, chiefs mandated the "capture" of unmarried women. The colonial government supported these detentions, believing that they were necessary to reduce venereal disease in young women. In reality, chiefs were actually disturbed by the new financial independence of Asante women who farmed cocoa. The prevention of venereal disease thus served as a cover for the reassertion of elite male authority "over women's productive and reproductive power" (Allman 1996: 212).

Colonial authorities often blamed indigenous peoples for the prevalence of venereal disease. Although medical authorities in German East Africa believed that venereal disease had been introduced into the colony by Europeans, they nevertheless asserted that the "loose morals" of indigenous women were responsible for spreading venereal disease. As one doctor stated, "civilisation is indeed responsible for bringing [diseases in], but not for their general dissemination. This requires a suitable soil, that is, 'loose morals' . . . that do not allow for immunity" (quoted in Walther 2013: 182). Likewise, some French doctors attributed many birth defects and skin problems to hereditary syphilis that they claimed was endemic in Morocco; blaming it on Arab customs, they wanted to inject pregnant women with the arsenic used to treat venereal disease. Fortunately, as Ellen Amster points out, the French government did not provide funding for these efforts (Amster 2016: 331; see also Clark 2013: 86–114).

Imperial governments were also concerned with regulating interracial sex: they feared that relationships between white men and colonized women would threaten racial purity, and reduce white "prestige" in the colonies. In 1905, for instance, legislation passed in colonial Eritrea banned marriages between Italian women and native men, and established that indigenous women who married Italian men would not be granted citizenship (Baratieri 2014: 366). Some governments instructed their officials to renounce their native concubines and marry white women instead (Conklin 1997: 169). In the East Indies, Dutch imperialists began to fear the consequences of concubinage: the increasing number of pauperized and discontented Eurasians. The Dutch increasingly resorted to a language of racial purity in the 1920s. As the nationalist challenge mounted, officials began to crack down on sex between Europeans and indigenous peoples. White women were given the responsibility to control the sexual drives of white men and to preserve the "race" in Indonesia and marry white men. But as officials discouraged concubinage, more Dutch men actually married native women, often their housekeepers (Stoler 1992: 530) (Figure 6.1).

Similarly, in Indochina French officials admonished European men to uphold their values of reason and self-restraint against what they regarded as the dissolute desires of the native population; they needed to preserve racial purity to preserve their imperial domination, which was becoming increasingly fragile. French authorities worried that in Indochina a European man might lose his inhibitions in the "heavy and odorous atmosphere of the opium den," becoming "incapable

FIGURE 6.1: Postcard of the colonies of the Netherlands, *c.* 1900. Credit: Culture Club/Getty Images.

of true desire," and masturbating himself, or even worse, being seduced by the boy preparing the pipes, who was much more "appetizing" than the native prostitute (Proschan 2002: 625). The French had long encouraged concubinage with Indochinese women, and even granted citizenship to their offspring if they could be seen to have assimilated into French culture, but in the interwar period they also became anxious that native women would accuse French men of fathering their children and disturb the racial order (Saada 2012: 121–47).

European authorities also tried to control poor whites, especially women, who defied convention and mingled with colonized peoples, thus endangering racial distinctions. During the 1938 election in South Africa, interracial marriage became a central issue; when the United Party refused to ban it, the "Purified" National Party (GNP) produced a poster depicting a white woman living in squalor with her African husband. Not only did they fear racial mixing, they also wanted to reestablish the gender hierarchy endangered by the increased independence gained by Afrikaner women during the 1920s and 1930s. As Jonathan Hyslop writes, by "portraying white women as sexually threatened by black men, Afrikaner males claimed the role of protectors of women, thereby reasserting their patriarchal control" (1995: 57–81).

Colonized peoples also sometimes opposed interracial relationships. In the Gold Coast in the 1920s, African nationalists deployed the specter of interracial sex both to assert patriarchal authority over African women, and to argue against colonial authority. "By casting European men as sexually promiscuous interlopers," Carina Ray notes, African nationalists "challenged the very idea that Europeans were morally suited to rule the colonial world" (2014: 82). Yet sometimes indigenous women may have been able to exploit interracial relationships to their own advantage. For instance, women in rural southern Mozambique pursued "strategic engagements" with Portuguese men to access economic opportunities, gain farming land, or learn a trade (Gengenbach 2010: 20). Robert Aldrich has made a similar point about relationships between European and indigenous men in French colonies: while "some relationships differed little from prostitution or included coercion and violence, yet many indigenous men could derive material and emotional advantages in the form of income, social promotion, or closer association with the colonial ruling order from partnerships with Europeans" (Aldrich 2002: 202).

In addition to trying to regulate interracial marriages, during the interwar period western governments and local reformers sometimes tried to change indigenous marriage customs as part of an effort to modernize these societies. They did not always agree on strategies, and their efforts often sparked nationalist objections. In Indonesia, the Dutch government tried to mandate monogamous marriages for non-Muslims married to Muslims, ostensibly to protect them. Some nationalists had demanded this change as part of their vision of a new, modern society. But Indonesian Muslims were affronted at this interference in their religious customs. They pointed out that polygamy prevented prostitution and adultery, and highlighted the hypocrisy of Europeans who failed to interfere in the practice of European men taking native concubines (Locher-Scholten 2000: 193–206).

Campaigns against child marriage, which had been prominent in the 1890s, were also revived in the twentieth century. This time, however, it was not just a matter of western governments imposing alien cultures; in many cases local reformers now advocated laws against child marriage.[1] In India, the American journalist Katherine Mayo (1867–1940) depicted child marriage as the epitome of "barbaric" Hindu customs that made Indians incapable of self-rule. Many female Indian nationalists rejected her negative attitude toward their culture but wanted to press for reforms themselves; they demanded that the nationalist movement take on women's causes. Despite resistance from the British government, who were interested in appeasing Orthodox Hindus as a way of dividing Indians to hinder the nationalist cause, child marriage became a major nationalist focus. Eventually, the British conceded and allowed passage of the Sarda Act of 1929, which set the age of consent within marriage 13, and consent to sex outside of it 14 (Mukherjee 2006: 233; Pande 2012: 206). This act applied not only to Hindus but to all marriages, and allowed for a notion of universal human rights for women who breached the assumption that religious communities should have a monopoly on control of personal lives. However, the act also sparked tensions with Muslim communities (Sinha 2006: 155–61).

In the nineteenth century, social purity campaigns used a rhetoric of "white slavery," but now, campaigns against sex trafficking had to fit with the notion of trusteeship. For European women activists, this fit well with the "maternalist" tradition of taking care of others, often in a condescending manner (Tambe 2009: 404–10). However, European governments sometimes objected to efforts to suppress trafficking. In the Straits Settlements, for instance, concern with venereal disease led some officials to propose the reintroduction of regulations that resembled the Contagious Diseases Acts in compulsory treatment. In Hong Kong, British officials at first resisted efforts to reform the *mui tsai* system in which young girls were contracted into domestic service and sometimes sex work (Gorman 2008: 186–209) (Figure 6.2). Furthermore, humanitarian activists and League officials did not always recognize that many female migrants were voluntarily seeking better opportunities in a new global labor market (Rodríguez García 2012). In West Africa, colonial officials failed to report the sexual trafficking of very young girls to the League of Nations, leading to a public outcry and new legislation. However, this legislation also cracked down on sex work by adult Nigerian women and stigmatized the broader patterns of women's labor migration that were impelled by the very developments of the modern economy that colonial officials were trying to encourage, as Saheed Aderinto notes (2015: 120). In France, colonial officials

FIGURE 6.2: *Mui tsai*, child slave. Credit: Anti-Slavery International.

pushed back against the League's efforts to suppress trafficking on the grounds that it would interfere with regulated brothels, which they insisted were essential to fight venereal disease.

For the French, regulated brothels were also important as a way of segregating sexual commerce in colonial North Africa, and in some ways the system intensified between the wars to provide sexual services to soldiers (Limoncelli 2010: 120–7; Amster 2016: 335). They even introduced regulated brothels to Syria and Cameroon (Camiscioli 2009: 104). Despite these efforts, the old system of the *maison tolerée* seemed increasingly outdated in the new more sexualized popular culture of urban Morocco, where clandestine prostitution flourished out of authorities' control (Taraud 2003: 143). The French colonial officials' insistence on the regulatory system undermined the moral authority of the French empire and further inflamed nationalist resistance.

In Egypt, Islamic nationalists and Egyptian feminists had long campaigned against the state regulation of prostitution, which had been imposed by the British in 1882. While the Ottomans had closely regulated the sexual behavior of their subjects, especially soldiers, the British were mainly concerned with the health of white soldiers, for women who sold sex to indigenous Egyptians only were not inspected. The Egyptian government, as part of its effort to display national independence, finally banned prostitution in 1951. The Egyptian opposition to prostitution was not, however, solely the product of western discourses; rather, Egyptian nationalists also drew on medieval Islamic texts to argue for the abolition of prostitution. In fact, nationalists viewed marriage as an important institution that would protect the sexual, moral, and mental health of Egyptian men, thus ensuring the success of the Egyptian nation (Kholoussy 2010: 677–91). Similarly, in the 1950s the members of the anticolonial FLN (Front National de Liberation) in Algeria viewed prostitutes as traitors to their cause, although some prostitutes actually aided the nationalists' movement by passing on information inadvertently given by their customers (Taraud 2003: 361).

For nationalists in the Islamic world, reforming sexual behavior was an important part of their cultural process. In the late nineteenth and early twentieth centuries, Egyptian and Iranian nationalists who visited Europe were shocked by what they saw as sexual immorality and the looseness of white women; they defined Islam as purer in contrast. In turn, these nationalists repudiated the long tradition of men keeping boy lovers and celebrating the beauty of male youths in poetry, declaring that these practices corrupted Islamic purity. Instead, they wanted to modernize relationships between men and women into a new form of heterosexuality suitable for modern nations (Massad 2008; Kholoussy 2010). Iranian constitutionalists at the beginning of the twentieth century criticized pederasty of boys and marriage of young girls as exploitative and undermining the brotherly bonds of nationalists because they were based on inequality of age (Najmabadi 2008; Afary 2009). Historians emphasize that these reform efforts were not primarily imposed by western Orientalist discourses, but were responses to internal dynamics within Iranian society.

The veil also became an issue in larger debates over women's work and education in the interwar and immediate postwar period. Some colonial officials and their supporters encouraged women to unveil as a sign of modernity and support for the French in Algeria. Some nationalists also promoted the unveiling, education, and employment of women in the interwar period as a means of modernity. However, the development of a commercial popular leisure culture where women worked in department stores, frequented cafes, and even sold sex, was both alluring and frightening to young nationalists (Taraud 2003: 357). Most Islamic reformers advocated more traditional religious measures about veiling and the female role. Colonial authorities sometimes went along with this populist conservatism to keep a lid on revolts (Thompson [2000] 2013: 87–120).

NEW DISCOURSES OF SEXUALITY

Although many of the old racial discourses of the nineteenth century remained intact, the first decades of the twentieth century also brought shifts in racial thought. Particularly after the horrors of the Great War, the image of European peoples heading a stately march toward an idealized civilization began to unravel. As Henrika Kuklick has written, the generation that came of age in the postwar period thus "regarded human nature as fundamentally irrational, and considered individual and social degeneration as just as natural as progress" (Kuklick 1991: 23). Simultaneously, the idea of essential racial difference was increasingly questioned by anthropologists, who began to move toward a "cultural relativist" position. Functionalists like Bronislaw Malinowksi (1884–1942), A.R. Radcliffe Brown (1881–1955), E.E. Evans Pritchard (1902–73), and particularly Franz Boas (1858–1942), began to argue that differences between groups of peoples were due to cultural variation, rather than biology. Meanwhile, sexologists like Havelock Ellis (1859–1939) and Sigmund Freud (1856–1939) increasingly worried about the negative effects of "civilization" upon the sexual health of Europeans; while the suppression of sexual instincts was viewed as essential for progress, it also created opportunities for the development of perversions or neuroses (Hoad 2000; Epprecht 2008). Thus, in the early twentieth century, artists, intellectuals, sexologists, and anthropologists increasingly advocated a return to the "primitive" as a cure for western ills.

Cultural modernists found what they imagined to be "oriental" or "primitive" sexuality to be inspiring; a fantastical image of "oriental" and "primitive" sexuality also began to dominate in popular and high culture. The bestselling novel by Edith Maud Hull (1880–1947), *The Sheik*, published in 1919 and made into a film starring Rudolph Valentino in 1921, epitomized this Orientalist trend (Figure 6.3). The novel tells the story of an Englishwoman, Lady Diana Mayo, who was raped by an Arab Sheik while traveling alone in Algeria. Lady Mayo falls in love with the Sheik, who luckily turns out to be an Englishman in disguise. The novel played with anxieties about interracial intimacies, and about the increased independence of European women in the interwar era (Chow 1999: 64–87; Blake 2003; Teo 2010). At the same time, racist images pervaded popular culture (Chase 1992: 256; Ellena 2004: 257). The African-American singer and dancer Josephine Baker (1906–75) was the toast of Paris and Berlin, but her popularity was predicated on her performance of a particular vision of "savage" sexuality (Figure 6.4); as Roman Horak notes, "Baker was presented over and over again as the Other of urban European modernity" (Horak 2013: 516). Similarly, the Cubists repurposed the conventions of African art to tap into an impulsive, sensual, and primal impulse that they felt was lacking in European life (Blake 1999). In both cases, the lack of restraint that supposedly characterized the "primitive" was seen as a cure for European over-civilization and neurosis.

Radical sex reformers believed that the West had repressed the art of love and idealized the "Orient" as a source of erotic knowledge. The German physician and sex educator Max Hodann (1894–1946) proclaimed "the world of the Orient, the Mohammedan-Arabian world, as well as the Indian and Shintoist, is today still free from this ban against sensuousness which oppresses

FIGURE 6.3: A scene from the film "The Sheik," in which Rudolph Valentino (1895–1926) embraces Agnes Ayres. Credit: Hulton Archive/Getty Images.

FIGURE 6.4: Josephine Baker posing with a tiger rug, *c.* 1925. Credit: Hulton Archive/Getty Images.

Europe and America, and prevents the growth of any love culture" (Hodann [1932] 1975: 12). In her 1937 marriage manual, the family planning pioneer Helena Wright (1887–1982) wrote, "there can be nothing impossible about the achievement of a successful sex act, because it is the universal experience of primitive peoples, and of Eastern civilizations," who treated sex as a cultural art and skill (Wright [1931] 1937: 85). The Dutch physician Theodore Van de Velde (1873–1937), author of the 1926 bestseller *Ideal Marriage*, explored "oriental" sexual manuals for new positions for intercourse, but he also believed that western women's sexuality was physiologically different and more complicated (Van de Velde [1926] 1930: 149). A male homosexual journal praised Islamic cultures for discreetly tolerating same-sex relations (Karsch-Haack and Stelter 2002: 25–30, 80–2). On the other hand, the "primitivity" of African sexuality continued to be stigmatized. As Keguro Macharia has put it, "The African appeared in sexology's archives as hypo- and hyper-developed: too uncivilized to be homosexual, a condition that afflicted the 'over-civilized' races, and too excessively bodily not to be queer (the too-large penises, too-large clitorises, too much appetite)" (Macharia 2014).

In African colonies, Europeans were less likely to view colonized peoples as possessing special sexual knowledge. As opposed to those in the exotic "East," where sexual expertise had supposedly been developed as a cultural form, Africans were generally viewed as being too "primitive" to have anything but heterosexual, reproductive sex. As Marc Epprecht has put it, African cultures were considered unique "in the[ir] absence of, ignorance about, or intolerance toward exceptions to the heterosexual norm" (Epprecht 2008: 25). However, this very adherence to "natural," "uncontaminated" sexuality was what made Africans virile and healthy; experts including Carl Jung (1875–1961) and Marie Bonaparte (1882–1962) proposed that data about the sexual practices of "primitive" peoples could thus be used to improve the sexual health of Europeans. Bonaparte was particularly inspired by the practice of clitoridectomy in some East African communities. A former patient of Freud's, she was disturbed by her inability to achieve a "mature" vaginal orgasm. As Bodil Folke Frederiksen has written, Bonaparte became convinced "that because of African free sexuality and possibly because of the prevalence of clitoridectomy, African women might be better 'vaginalized', as she expressed it, and thus more feminine than European women" (Frederiksen 2008: 26). She subsequently underwent several operations to move her clitoris closer to her vaginal canal in an effort to cure her supposed sexual dysfunction, before ultimately deciding that psychoanalysis was a more effective treatment.[2]

This is not to say that the idea of the "primitive" as sexually pathological entirely disappeared; rather, it existed alongside the newer discourse stressing the dangers of civilization for sexual health. Furthermore, the sexual dysfunction of Europeans posed a direct threat to colonization. As colonial possessions increasingly challenged imperial authority, western imperial powers became ever more concerned about their ability to exert control over seemingly more virile and sexually functional peoples (Davin 1978). The sexual discourses of the nineteenth and twentieth centuries thus represented a curious Catch-22: the lack of sexual restraint that supposedly rendered "primitive" peoples incapable of self-rule also guaranteed that they would produce larger and less neurotic populations than those who ruled them.

The idea that African sexual norms and practices must be protected from "contamination" by more "civilized"—and hence more deviant and neurotic—cultures served as a justification for keeping colonized people out of cities, schools, and politics. The "detribalized native" was viewed as particularly prone to adopting criminal or immoral behaviors, or succumbing to madness (Vaughan 2004: 100–28). In British colonies, regimes were thus able to justify the segregation of colonized peoples in rural "Native Reserves" as an extension of their duties as guardians of vulnerable wards; as Mahmood Mamdani notes, "the essence of protection [of natives] was not to guarantee rights but to enforce custom" (1996: 70).

Despite the insistence on the need to preserve indigenous sexual practices from "contamination," scholars have shown that colonialism dramatically altered African sex/gender norms. Oyèrónkẹ́ Oyěwùmí has argued (controversially) that the very category of gender did not exist in Yorubaland prior to European colonization: in precolonial Yoruba society, she writes, "the body was not the basis of social roles, inclusions, or exclusions" (Oyěwùmí 1997: x).³ Colonization, she argues, thus introduced patriarchy to a space where seniority had previously been the most significant category of difference.

Indeed, the mandate to preserve indigenous cultures and mores often served as a cover to do just the opposite—to recreate "customs" to meet the needs of a particular moment. In accordance with the doctrine of indirect rule, authorities in colonial Africa sought to rule through indigenous institutions. In reality, these institutions were often invented or transformed through the process of colonization (Hobsbawn and Ranger 1992; Spear 2003). Customary law proved a particularly useful tool for controlling the behavior—both sexual and economic—of indigenous women in Northern Rhodesia (Chanock 1982). Yet non-elite men and women were also sometimes able to exploit disputes among various authorities (missionaries, administrators, and chiefs and other African elites) in defining customary law to pursue their own agendas. Thus, argues Rachel Jean-Baptiste, "The colonial state and African male political leaders were constantly shifting their articulations of customary law in response to the unanticipated ways in which ordinary men and women defined, engaged in and were in conflict over matrimony and sex" (2008: 240).

Similarly, in Kenya in the 1920s and 1930s, attempts by missionaries and humanitarians to ban the custom of clitoridectomy backfired as Gikuyu nationalists embraced the custom as essential to the social structures of their community. As Susan Pedersen explains, "As a defense of clitoridectomy became entangled with long-standing Kikuyu grievances about mission influence and access to land, clitoridectomy ... came to be seen as a mark of loyalty to the incipient, as yet imaginary, nation" (Pedersen 1991: 651). The trained anthropologist (and later first president of independent Kenya) Jomo Kenyatta (1891–1978) "defended the positive function of initiation rites, particularly clitoridectomy, in direct response to missionary attacks on their supposed barbarity and encouragement of sexual promiscuity by claiming instead that they actually turned children into socially and sexually responsible and disciplined adults" (Berman 1996: 334). When missionaries began to refuse to let circumcised girls attend their schools, Gikuyu nationalists set up their own "independent schools." These schools in turn helped build nationalist sentiment.

POSTWAR MORAL IMPERIALISM AND DECOLONIZATION

Just as the process of building up colonial regimes drew on sexual rhetoric and practices, sexuality also influenced the process of tearing them down. Decolonization brought with it particular kinds of sexual violence, as colonial regimes sought to retain control. Men and women detained by the British colonial government during the suppression of the Mau Mau rebellion in Kenya faced sexualized torture—in June 2013, the British government agreed to pay compensation to over 5,000 of these torture victims (Elkins 2005b; Anderson 2011; Parry 2016). In his study of the Algerian War of Independence, *The Wretched of the Earth* ([1961] 2004), Frantz Fanon (1925–61) highlighted the sexual humiliation of colonized men; attacks on the virility of Algerian men signaled more foundational anxieties about the ability of the French to defeat an enemy often perceived as more martial, sexually powerful, and potent than his colonizer (Fanon [1961] 2004). Algerian nationalist women were also raped in prison; the sexualized torture of FLN militants like Djamila Bouhired and Djamila Boupacha attracted the attention of major French intellectuals like Simone de Beauvoir (1908–86) and her partner Jean-Paul Sartre (1905–80), who viewed torture as a source of national shame for the French (Surkis 2010). Yet, as Todd Shepard has argued, sexual stereotypes also created possibilities for Algerian nationalists to resist: "During the Algerian War," he writes, "the implicit reliance on the sexualized and gendered understandings that had so underwritten colonialism's role in building modernity became manifest," opening opportunities for anticolonialists "to draw much attention to the French use of such tactics and to offer convincing rebuttals" (2008: 186) (Figure 6.5).

Sexual violence was also perpetrated by colonized people against one another. Members of the FLN targeted Algerians who were viewed as

FIGURE 6.5: A man sits in front of OAS graffiti in Algeria, c. 1962. Credit: Dominique Berretty, Gamma-Rapho Collection/Getty Images.

collaborators; victims were sometimes castrated, symbolizing their emasculation under colonial regimes (Shepard 2008: 44). During the Partition of India and Pakistan, thousands of women on both sides of the border were abducted, raped, mutilated, and forcibly married and/or converted as the two states sought to establish their geographic and semantic boundaries. Women's bodies became a battleground upon which the tensions between religious groups were fought out; nevertheless, women were also agents (and sometimes agents of violence) during Partition (Butalia 1993).

The postcolonial period saw increases in migration from former imperial possessions, with parallel anxieties about its effects. In France, workers were imported from the former colonies to fill labor shortages. French authorities blamed the poverty of the Antilles on the excessive sexuality and fertility which supposedly characterized Guadeloupean and Martiniquan women, and viewed immigration as an opportunity to defuse population pressure, employ these women, and reform their sexual mores by introducing them to French society (Germain 2010: 476).[4] Once in France, Antillean women were funneled into domestic work, and, faced with insufficient state support, some turned to prostitution to earn a living. Nevertheless, today Antillean women play a key role in French politics. As a member of the French Parliament, Christiane Taubira, a French Guianese women, crafted legislation which recognized the Atlantic slave trade as a crime against humanity and required school curricula to discuss this history; hers is a prominent voice in debates about citizenship, race relations, and negritude in France (Wilks 2015: 97).[5]

In Britain, Clive Webb has found that mixed-race couples in the 1950s often fared better than their peers in the United States; although discrimination was not illegal and couples certainly experienced it, interracial marriage was not prohibited unlike in the United States with its Jim Crow laws (Webb 2017). But in 1958 the Notting Hill riots in London erupted, as white people alleged that black men were pimping white women in order to excuse white assaults of their black neighbors. A murderer even covered up his crimes by deflecting attention away to prejudice against Jamaican immigrants (Mort 2006). In 1968, the Conservative British politician Enoch Powell infamously predicted that the streets would run with "rivers of blood" if the migration of non-white people was not stopped (Bailkin 2012: 23).[6] In the 1970s, women from South Asia were subjected to virginity tests at Heathrow if they were arriving to join their husbands (R.A. Hall 2002: 55–68).

In the present moment, rhetoric about the sexual and gendered cultures of non-western people has become a particularly useful tool for the rejection of multiculturalism in Europe. Both queer folks and Muslim women are depicted as vulnerable populations who must be saved from their culture and their menfolk respectively. Conversely, former imperial nations in Europe define themselves in terms of "homonationalism," claiming that their toleration of multicultural populations and gay people indicates their modernity and their "superior ability to tolerate difference" (El-Tayeb 2011: 83). While it is true that some predominantly Islamic countries have adopted repressive legislation limiting the rights of women and GLBTQ people, the discourse of homonationalism problematically generalizes across nations, and reiterates an Orientalist tradition of portraying the Muslim Other as superstitious, premodern, culture-bound, and out of step with supposedly universal norms of tolerance and human rights (Puar 2007: 39; El-Tayeb 2011, 2012). As El-Tayeb notes, when queer activists join this project, they "assure the nation of [their] loyalty." But such "conditional inclusion" can readily be revoked if members of marginal communities refuse to assimilate to national norms (El-Tayeb 2012: 83). At the same time, Jasbir Puar notes that homonationalist discourses continue to feature the terrorist Other as both particularly virulent in his homophobia, and suspiciously prone to queer tendencies (Puar 2007: 37).[7]

Homonationalist discourses have also been applied to spaces in sub-Saharan Africa, where both conservatives and progressives have expressed opposition to the "exportation" of GLBTQ identity to Africa.[8] African leaders in Zimbabwe, Uganda, and Nigeria and elsewhere have attempted to legitimize anti-gay policies and legislation on the basis that homosexuality is not an indigenous practice.[9] The response of western progressives to such rhetoric has often recirculated ideas about the "backwardness" of the "dark continent"—while ignoring the fact that fundamentalist Christian organizations from the US contributed heavily to anti-gay campaigns in Africa (Baptiste 2014; Walker 2014). LGBTI activists in Africa have opposed policies that seek to limit or stop aid to countries with anti-gay policies, pointing out that donor sanctions reproduce power imbalances between countries, ignore the fact that LGBTI Africans also depend upon foreign aid, and often "exacerbate the environment of intolerance in which political leadership scapegoat LGBTI people for donor sanctions in an attempt to retain and reinforce national state sovereignty."[10]

More progressive voices have, however, also expressed reticence about the applicability of GBTQI identities in the African context. In a ground-breaking book which established the long history of marriages between Igbo women in precolonial Nigeria, Ifi Amadiume chastised black lesbians in the West for making connections between such marriages and their own relationships. "Such interpretation[s]," she noted, "would be totally inapplicable, shocking and offensive to Nnobi women, since the strong bonds and support between them do not imply lesbian sexual practices" (Amadiume 1987: 7).[11] Of course, as Kathryn Kendall notes in her study of same-sex love among women in Lesotho, the absence of a sexual connotation may actually enable women to pursue same-sex relationships: "The fact that these activities are not considered to be 'sexual' grants Basotho women the freedom to enjoy them without restraint, embarrassment, or the 'identity crises' experienced by women in homophobic cultures like those of the United States and Europe" (Kendall 1999: 161–5).

More recently, Neville Hoad has expressed concern that attempts to fold those who engage in same-sex practices in Africa into the universalizing language of gay rights has the effect of "closing down spaces for these participants without replicating the set of historical circumstances which allowed gayness to have historical agency in the west" (Hoad 2007:153). Joseph Massad has raised similar concerns about use of GLBTQ rhetoric in the Middle East, suggesting that sexual practices and identities that do not fit a western vision of "queerness" may be made invisible in the process (Massad 2008: 16). However, the notion of a western importation of sexual identities may not be particularly accurate. In the case of Thailand, ideas about sexual identity were being imported from China and India long before the advent of western imperialism in south-east Asia. Furthermore, Thai people adapt and transform "western" identity categories to meet their own needs and expectations (Jackson 1997).

We also need to attend to the flow of identities in the reverse direction, from the Global South to the West. Western transfolks have borrowed the concept of "third gender" identities such as the *berdaches* of North America, *hijras* of India, and the female husbands in parts of West and East Africa to describe their own experiences. Just as the term "transgender" has roots in a particular set of western discourses, each of these third gender identities emerged in the particular and specific context of space and history (Towle and Morgan 2002;

see also Dutta 2012). The western embrace of "third gender" identities often recirculates problematic anthropological discourse about a more "natural," "intuitive," or "primordial" approach to gender identity. Aren Aizura has observed that Thai clinics may intentionally reproduce the Orientalist fantasies of western transwomen who visit the clinics for gender reassignment surgery (Aizura 2010).

These observations about current debates surrounding sexuality and race in the Global South underscore the extent to which the complicated sexual politics of imperialism have survived in different guises in the neocolonial world. At the current moment, a new wave of conservativism that rejects globalization and multiculturalism is sweeping across parts of Europe and the United States. In each case, claims about the sexual and gendered mores, practices, and typologies of people of color are being circulated to oppose their presence in the wealthiest parts of the world. Far from a new phenomenon, this set of racial and sexual scripts draws strength from a much longer genealogy that tied sexuality to the West's right to colonize and rule. However, as we have attempted to show here, the metaphors of gender and sexuality have also been available to those who used them to resist imperialism, to assert agency, and to undercut the claims to supremacy implicit in colonial projects. As we prepare to challenge this political turn in the coming years, we would do well to keep in mind these twin histories of repression and resistance.

CHAPTER SEVEN

Resistance

ROLAND BURKE

Resistance to empire sits among the richest fields of contemporary historical scholarship. A generation of innovative inquiries, and the explosive growth of a sibling field, international and transnational history, has transformed understanding (Clavin 2005, 2011; Sluga 2013). Half a century of historical investigation has resolved, in ever finer detail, the ways in which empires exerted their power culturally, socially, and politically, and the concomitant damage they wrought upon the peoples subjected to them, both direct and mediated (Mamdani 1996). Academic approaches to empires and their dissolution are now less constrained by narratives of incremental progress from colonialism to a single terminal point, that of independent statehood, with the arrival of recent transformative works from Antoinette Burton (2015), Heather Streets-Salter and Trevor Getz (2015), and Tracey Banivanua Mar (2016). An efflorescence of literature on the cultural and social interface between colonizer and colonized has demonstrated the means by which imperial projects were enacted on the ground, on the page, and in the mind. This revolutionized understanding of how empire functioned has been accompanied by a corresponding revolution in understanding of resistance to it (Taylor 2002; Pannikar 2009).

The relevant chronology has been extended further back than the once orthodox focus of the 1940s to 1960s, revealing traditions of resistance, cultural and social, that were continuous. Older classifications of "primary" resistance, occurring around the time of conquest, and "secondary" resistance, proximate to independence, have been supplanted by a complex picture of ongoing contestations of imperial control which varied in intensity, quality, and scale. Whether it was the passive resistance of a sluggish work rhythm or the withdrawal into traditional religious or social frameworks, resistance was not only dynamic. Thus, resistance itself has become a more capacious and nuanced category—including phenomena less conspicuous than the intuitive examples of mass protest and outright insurrection (Sharpe 1989; Taussig 1993; Bahba 1994; Wolski 2001: 216–36). Greater understanding of the role of women and a gendered frame of analysis has refurbished the staid and partial pantheon of masculine anticolonial actors and archetypally masculinist actions (Chatterjee 1989: 662–83; Chaudhuri and Strobel 1992; Sinha 1995, 2006; Cooper 2009: 129–45; Boittin 2010). A more expansive map of the sites of resistance has also been cultivated, with the international and transnational connections between anticolonial movements among the most vibrant areas of study (Paisley 2012; Carey and Lydon 2014; Manjapra 2014; Goebel 2015: 1–21). Finally, the purpose of resistance has been broadened away from narrow nationalist ambitions. Resisting imperial injustice did not automatically entail a wholesale pursuit of independence. Nation-states were often an anomalous and poor fitting schema for peoples and territories fighting colonial abuses (Lorcin and Shepard 2016). Embracing empire, and resisting instead its hypocrisies and harms, both cultural and political, was an orientation adopted by a number of movements, and retained well into the peak years of decolonization between 1950 and 1960.

RIGHTS, REFORMISM, AND REVOLUTION: VARIETIES OF OPPOSITION TO EMPIRE

No single mode of resistance defined the twentieth-century's anticolonialisms. Even within the arc of a single (and singular) career, that of the legendary W.E.B. Du Bois, plural frameworks for understanding empire's abuses, and the racism that attended them, were pursued. Du Bois, for instance, pioneered international solidarity movements, organized around the shared global experience of empire's oppression in the general case; more materialist and Marxian influenced anti-imperialism; conventional, collective national self-determination, and racialized anti-imperial internationalism, in several iterations of Pan-Africanism. Throughout his life, his command of the interior resistance to racism, or "mental colonization," and the scope of forums provided by culture and everyday praxis, was never absent. In the mid-century, Du Bois experimented with institutional mechanisms for reform in legal initiatives, including a brief but striking effort to hold the newly formed United Nations to its loudly proclaimed promises of human rights. It typified not only his ecumenical and agile contestation of empire, but a larger innovation that intersected and reshaped much of anticolonialism in the postwar period (Figure 7.1).

The transformational middle decades of a century of anticolonial resistance were coincident with the institutionalization of human rights as a notionally

FIGURE 7.1: Dr W.E.B. DuBois of the United States, after his speech before the World Congress of Partisans of Peace in Paris. Credit: Bettmann/CORBIS/Bettmann Archive.

universal norm for everyone—an epoch which began with the adoption of the Universal Declaration of Human Rights (UDHR) in December 1948. Both crusades crossed and informed each other—sitting firmly in alignment for a period, and then diverging drastically in the 1970s. In the 1940s, human rights arrived as one of the default languages for expressing resistance to colonial rule, and calling into question the cultural conceits of the "civilizing" project of the imperialists. Established as the ascendant moral lingua franca of the world, and one proclaimed (albeit with hesitation) by the imperial powers, human rights critique afforded ample capacity for destroying European claims to humane rule. Empire rested on a presumption, the supremacy of one peoples over another, which was flatly incompatible with the most fundamental precept of Article 1 of the UDHR, a sweeping statement of human equality. Colonial administration violated, at best episodically, at worst grossly and systematically, almost every one of the provisions that followed: on freedoms of movement, assembly, association, expression, conscience, fair justice, and political participation. It failed dismally on economic and social rights—sustenance, education, health, welfare, and housing—the very substance of "civilization" which liberal colonial development purported to advance as its primary purpose.

This rights-based critique of imperialism had a deeper lineage in the liberal nationalist tradition, but its post–1945 revision was a meaningful shift insofar as individual rights were established as a legitimate, explicitly universal, aspiration. Although the romantic and liberal nationalist creeds of the two preceding centuries did have a significant international component, and did pretend to universal application, they lacked the formalized codification that attended the modern refurbishment of human rights. Rejecting human rights standards on grounds of race, or its coded interwar equivalent, "backwardness of civilization," was, accordingly, a less viable option for imperial administrations.

While human rights was a powerful shaping language for resistance, both cultural and political, it remains clear that throughout the twentieth century, nationalism in a *collective* sense was the dominant mode of anticolonial struggle, and some species of social democracy were the preferred model for a postcolonial state (Afshari 2007; Moyn 2010; Klose 2013). By the end of 1950, the existence of colonialism was itself being cast by many as a human rights violation outright, but one which abused whole nations, and not merely their constituent individuals. The only effective remedy was held to be national self-determination, which was written into the draft human rights covenant as the very first article. From Accra to Zanzibar, the genealogies drawn upon resided, broadly speaking, within traditions that dated to the foundational anti-imperial moment of 1776 (cf. Breuilly 2013: 1–20). Anticolonial leaders cast themselves as the heirs to a celebrated democratic nationalist canon, often quoting the heroes who defined an emancipatory heritage the West had claimed as its own. Animated by the same spirit that had inhabited Thomas Jefferson and Giuseppe Mazzini, African, Asian, Oceanic, and Arab struggles were, at least to liberal opinion, both comprehensible and legitimate (Emerson 1962: 222–4).

The eventual success of these nationalist campaigns was the product of incremental reform, wholesale revolution, and, in some cases, sustained armed rebellion. Typically, each of these elements was interlaced in a chaotic dialogue of indigenous resistance and imperial reluctance—and only rarely unfolding according to a systematized plan. In the main, a greater role for reformist gradualism was the pattern exemplified by the closing decade of US administration in the Philippines in the 1940s, the British in south Asia and parts of Africa in the 1940s through the early 1960s, and France in some of its African territories. By contrast, revolution—often involving immensely bloody and protracted insurgencies—was the primary driver in Algeria, Kenya, Indonesia, and French Indochina across the 1940s and 1950s, and much of southern Africa across the 1960s through the 1990s.

At the sharpest edge of these revolutions, the whole notion of resistance was reconceived beyond the accession to sovereignty. The pioneer of this new kind of revolutionary resistance, the Algerian National Liberation Front (FLN), pressed the case for a more total vision of "national liberation"; a liberation not just from the political yoke of the French but also from its cultural impositions and anti-Islamic practices. After a decade of ever-escalating imperial violence and dilatory promises, Algerian nationalist ideologues, along with a chorus of European disciples, evangelized a bloodier campaign against empire (Hamon and Rotman 1979; Charby 2004; Byrne 2016). Famously articulated by Frantz Fanon in his exceptionally influential *Wretched of the Earth* ([1961] 2004), and amplified by a militant foreword from Jean Paul Sartre, the cleavage between colonizer and colonized was cast as total. Even Albert Camus, caught between the Syclla and Charybdis of cultural and political tensions of decolonization, was unable to promote his *trêve civil* and ended a temporary cultural pariah in France. Along with the insurgency in French Indochina, which won its first major success in May 1954, Algeria's revolution set anticolonialism in a new key—less liberal, less consensual, and much more maximalist in how the conflict was conceived. Pioneering early work from Alistair Horne (1977) revealed the depth of polarization, and the brutality and complexity of the Algerian conflict (Thénault 2011)—and its international repercussions (Connelly 2002: 1–17, 276–85). Numerous successor struggles, and a veritable generation of western European and American intellectuals, would be inspired by the cultural and political creeds of Algiers, extending the particular nationalist resistance in North Africa to a world-spanning revolutionary cause. Militant anticolonial nationalism, whether political or culturally anchored merely in ideology, became, strangely, a transnational movement. Its icons, Regis Debray, Amilcar Cabral, Samora Machel, Ho Chi Minh, Leila Khaled, and—above all others—Che Guevara, would adorn university halls and inhabit student hearts across both West and South (Figure 7.2).

If sovereignty in the form of independent statehood, acquired either through reformism and non-violent mobilization, or revolutionary violence, ultimately outcompeted alternative avenues, it was by no means the inevitable course. In a substantial swathe of territories, most strikingly across Francophone Africa, a democratic reformation carried within empire was a credible alternative, sincerely pursued by local freedom movements (Wilder 2015; Stromberg Childers 2016). New imperial federations were sketched out, with assurances of genuine cultural and economic solidarity, equality, and regional autonomy. Such architectures of colonial freedom within empire never eventuated, but for those which envisaged them, almost as often African leaders as French metropolitan politicians, their failure was not celebrated—freedom and equality within empire was a goal, not a consolation (Cooper 2008: 168). The contours of this vision were set out in the Brazzaville Declaration, which was concluded by Free French leader Charles de Gaulle in January 1944.

Although the Brazzaville text ultimately found vastly less influence than the earlier nationalist touchstone, the 1941 Atlantic Charter, its federalist sentiment

FIGURE 7.2: Vietminh poster celebrating the victory of Dien Bien Phu. Credit: Photo by Apic/Getty Images.

did hold meaning for many (cf. Jennings 2015: 250–2). Two of the most eminent figures in African literature and philosophy, Aimé Césaire and Leopold Senghor, were not, initially, nationalists in the conventional sense—much as they abhorred French oppression, and the perennial hypocrisy of French professions of liberty, equality, and solidarity. With its diminished emphasis on independent statehood as the prime means for emancipation, indigenous activists and politicians who engaged with these schemes (or proposed their own) often grasped a wider set of means for redress against imperial injustice (Cooper 2014).

Across this chapter, the creed of anticolonial nationalism will constitute the dominant strand of opposition to empire, but it is not taken as the highest expression of resistance. Given the depth of its influence and impact, anticolonial nationalism is inescapably prominent in any narrative of twentieth-century resistance—yet sovereignty in the form of statehood proved an insufficient remedy to the lasting sequelae of colonization. By the late 1970s, sovereignty itself, which had been so hard fought, and so recently won, was increasingly showing its limits for every state. The cumulative harm of empire had not been ameliorated, but statehood—the purported means for addressing it was receding from its peak moment of power. There would be no elegant resolution to empire's miserable legacy. The triumph of independence was a waypoint, a fractional increment of successful resistance, one which more often revealed the extent of the injuries, and compelled the pursuit of a constellation of alternative means of opposition.

THE DISAPPOINTMENTS OF THE "WILSONIAN MOMENT": INTERWAR RESISTANCE TO EMPIRE

As the first apocalyptic slaughter of the industrial age drew to its close in November 1918, the world that would emerge from the First World War seemed to hold considerable promise for those arrayed against imperialism. With Britain and France, the two foremost western European empires, deeply shaken by the scale of both mobilization and destruction, the prospect of a radically reordered world seemed certain (Gerwarth and Manela 2014a: 786–800). US President Woodrow Wilson ascended as the new global architect, with a vision which looked, initially, like a promise of nation-states for the world's peoples and with it, a repossession of their culture and politics. Wilson's exaltation of self-determination as a privileged principle rallied a wave of anti-imperial claims, and promptly disappointed virtually all of them (Manela 2007: 3–37, 197–226). Ultimately, the 1919 Paris Peace Conference offered half-measures and accommodation for Britain, France, Belgium, and the Netherlands. At best, the new League of Nations system promised mild scope to hold the administering powers to account in some limited set of territories, via the Permanent Mandates Commission.

Despite the manifest disappointments of 1919, the frayed hold of empire was tested during the interwar years. Even if equality of citizenship or national independence seemed barely any closer than they had been in 1913, more assertive forms of resistance contested European power, and more confident arguments hammered relentlessly against imperial claims across the second-half of the 1920s and 1930s. For the subset of territories overseen as Mandates, there was now a permanent forum for interrogating imperial practice. Weak and ritualized as it was, the requirement to respond to dissent in an international forum was unprecedented (Pedersen 2015: 44–76; Wheatley 2015: 205–48). Colonized peoples could seek to have their claims heard, and in a handful of cases, even speak back to the dissembling French, British, and Australian legations in Geneva.

If the Mandates system was symbolically potent, it was mostly ineffectual outside its native habitat in the Palais des Nations. Less easily dismissed with diplomatic élan and procedural obfuscation was the surging resistance on the ground. In the December 1921 settlement of a bloody civil war, a large section of Ireland won its independence—the Irish nation's first large-scale success against English rule since the age of the Tudors. Egypt negotiated improved autonomy, and a formalistic independence from Britain in 1922. Across Africa and the Arab world, local strikes, tax revolts, and insurrections unfolded in staccato fashion; never reaching the threshold for genuine crisis, but disproving the secure equilibrium that professionalized colonial administration had posited (Bush 1999; Derrick 2008). Ethiopia, never colonized, fought valiantly against the first expansionistic outbreak of interwar Fascism—winning worldwide sympathy as it withstood the onslaught of Italian dictator Benito Mussolini, a campaign that was notorious even in the 1930s for its use of chemical weapons.

Although Ethiopia unmasked the rising brutality of a new kind of fascist empire, with its cultural and political impositions, India was the epicenter for a renewed contestation of the fundamental claims of imperialism. Wartime repressions and extractions, which crystallized in the extraordinarily broad authoritarian license enacted through the 1915 Defense of India Act and the murderous brutality from British authorities at Amritsar, were indicative that whatever was agreed at Whitehall would now be tested by the people of India. Resistance flourished in the interwar milieu. Indian nationalists were provoked by the twin imperial impulses—crackdown and prophylactic concession. The former, the impulse to intensified repression, was abundant in the 1919 Anarchical and Revolutionary Crimes Act; the latter, grudging professions of reform, was threadbare but visible in the 1919 Government of India Act.

Amidst the reconfigured conditions of the interwar years, India's resistance began to break out of the grooves which had limited its transformative effect for over a century. Gandhi, who had already built a career in leading local movements for justice against exploitation in South Africa before the First World War, served to catalyze successful campaigns against crushing taxation assessments in 1918. Navigating a new path of resistance, which refurbished the tired political armamentarium of the Indian National Congress, while simultaneously eschewing sporadic popular insurrectionism that followed the April 1919 massacre, Gandhi inaugurated a qualitatively different campaign against empire. Working at the level of community activation, with its emphasis on local cultural traditions, as opposed to elite political negotiation, Gandhi proposed techniques which embedded the practices of national resistance into the everyday individual cultural and economic actions and outlook of India's peoples. More than dissent, Gandhian practice furnished the capacity to enact forms of daily practice that transcended empire's cultural, political, and economic tendrils.

The measures he popularized constructed sub-state domains of independence—a sovereignty of spirit and personal industry beyond empire's reach. Traditional fabric production decoupled those who practiced it from imperial trade networks, a measure so successful it remains the centerpiece of the Indian national flag. Salt production evaded empire's mercantilist hand, and delivered independence of supply in a vital commodity—while simultaneously opening an opportunity for communal solidarity and purposive mobilization of traditional cultural practices. Bodily agency and corporeal sovereignty, typified by hunger strike, carved out the most elemental sphere of independence and personal autonomy. As a powerful means for communicating resolve without extrinsic violence, the hunger strike was a technique that had been used adeptly by suffragists in Britain, and, later and controversially, by imprisoned Irish Republican Army cadres in their campaigns for Northern Irish sovereignty in the 1980s. For Gandhi, while never the mainstay option, it was a recourse that often held potency, particularly at key moments when the grander cause was *in extremis*. By 1930, the risk these new isomers of resistance posed was abundantly clear to the British authorities, who struggled to craft a response from the standard set of repressive tools.

"A WORLD MADE NEW"? THE ANTI-IMPERIAL FOUNDATIONS OF THE POSTWAR GLOBE

Where the First World War had strained, transiently, the fabric of imperial control, the Second World War precipitated the terminal crisis of Western empires. If their complete disintegration was not necessarily inevitable, radical alteration in some form was inescapable. The postwar United States, now the unquestioned hegemon, was ill-disposed to the persistence of European empire. Its principal rival, the Soviet Union, had been reliably hostile to western imperialism since its birth as an organized state in the 1920s, and devoted much of its international policy to anticolonial agitation and providing many anticolonial movements in the colonies with an ideological springboard. The blueprints for the new postwar world, set down in the Atlantic Charter, intra-war Allied communiqués, and the establishment of planning meetings for the United Nations Organization, all tilted the globe away from empire (Borgwardt 2005: 14–86). In the 1945 United Nations Charter, the assumed pattern for world organization was the sovereign state—whatever permission existed for empire was in ellipsis, namely, the absence of explicit condemnation. Racial equality, which had been rejected, even in a problematically constrained form, when proposed in the League of Nations Covenant, was now a bedrock principle. Human rights, their content as yet undefined, were a notional peer to the highest priorities of the new system, alongside sovereignty, peace, and collective security. A dedicated Trusteeship Council, successor to the Mandates Commission, was augmented—and less likely to allow the cozy ententes and easy evasions of the 1920s (Haas 1967: 292–300). At a grand political and ideological level, the currents of the world no longer ran with empire.

In the immediate postwar years of the late 1940s and early 1950s, conditions for the major imperial powers were austere in the metropole, and often disastrous in those territories in which they were seeking to reestablish control. Dramatic defeats in the Asia-Pacific and North Africa demonstrated the vulnerability of western armies. Britain's catastrophic and precipitous defeats in south-east Asia, exemplified by the fall of Singapore in 1941, shattered any illusion as to white martial and cultural supremacy. So, too, the near wholesale destruction of Australia's air defenses by the technologically superior Mitsubishi Zero, an aircraft that was much more advanced than its western counterpart. The complex and superbly executed surprise attack at Pearl Harbor completed a year of unhalted Japanese military triumph. Its cumulative impact vastly exceeded the only major precedent, Japan's victory over the Russian Imperial Navy earlier in the century. The attitudinal consequence of these defeats was compounded in the Pacific theater, as they had been inflicted by a non-European military, and one which proselytized its own self-serving Pan-Asian vision in an attempt to coopt local peoples. The cultural superiority, as expressed by attitudes to "inferior" races, was thus seriously undermined. The Axis-supported Indian National Liberation Army, and Indonesian nationalist groups, gained military and organizational capacity as a direct consequence of the war.

In those colonial territories which the western allies managed to hold against the Axis, urgent imperial demand for resources produced chaotic mobilization and local capacity-building. Desperation produced disinhibition, and opened a window for coercing concessions—not least in India, where the war marked the final spasm of British repression: the setting for a dynamic mixture of uneasy cooperation against Fascism, hastily expedited initiatives on imperial reform, and continent-wide activism and rebellion (Khan 2015). The August 1942 Quit India campaign, which inaugurated almost population-scale mass resistance and non-cooperation, was the flagship case—one well addressed in the magisterial study of Francis Hutchins (1973). Despite engaging all of its repressive apparatus, with over 100,000 imprisoned, and the entirety of the Indian National Congress jailed, the British authorities, already at the outer limits of capacity, had little prospect of maintaining the status quo.

Above all, the scale of disruption, and the existential quality of the struggle against the Axis, had revealed that even those cultural structures and systems of power which seemed impervious to change could be brought to crisis. Indonesia's independence movement was among the first successes—from March 1942 to December 1949, it traversed the distance from precarious and persecuted dissident movement to presidency and parliament. Seizing on the circumstances opened by Japan's invasion of the archipelago, and an ideological framework that drew on multiple threads of anticolonial thought, pragmatically weaved by Ahmed Sukarno, resistance transitioned from cultural and political dissent to full-scale systems of parallel government. Fellow nationalist leader,

Mohammed Hatta, arguably the co-equal founder of the new Indonesian nation, having experienced Dutch colonialism and Japanese militarism, became an ardent champion of a different course: an Indonesian state, with its citizens protected by the individual freedoms enumerated in the 1948 UDHR (Hatta 1960; see also Feith and Castles 1970).

THE ZENITH OF ANTICOLONIAL RESISTANCE: A WORLD AGAINST EMPIRE, 1945–60

While there were innumerable moments and planes of resistance well before 1945, the peak years of successful contestation of imperial control were concentrated into the two decades that followed the Second World War. In three years alone, a major swathe of the world's colonized population won independence, principally in Asia and the Arab world: Syria and Lebanon in October 1945, the Philippines in July 1946, Burma (Myanmar) and Ceylon (Sri Lanka) in early 1948, and the Dutch East Indies (Indonesia) in December 1949 (Young 2001: 159–316). The largest and most traumatic was the conjoined independence and partition of British India. Freedom from colonial rule was commingled with immense misery, with intercommunal violence and administrative chaos accompanying the birth of India and Pakistan in August 1947. The differences of religious culture and practice, which were at the root of the decision to create a separate Muslim state, led to hundreds of thousands being killed, and still more displaced and injured. Although it heralded the cultural and political disintegration of the British Raj, it was also a demonstration that accession to statehood was not the end of colonially produced violence: imperial rule had lasting political and cultural sequelae, and was not elegantly unstitched, despite the eloquent use of "Partition."

Africa's surge to independence was concentrated in the decade between 1955 and 1965, with abbreviated transitions from outright imperial administration to full statehood (Birmingham 1995). The gradient was especially steep for the Belgian Congo, where the transfer of power in June 1960 was so precipitous and flawed that massive disorder ensued. International intervention, widespread violence, and a legacy of state incapacity demonstrated types of lingering damage that were frankly beyond effective resistance. Marginally less catastrophic was the resentful French withdrawal from Guinea in October 1958. Incensed by the success of nationalist Ahmed Sékou Touré and his Democratic Party (PDG), who successfully carried a vote for independence, as opposed to autonomy within a greater France, thus administering a slap in the face to the "mother" country, the administration destroyed the territory's infrastructure, including medical facilities. A capable political movement to resist French imperialism could win statehood, but could not resist the fury of a France culturally repudiated, or its immiserating material sequelae.

The mood of the anticolonial peak was captured at its midpoint, in the landmark April 1955 Asian-African Conference in Bandung, Indonesia. Assembling almost every nationalist hero, from Jawaharlal Nehru to Gamal Abdel Nasser (Figure 7.3), Bandung was the crystallizing moment, when the first, relatively liberal phase of anticolonial nationalism reached its zenith (Kahin 1956: 3–28; Burton et al. 2006; see also Wright, 1956). Much mythologized as the birthplace of the Third World, the actual proceedings of the meeting were more fractious and cautious (Vitalis 2013: 261–6). Nevertheless, unalloyed opposition to empire, and the racial discrimination which subtended it, provided a unifying theme for the otherwise fissiparous assembly of nations. All twenty-nine delegations, while divided on much, were unanimous in their condemnation of colonialism "in all its manifestations" (Asian-African Conference 1955). Less prominent was the unanimous support for the 1948 UDHR, recognized as "a common standard of achievement for all peoples and all nations," an indication of the optimistic, and democratic, disposition of anti-imperialism in the 1950s (Burke 2006: 961–5).

In retrospect, Bandung was an inflection point. The democratic, rights-oriented, anti-imperialism had crested, and receded into near oblivion by the late 1960s. The human rights dimension remained in recession until the revival

FIGURE 7.3: Gamal Abdul Nasser of Egypt (center left) talking with Jawaharlal Nehru of India during the Bandung Conference. Credit: Howard Sochurek/The LIFE Picture Collection/Getty Images.

of popular mobilizations in the 1980s and 1990s, this time, directed at casting out endogenous tyrants, or in the evocative phrase of the 1950s, "internal colonialism." The spirit of the late 1940s and early 1950s persisted for a decade, acquiring the status of a global orthodoxy by the dawn of the 1960s. In December 1960, a General Assembly populated by newly independent states advanced the Declaration on Colonialism. Proclaiming the sovereign state the default option for ordering the nations of the world, the Declaration was a breviary of Third World aspiration, largely drawn from the language and mood of the epochal Bandung Final Communiqué. A substantial set of Asian and African legations made a conscious attempt to place the Declaration within a universal, democratic tradition, and a kind of collectivist complement to the individual web of freedoms enunciated in the UHDR (Burke 2010: 35–58).

The gains achieved through predominantly non-violent strategies had forestalled any widespread embrace of revolutionary warfare for the first two decades of nationalist crusading. The two signal successes of the early phase of resistance, India's Congress Party and Ghana's Convention People's Party, had relied on massive popular pressure. Yet, as the cases where non-violence failed began to mount across the 1950s and through 1960s, where mobilization had found an unrelenting escalation in repression, as opposed to reluctantly conceded reforms, philosophical choices which had been mostly deferred became inescapable.

The shift in the nature of anticolonial techniques was, in substantial part, determined by the nature of the colonial regimes they were arrayed against, and in particular, the presence and intransigence of a settler colonial population. Despite its self-cultivated reputation as the most humane of imperial custodians, there were myriad examples where postwar resistance to British rule was met with severe and systematic policies of repression and terrorization. Kenya, with a powerful and uncompromising settler community, and profoundly inequitable land distribution, was perhaps the most grotesque example. In response to the violence and perceived cultural excesses of the Mau-Mau, across 1952–6, a program of mass internment without trial, executions, rape, and torture was enacted. Although only fully appreciated in recent years, with the revelations from Caroline Elkins (2005a, 2005b) and David Anderson (2005), the accession of Jomo Kenyatta to power in December 1963, amidst much ceremony, was the capstone atop a foundation of authoritarianism and bloody counterinsurgency.

Algeria was still more protracted and polarized, with an escalatory spiral between terror, French imperial repression, and, eventually, reactionary settler colonial counterterror. Fealty to the revolutionary violence exalted by Fanon and Sartre, and practiced with bloody success by the FLN was the cardinal rule for this new era (Museveni 1971: 1–24). It would find able practitioners, and despicable target regimes, further south—in the desperate wars of national liberation fought in white supremacist Ian Smith's Rhodesia, the settler culturally repressive system of apartheid South Africa, and Portugal's territories of Cape Verde, Angola, and Mozambique. Here, a collection of protest movements transitioned to armed struggle, with varying degrees of enthusiasm: little in South Africa, rather more in Angola. In Rhodesia, the Zimbabwe African National Union (ZANU) and Zimbabwean African People's Union (ZAPU) carried slow, attrition-based guerrilla struggles against the isolated and archaic Smith regime (Figure 7.4). From June 1961, in South Africa, after anguished deliberation, Nelson Mandela was authorized by the African National Congress (ANC) to operate a dedicated armed wing, *Umkhonto we Sizwe* (Spear of the Nation).

Portugal's African empire, the last bastion of formal imperialism on the continent by the late 1960s, was administered by a metropole that was radically dissimilar to those in France and Britain. British and French empires had been secured, retained, and eventually—and reluctantly—decolonized, by polities that were notionally committed to universalistic democratic philosophies. There had always been a degree of tension between their self-fashioned identities as democratic standard bearers, and the reality of racism and

FIGURE 7.4: Victory of Robert Mugabe in Rhodesia, 1980. A supporter of Robert Mugabe holding a cock, symbol of the Zanu Party. Credit: Keystone-France/Gamma-Keystone via Getty Images.

authoritarian rule abroad. This kind of contradiction was much less apparent in Portugal, not because of a more enlightened colonial administration, but rather, a more repressive domestic government. Salazar's government did not face the perilous asymmetry of ideals that beset French and British imperialisms—it was fascist at home, and somewhat more fascist abroad. Southern Africa became an almost contiguous and continuous war zone, with the African Party for the Independence of Guinea-Bissau and Cape Verde (PAIGC) evicting Portuguese administration from huge tracts of the country—decolonizing the territory by halting increment across the late 1960s. Mozambique's Liberation Front (FRELIMO) and the Popular Movement for the Liberation of Angola (MPLA) outlived the departure of Portugal in 1975, and engaged in relentless civil and proxy wars well into the 1980s.

THE "POLITICAL KINGDOM" REALIZED: DISCOVERING THE LIMITS OF SOVEREIGNTY

National cultural and political mobilization, which was predicated upon a culturally united people, with single, monolithic purpose, was an exquisitely effective instrument for advancing sovereignty. It was much less adept at cultivating the lasting freedom of the citizens its new national culture would create. Total subordination to the goal of ridding empires too often transmuted into a more permanent total discipline, carried out in the name of development, national integrity, or internal security. Liberation movements, which typically won a period of grace and popularity, conflated party with nation, nation with people, and people with president. New elites ruled, with an inheritance of repressive tools that were transferred along with sovereignty. One of the first beacons of freedom was the first to dim, with Ghanaian independence the paradigmatic case of post-colonial disappointment. Kwame Nkrumah, who had exhorted colonized people to focus first upon the "political kingdom" as the gateway to full freedom and welfare, had been celebrated as the liberator of a nation, and the prophet for a continent, in March 1957. Yet his own "political kingdom" started to show a worryingly authoritarian disposition only a handful of years into his tenure.

Soviet-style developmentalism, and the still more appealing and still more fraudulent promise of Maoist single-bound leaps into modernity, captivated many among postcolonial elites and western intellectual circles, providing a counterpoint culture to those of the departing colonial powers. Each proposed massive fixed investment and industrialization effort, seeking to "break out" of the impoverishing quicksand of commodity export. Nkrumah became an energetic and outspoken convert. As the first leader to describe "neocolonialism," in terms highly favorable to his own accumulation of power, the Ghanaian icon embarked on extremely ambitious plans—for electrification, metallurgy, and all of the trappings of an industrial economy (Nkrumah 1965: i–xx). These were not ephemeral quests, and presumed decades-long servitude, and the coerced sacrifice of individual freedoms reminiscent of imperialist development programs. Methods redolent of the worst features of alien domination were defended vigorously—with hated impositions like labor conscription baldly justified to bodies like the International Labour Organization (ILO) purely on the basis that their extractions were now being directed by a nationalist government, and not an imperialist governor-general (Maul 2012: 6–7, 17–27, 179–90, 269–77). The yoke of colonial culture, it seemed, was difficult to discard.

Acquisition of political sovereignty and cultural autonomy, momentous achievements, tended to be followed by disappointments as their limits were revealed. Economic agency did not accompany the accession to independence, and indeed, often there was almost no change at all in the material limits placed on the peoples within them. Structural transition from the extractive-type, export-oriented, culture of colonial economies that had been created to serve the greater imperial system was an almost impossible undertaking, one even more fiercely resisted than a shift in political control. Western powers acquiesced to political self-determination by the late 1950s, but demands for economic self-determination, under the banner of "Permanent Sovereignty Over Natural Resources," were bitterly rejected. Although much of this had been appreciated for decades, and development had been a key pillar in arguments for political decolonization, the magnitude of the challenge exceeded even the most pessimistic forecasts.

Resisting colonial head-taxes, launching general strikes, and pressing for self-government had no equivalents in the economic sphere, where former colonies were compelled to remain in the status of grateful supplicants. Imperial authorities could be compelled to leave, but economic resistance to empire was predicated on positive engagement. Any major effort to create economic sovereignty required massive cooperation, and a willingness to extend such cooperation even in circumstances where indigenous governments held control. Despite some piecemeal efforts, this was rarely in evidence. More radical proposals were advanced to decouple the former colonies from the imperial economies they had been culturally deformed to serve. Detailed ideological and theoretical disquisitions were prepared, in various keys: "neocolonialism," "dependency theory" in the 1960s, and, later, in the 1970s, an elaborate program for "a New International Economic Order," proclaimed by the Non-Aligned Movement and the UN in 1974 (UNGA 1974a, 1974b). Common to all of these exhortatory crusades for economic justice was the assertion of a right to international economic redistribution—as distinct from charitable dispensation. Masters of their own states, postcolonial leaders appealed to the world community as wronged peers, not mendicants. The capitalist culture that had been imposed by the imperialists was nigh impossible to circumvent. Fierce rhetoric from postcolonial leaders could, and did, win General Assembly vote, but delivered little more. Performing the optics of resistance to the "existing unjust international economic order" became an annual mainstay for the postcolonial bloc at the UN, its symbolism increasingly hollow as little was won, and the emancipatory credentials of postcolonial governments continued to corrode with ever longer records in power.

Few obvious solutions were available to dependency and economic marginality. Tanzanian President Julius Nyerere's autarkic self-development, articulated in the February 1967 Arusha Declaration, was perhaps the most culturally or ideologically coherent—though its conceptual appeal was matched only by its abysmal consequences for Tanzania's people (TANU 1967). Countering both the global market and Leninist heavy industrialism with the syncretic model of "African Socialism," Nyerere claimed to fuse the traditional communalist, agrarian ethos of the continent with features of modern welfare states. Nyerere's communalistic "Villagized" national development, or *ujamaa*, while carried out in the name of authentic traditions of African culture, rested on an assumption of backwardness that licensed the same mass social engineering and wrenching displacement of communities practiced by colonial administrators—with individuals seen through the prism of economic instrumentalism. Unlike the tax resistance of the 1930s against British rule, there was little recourse against zealous Tanzanian party officials loading families into trucks, all in the name of the nation.

ANTI-IMPERIALISM OR HUMAN RIGHTS? THE COLLAPSING MORAL CLAIMS OF POSTCOLONIAL NATIONALISM

By the later 1970s, the whole edifice of nationalist, statist anti-imperialism as an emancipatory project was in crisis. Nyerere's *ujamaa* was, by the standards of most postcolonial rulers, especially in Africa, among the least of the worst human rights abuses. Only a handful of even vaguely democratic governments had survived, with Botswana's Seretse Khama and Senegal's Leopold Senghor standing out amidst a cohort of corrupt and repressive rulers. Two extraordinarily brutal civil wars, both directed against minority populations seeking their own national freedom—the federal government of Nigeria's crushing encirclement of the Biafran secession (1967–70) and Pakistan's genocidal assault on Bangladesh (1971)—rendered the last moralistic vestiges of postcolonial nationalism deeply suspect (Figure 7.5). While opposition to imperialism and support for universal human rights were almost superimposable struggles between 1945 and 1965, increasingly, postcolonial nationalist leaders were emerging as peer-competitive with imperial administrations in their paternalist rhetoric and repressive conduct. Indonesia's subversion of West Papua's independence movement in the infamous

FIGURE 7.5: Four starving Biafran children sit and lie around a bowl of food in the dirt during the Nigerian-Biafran civil war. Credit: Hulton Archive/Getty Images.

"act of free choice" in July 1969, and its subsequent invasion and annexation of East Timor in December 1975, were quintessentially imperialist. Carried out by the New Order regime of General Suharto, they seemed little different to nineteenth-century territorial seizures. For many, particularly intellectuals, the disastrous second decade of postcolonial rule required an agonizing fractionation of what had actually been the purpose of resistance—opposition to the abuses of empire, or ending the abuses characteristic of imperialism.

Even India, the first of the great democratic anti-imperial crusades of the twentieth century, had departed from the original vision of indivisible partnership between individual rights and sovereignty. Prime Minister Indira Gandhi, after several years of wandering toward authoritarianism suspended democratic rule in June 1975, during which human rights abuses soared, most strikingly in the coercive sterilization program, which partnered an unaccountable state with foreign donors and technocrats. The same society, and a number of the same personnel, who had carried the struggle against Britain, generated the groundswell of protest which restored Indian democracy in March 1977. It would be among the few postcolonial societies to manage such a rapid revival of resistance to dictatorship.

At the dawn of the 1980s, the revelation of the depth of the genocide in Cambodia, and the Stalinist tyranny of General Haile Mengistu Mariam in Ethiopia, who had seized power and enacted a regime of "Red Terror" in February

1977, obliterated the last remnants of postcolonial exceptionalism (Davey 2015: 220–46). Support for postcolonial citizens, as opposed to lauding the now shop-worn anti-imperialist speechifying of tyrannical postcolonial states, became the default option—now definitively expressed in the language of universal human rights. Crucially, it was a language that was open to all: oppressed individuals, minorities, and First Peoples seeking justice within settler colonial states. It held the flexibility to seek more than the end of imperialism, privileging instead the acquisition of freedom, not the mere absence of alien rule.

The first resistance movement to fully reflect the synthesis between transnational human rights activism and older traditions of anti-imperialism, was also one of the oldest and hardest fought—the national, regional, and eventually worldwide battle against South Africa's apartheid system. Apartheid, a pathological edge case of settler colonialism and its culture had evolved out of both British settler patterns, and a distinctive Dutch and French colonial tradition, that of the cultural concept of Afrikanerdom. With the electoral victory of the Afrikaner-based National Party in 1948, apartheid was declared South Africa's guiding policy (Dubow 2014: 12–27). The country's premier resistance movement, the ANC, was confronted with an ever-more elaborate set of repressive laws (Posel 1991; Clark and Worger 2004). Multiracial and social democratic in orientation, the ANC was skeptical of the racialized nationalism exemplified by Pan-Africanism, and had been an early proponent of a human rights approach to opposing settler colonial repression, a vision enunciated in its June 1955 Freedom Charter.

ANC operations encompassed an immense range of techniques and guiding ideologies. Developed in response to a *sui generis* form of colonialism, which itself was impressively sophisticated in its techniques, South Africa's freedom movement drew upon essentially every strand in the repertoire of contention: industrial action, mass demonstration, petitioning, consumer boycott, work stay-away, non-violent civil disobedience—followed by non-lethal armed sabotage, and finally, lethal guerrilla warfare. The complexity of the colonial structure, and its astonishing resilience, allowed a depressingly long time horizon for forced experimentation. In essence, the sheer persistence and metamorphism of colonial structures, spanning an era when so many had disintegrated, afforded an unwelcome opportunity for South African liberation movements to pioneer new kinds of resistance *de novo*.

Apartheid's durability also meant that South Africa's freedom struggle was the only major case where an anticolonial movement would remain fully engaged in struggle after the rise of global human rights activism. After brief excursions into the harder edges of Algerian-influenced "National Liberation" philosophy, Stalinism, the more exclusivist culture of Africanist collective sovereignty, and the interiority-focused Black Consciousness Movement of Steve Biko, its closing decade was characterized by the revival of an emphasis on universal human rights as the basis for a new settlement—particularly after the 1983 birth of the United Democratic Front. Drawing upon a growing reservoir of support from a world-spanning Anti-Apartheid Movement, the final settlement across 1991–3 rested on equal human rights for all South African citizens, a solution which, for all of its flaws, held the country together for the first decade of its transition from racialized dictatorship.

The dawn of the 1990s demonstrated the new configurations indigenous peoples had created within the emergent global human rights milieu. Alongside the hopes of South Africa's "miracle" transition, and the independence of its near neighbor Namibia in 1990, the early years of the decade were dense with events which refocused attention on the plight of colonized peoples. The year 1992 alone witnessed the nation-changing Mabo land rights judgement in Australia, renewed attention on the genocidal impact of the Conquest, evident in the events surrounding the quincentennial of Columbus in 1992, and growing recognition of the intersection between environmental destruction and indigenous dispossession, debated at the first Earth Summit in Rio.

At the June 1993 World Conference on Human Rights, held in Vienna, new agendas coalesced—commingling the wider HRNGO movement and more specific indigenous activist groups (Figure 7.6). The "s" campaign, which referred to the need to protect the rights of "peoples" in the plural, as opposed to "people," won substantial traction in an otherwise fractious conference. Alongside the only major success of an otherwise disappointing meeting, the

FIGURE 7.6: UN Human Rights Conference in Vienna. Credit: Leopold Nekula/Sygma via Getty Images.

strengthening of the women's human rights network, indigenous rights activisms found cultural and political affinities with each other, and other marginalized communities in the postcolonial world. With independence achieved, and its limits revealed, the early 1990s were a site for sub-state and transnational resistance-building (Jhappan 1992; Coates 2004; de Costa 2006a). Across the first half of the decade, a deepened connection between the world's First Peoples and their shared struggle against settler colonial structures revivified indigenous activism, and placed it within a human rights-based institutional framework. Attitudinal, social, and cultural spheres of resistance were expanded; and, in increments, some useful reforms were won, often by a broad-based activist coalition of human rights, indigenous peoples, and environmental NGOs. Transnational connection of the sort exemplified by the 1990s was certainly not new, the difference was one of scale and persistence, as well as a new latticework for institutional foothold (cf. Paisley 2006).

RESISTING THE NEBULOUS OPPRESSION OF THE CONTEMPORARY WORLD ORDER, 1989–2016

As the century closed, and the last formal vestiges of empire were relinquished in Hong Kong (1997) and Macau (1999), many of the injustices once properly attributed to empire persisted, even if empire as a recognizable entity had dissolved. Sites and sources of misery were real, but their provenance was vague. Oppressors were abstract, even if the oppressions were not. So, too, the unadorned legacy of empire's violence and continent-scale social engineering; which bequeathed terrain, mental and national, upon which new actors would carry out massive and grotesque human rights violations, not least in the Middle East (Hardy 2016). Three decades after the disappointments of political self-determination became inescapable, the meaning of resistance was no longer clear, primarily because the injustices were no longer mapped to a physically present alien domination (Hardt and Negri 2000). Hands dispensing repression in the most immediate sense were almost always indigenous, not foreign. Material impoverishment was structural, a consequence of economic forces that seemed impossible to avoid—and frequently, had slipped the bonds of any national government, developed or developing.

Identifying a means for resisting the negative state of extreme poverty, produced by agents that were distant and opaque, was the kind of challenge difficult to resolve in the fantastical realm of academic symposia, let alone on the ground. Points of direct interface between foreign capital and repression, primarily in mining and extractive industry, could serve as a galvanizing nucleus, but even there, the requirement for technical specialization, and the subterranean quality of foreign control, made recourse to obstructionist protest or disobedience infeasible in a great many cases. Cast in the grim role of supplicants, for capital, specialist input, and strategic security, the scope for exercising collective agency had narrowed. Salt marches and autarkic impulses had no equivalent when the resources at issue were advanced antiretroviral medications and fiber-optic communications infrastructure. One of the few meaningful acts of resistance here was the mandatory licensing of essential medications for domestic manufacture, led by India—a case where global activism compelled transnational pharmaceutical giants and their political patrons to accept limits to their power in 2001.

The heroic age of resistance, characterized by bold, imposing national movements, clarity of purpose, and utopian optimism of spirit, was now heritage—not hope. Injustices were exerted by variegated phenomena, and transnational entities that bore only partial resemblance to formal colonialism—and resistance was distributed accordingly. Smaller-scale struggle, fought by increment, and organized at the sub-state and translocal level, represented the face of the approaching millennium. Affinities were intricate, created with peer struggles, and not the automatic association provided by co-nationals. Forums were more dispersed, and resided just as much across borders as within them. National liberation was mostly moribund, replaced by international and transnational activism and advocacy. The high tempo of the crusades of the 1940s, 1950s, and 1960s had a less glamorous afterlife, marked by endless engagement, negotiation, and travel. This was a grinding and attritional process, of calendars punctuated by conferences, countless working groups, programs of action (or inaction), and compromises. The comfort, as modest as it was, could be found in the convergence between anti-imperialism and the expanding armada of movements which fought injustice in the general case: human rights, women's rights, environmentalism, and human-centered development. This was the perhaps the single consolatory paradox of the now diffuse cause of global justice—the abuses were wider and more complex, but the catchment for human solidarity, and the mechanisms for connecting with it, had become equally networked and globalized. The struggle for "political kingdom" had become planetary.

CHAPTER EIGHT

Race

BRUCE S. HALL

INTRODUCTION

The category of race has come to be used more and more often by anglophone historians over the last couple of decades to analyze an increasing number of historical situations outside of the traditional areas where race has long been understood as important (Atlantic slavery and post-slavery, settler colonialism, modern eugenics, etc.). Critics of this increasingly capacious use of race in historical writing fear that deploying race in such diverse contexts dilutes the value of the concept in its modern western "home," while at the same time imposing a modern western category on histories for which this term had no meaning. Essentially, what is at stake is whether historians want to understand race as the exclusive province of modern western historical formations, or whether the category can be used more analytically than homiletically, as a tool of historical explanation instead of (always) as a tentacle in the web of modern western power. This chapter will examine some of the different ways that race has been used in recent historical writing on twentieth-century colonial and postcolonial settings outside of Europe and North America.

One important early work in the effort to isolate a racial dimension from a broader non-western cultural context was Frank Dikötter's *The Discourse of Race in Modern China* (1992). Dikötter managed to overcome several problems that critics often point to when the language of race is used in seemingly unfamiliar settings. First, he borrowed the sociologist Michael Banton's (1987) typology of racial ideas in order to show the different things that race was made to do in various Chinese contexts at different historical moments. For example, early Chinese discourse about race was bound up with theories of Chinese imperial lineage. Later iterations of race were tied to distinctions of physical type, of status hierarchy, of ethnicity. By approaching race as a dynamic tool capable of articulating with other forms of hierarchy and inequality, Dikötter (and Banton) made clear that race was not a single, unchanging idea. It was a way of applying Stuart Hall's insight that, in the case of modern Britain, race is "the modality in which class is 'lived', the medium through which class relations are experienced, the form in which it is appropriated and 'fought through'" (Hall 1980: 341). If race could be different things, articulated to different social structures, then it also must necessarily be a set of ideas subject to historical analysis. It was in tracing the change in racial ideas over time in China that Dikötter's work proved so original—and controversial (Liu 2004: 72–3)—largely because he refused to accept a historical process limited to Chinese borrowings of western racial ideas.

> Chinese reformers in the 1890s were active agents who participated in the invention of their identities. They were not the passive recipients of a "derivative discourse", but creative individuals who selectively appropriated elements of foreign thought systems in a process of cultural interaction. More important, the reform movement which contributed so much to the invention of racial identities in China was largely the product of complex interactions and features of different indigenous schools of thought, such as New Text Confucianism, statecraft scholarship, classical non-canonical philosophies and Mahayana Buddhism, all of which had virtually nothing to do with Western learning (Dikötter 1997: 13–14).

Dikötter's book is an intellectual history of racial ideas in China, and as such is limited in some respects. But it showed how one might approach race historically and analytically in ways that opened up new areas for research.

CONTROVERSIES

Historians who choose to work on race in fields outside of the modern West often feel the need to defend their analytical choice. By this point, the extent to which this work is controversial is perhaps overstated as more and more historians accept race as a valid analytic in diverse settings, but it has nonetheless become one of the main tropes of this sub-field to defend the choice of analyzing race in histories of premodern and non-western contexts against imagined critics who would insist on understanding race as a modern western phenomenon. It is useful to examine the critique of this use of race, before moving to discuss the historiography itself.

The argument that race is quintessentially a modern idea that developed in Europe and the Americas beginning in the eighteenth century is certainly the most stubborn objection to histories of race outside of the modern West. There are any number of originary moments for the emergence of the modern idea of race—in the philosophy of Immanuel Kant, or in the biological typologies of Georges Cuvier, or in the early anthropology of Johann Frederick Blumenbach—but in one way or another, it is understood by many people as a product of the rational sciences (see Banton 1987; Hannaford 1996). Proof of this is sometimes said to lie in the difficulty of translating these terms into non-European languages, where race, as an idea, is said not to have existed. When Chinese or Arab intellectuals—to take just two important examples—embarked on the large-scale translation of important European-language texts into Chinese and Arabic beginning in the second half of the nineteenth century, they encountered the term "race" in the context of the reception of Darwin, and in the post-Darwinian social science in the works of people like Herbert Spencer, Gustav Le Bon, and Ernest Renan, among others (Dikötter 1992: 98–101; Elshakry 2014). In Arabic and Chinese, translations of the term "race" tended to be some equivalent of "types of people," "kinds of peoples," or single words derived from existing terms for peoples, stock, breeding, etc. (Dikötter 1992: 105, 109; Elshakry 2007: 55–86). As Marwa Elshakry puts it, "Discussing Darwin in Arabic occurred through a process of literally grafting new terms onto older ones" (2014: 17). But the fact that Chinese and Arabic reading publics received these European works, which included ideas about race, does not mean that these cultures had no preexisting racial ideas, or that elements of Egyptian or Chinese social hierarchy cannot be reasonably interpreted using the conceptual tools associated with race. These are, of course, empirical questions. It is clear that Arab and Chinese intellectuals absorbed late nineteenth-century usages of the term race and deployed them in complex ways in their own language and cultural context. How they did so is again a matter of empirical investigation. But the historical complexity of the translation of the term "race" in no way demonstrates that there was no such idea in the non-western societies where these ideas were being received.

One of the most popular approaches to the study of race historically has been to trace the genealogy of the word "race" or its cognates in different European languages. Done well, this illustrates the extent to which the meanings of the term "race" have changed over time. But done poorly, it can seem to suggest that the idea of race could only be carried by the term used to refer to it, or by another such as "black" (Banton 1987; Taine-Cheikh 1989: 90–105; Wheeler 2000; Boulle 2003: 12; Hall 1996: 28). Whether an idea, or a social or cultural formation, is "racial" does not depend upon the terminology, otherwise we are dealing with a form of historical nominalism. As the medievalist David Nirenberg has written, it is as if, in a European context, one argued "that because the word *Rasse* did not enter German until the eighteenth century and the word *Anti-Semitismus* until the nineteenth, we need not look for these concepts in the earlier history of German-speaking lands." As Nirenberg puts it, we should not be surprised that

> those who define race as the application of eighteenth- and nineteenth-century vocabularies of biological classification to human populations differentiated by skin color are certain that it cannot be found in earlier periods. Such definitions fail to make sense even of modern racial ideologies, which are themselves not only tremendously diverse but also change a great deal over time (2007: 73–4).

It is the purported contrast between "real racism" and some faux version which organizes many critiques of the uses of race in historical writing. This, as Ann Stoler points out in making a similar point with respect to European colonial officials in Indonesia, is usually based on an ideal-typical form of racism rather than real historical manifestations of racial thought in the past. Such a move is especially clear in efforts to contrast contemporary, apparently fuzzier forms of racism in the present of American and European societies with "fuller" or "truer" iteration of race in the past. According to Stoler,

> [t]he observation that racists in the postmodern era are encouraged not to see themselves as such may capture something significant about how racial discourses operate today, but it again flattens history in the service of a spurious contrast; namely that earlier racisms did nothing of the sort, that those racisms were candidly embraced by their advocates. But this is a caricature of colonial racial sensibilities, not a description of them. Dutch colonials in Indonesia in the late nineteenth and early twentieth century were not alone in adamantly declaring that they did not subscribe to racism and emphatically did subscribe to the equality of human rights (1997: 195).

Many critiques of efforts to find race in non-western (or pre-modern) contexts are based on these sorts of ahistorical comparisons with some purportedly "truer" form of racism.

Objections to the use of race in non-western contexts can have national peculiarities as well. In 1998, Pierre Bourdieu and Loïc Wacquant (1999) published an article in which they argued that American and American-trained scholars have imposed a highly ethnocentric model of race drawn from the particular, rigid dichotomy between blacks and whites in the United States, and imposed it as a universal analytic tool on societies which had very different histories and social realities. They cited the example of Brazil, and claimed in a scathing attack on the American political scientist Michael Hanchard's book *Orpheus and Power* (1994) about Brazilian black consciousness movements (Figure 8.1), that he "makes the particular history of the US Civil Rights

FIGURE 8.1: Black Brazilian women protest. Credit: EVARISTO SA/AFP/Getty Images.

Movement into the universal standard for the struggle of all groups oppressed on grounds of colour (or caste)." Furthermore,

> [i]nstead of dissecting the constitution of the Brazilian ethnoracial order according to its own logic, such inquiries are most often content to replace wholesale the national myth of "racial democracy" . . . by the myth according to which all societies are "racist", including those within which "race" relations seem at first sight to be less distant and hostile. From being an analytic tool, the concept of racism becomes a mere instrument of accusation; under the guise of science, it is the logic of the trial which asserts itself (and ensures book sales, for lack of success based on intellectual esteem) (Bourdieu and Wacquant 1999: 44–5).

The venom of Bourdieu and Wacquant's argument can perhaps be understood in part as reflecting a decade of significant anxiety in France (and other places) about processes of globalization and apparent Americanization of global cultural and intellectual forms. But their critique of the expansion of the academic deployment of race in different contexts is one that has been repeated often. They argue that the model of race in American scholarship is particular to the United States where race is (purportedly) dichotomous between black and white, where there is no mixed-race category, where the one-drop rule assigns everyone, with some lineal connection to enslaved Africans, the identity of black. But it is not just an intellectual error; it also is a product of the power of American institutions in the world.

> The fact that this racial (or racist) sociodicy was able to globalize itself over the recent period, thereby losing its outer characteristics of legitimating discourse for domestic or local usage, is undoubtedly one of the most striking proofs of the symbolic dominion and influence exercised by the USA over every kind of scholarly and, especially, semi-scholarly production, notably through the power of consecration they possess and through the material and symbolic profits that researchers in the dominated countries realize from a more or less assumed or ashamed adherence to the model derived from the USA (Bourdieu and Wacquant 1999: 45–6).

In criticizing the American sociologist Howard Winant, they write that "the 'globalization of race' results, not from a sudden convergence of forms of ethnoracial domination in the various countries, but from the quasi-universalization of the US folk-concept of 'race' as a result of the worldwide export of US scholarly categories" (Bourdieu and Wacquant 1999: 48).

The core of this argument had been put forward earlier by both Bourdieu and Wacquant. Bourdieu's argument was made in reference to sub-nationalist discourse in southern France (Bourdieu 1994: 220). Wacquant addressed himself specifically to race, arguing that academic work on race has consistently confused folk and analytical notions of race.

> For, with precious few exceptions, students of "race" have accepted lay preconstructions of the phenomenon. They have been content to tackle "race" in the manner in which it has been constituted as a "social problem" in reality itself. Worse yet: they have taken over as tools of analysis the reified products of the ethnoracial struggles of the past. In short, they have failed to establish a clear demarcation between folk and analytic understandings of "race" (1997: 222).

Wacquant argues that this confusion is intrinsic to the category of race because from its inception, science and common sense have mixed.

> The result of this ongoing traffic between folk and analytical concepts is that the history of racial domination is inscribed in the scientific unconscious of our disciplines and acts as a powerful censoring mechanism upon all researchers, including those who do not ostensibly study "race". This is visible in the categories we use, namely, the scientifically inept but socially

powerful differentiation between "race" and "ethnicity"; in how we organize our inquiries by reference to groups as they appear in the official taxonomies of the state; and in the structure of each national social scientific field, wherein "race" is alternately dissolved under another rubric, coupled with germane issues, or set apart for special examination (1997: 223).

Brazil is, of course, the home of the largest African-descended population in the Americas, and there is a long tradition of scholarship both inside Brazil and by outsiders (especially Americans) seeking to understand the particularities of the Brazilian racial story, and to find points of comparison and contrast with the situation in the United States. In fact, the earliest efforts to think about race comparatively were focused precisely on Brazil. The leading Brazilian sociologist of race Gilberto Freyre was trained in the US under Franz Boas and made much of the difference between the slave systems and the post-emancipation place of blacks in the US and Brazil (see Freyre 1986).[1] Frank Tannenbawm's *Slave and Citizen* (1946) was another important early work comparing so-called race relations between the US and Latin America. The comparison has been followed up many times since (see Degler 1971). So to suggest that Hanchard and other American scholars had blindly applied American-derived models on the Brazilian context is completely incorrect, even if there is much to criticize in some of this scholarship (French 2000).

The Bourdieu and Wacquant critique has become somewhat modular in that it has been repeated, in slightly different forms, in a number of other contexts. It is not just American academics importing race that is the problem, but the fact that many marginal groups in societies like Brazil have sought to use more explicitly racial language, often drawn from American examples, in their politics. In India, for example, the effort by Dalit (Untouchable) activists to have caste discrimination recognized as a form of racism by an important United Nations conference devoted to racism in Durban, South Africa in 2001, provoked much debate in India (Figure 8.2); with many interventions aimed at refuting the idea that race and caste could be understood as closely related. An example of this effort to pour water on the idea that caste was a form of race—or could usefully be analyzed as such—is an article written by Dikankar Gupta intended for a sophisticated, but not exclusively academic, audience.

Why is caste so often mistaken to be another kind of racism? There are two reasons for this. One is a misreading of Vedic texts inspired by the distinction made by early Indologists between fair Aryans and dark Dravidians. The other reason for equating caste with race comes about because there are some similarities between the ways blacks were treated in the southern United States, or in apartheid South Africa, and the treatment meted out to so-called "untouchables" in caste Hindu society (Gupta 2001).

FIGURE 8.2: A dalit with a poster of Dr Ambedkar in Chennai. Credit: Claude Renault/Getty Images.

We will leave aside the question of the "misreading" of the Vedic texts—while noting that they can certainly be read in ways that suggest a racial element (Robb 1995)—and focus instead on Gupta's argument about the distinction between Indian caste and US race. Gupta argues that studies have shown that there are overwhelming physical similarities between high and low castes within the same geographical region in India. Conversely, strata based on race are arranged along a continuum of color, whereby whites occupy one end and blacks the other of this hierarchical ladder, with the colors in between positioned accordingly along this scale. The color continuum is, he argues, objective and demonstrable so that there is little point in a black person claiming to be white if the person's skin color and features do not help to back this claim. To make the claim that caste and race are the same would require one to demonstrate that caste categories are fixed and immutable. But because there is evidence that formerly low castes have become kshatriyas (military elite), and sudras (laborers) have become elite pen-pushers, caste cannot be understood as immutable in the same way as race is.

I cite Gupta's argument at such length because I think it is representative of the kinds of objection that recur in response to work on race in non-western contexts. Race is simple, permanent, and natural; caste by contrast is highly complex, mutable, and requires a particular Indian politics to overcome. That Dalit activists in India have grabbed onto models of emancipatory politics aimed at overcoming racial oppression, whether from the United States or South Africa, is viewed with the same suspicion that Bourdieu and Wacquant saw self-consciously black Brazilian activists.[2] Taking this critique a little bit further, the fact that their racial ideology is "borrowed" renders it inauthentic, or at least inorganic, when held by non-Europeans (Mamdani 2001: 190; 2009: 147–52). But this is surely a refusal to acknowledge the choices made by subaltern intellectuals in how they represent and position themselves *vis-à-vis* other emancipatory struggles, and to fail to recognize the difficulty of subalternized minorities in carving out "a sequestered domain of an autonomous 'culture'" (Pandey 2013: 53). The denial of a racial dimension to caste in India is also part of a contemporary political struggle over the meaning of caste, as the tensions in Indian anticolonial and postcolonial politics around the life and career of the great Dalit intellectual B.R. Ambedkar (1891–1956) attest (Pandey 2013: 61–96). Or, more recently, the caste wars in Bihar in the 1990s.

CATEGORIES OF PRACTICE

So far, we have offered a critical review of the kind of argument raised against the use of race in non-western contexts without saying very much about what criteria should be employed to determine whether race is an appropriate framework in particular situations. This is a more complicated question than it might at first appear to be. Let us begin by looking at a representative definition.

> For the present study I shall define race as "a group of people who are believed to share imagined common characteristics, physical and mental or moral which cannot be changed by human will, because they are thought to be determined by unalterable, stable physical factors: heredity, or external, such as climate or geography." A belief in the reality of race in itself is always misguided, but it is not necessarily racism. It becomes racism if the ensuing differences between peoples are the basis for the division of individuals into superior and inferior racial groups (Isaac 2004: 34–5).

Most definitions of race show two features: that race requires a claim about immutable human difference grounded in biological reproduction, and that racism refers to using race to justify inequalities of some sort on this basis.

The value of such a definition is that it offers a starting point for the recognition of racial arguments, and their relationship to political and social structures. But this is not exactly an analytical framework. What would an analytical framework for race look like? We can usefully turn to debates within sociology in trying to arrive at such a framework. Eduardo Bonilla-Silva has argued that most social scientific work on race treats it as a purely ideological phenomenon, and that this is reflected in most definitions of racism (1996: 465).

Instead, Bonilla-Silva proposes an analytic model of race that stresses the reality of the category on group association, identity, and life chances: "After racial categories were used to organize social relations in a society, however, race became an independent element of the operation of the social system" (1996: 473). In his more recent work, Bonilla-Silva has taken this model to make a racial analysis of precisely the opposite kinds of discourse discussed in the definitions: viz. what he calls "color-blind racism," which he takes to be an ideology of white supremacy in the modern United States (2014: 10). By turning around the constructivist approach to race, Bonilla-Silva makes of race a social fact prior to language, and as such racial ideology in his analysis is a rather crude superstructure justifying white privilege.

But Bonilla-Silva's argument may seem stronger when understood as part of the debates over the "new racisms" that have emerged since the Civil Rights era in the United States, and as a consequence of anxieties over non-European immigration in Europe (Balibar 1991). Michael Omi and Howard Winant's influential formulation of "racial formation" captures some of the difficulty that historians of race face: "[R]ace is a matter of both social structure and cultural representation. Too often, the attempt is made to understand race simply or primarily in terms of only one of these two analytical dimensions." What Omi and Winant call "racial projects" connect "what race means in a particular discursive practice and the ways in which both social structures and everyday experiences are racially organized, based upon that meaning" (1994: 56). Because in this diachronic sense, race as a social fact matters in so many places around the world, efforts to define race or racism as a complex of ideas that invoke biological inferiority and immutability very often miss their mark. It is really impossible to make sense of racial phenomena unless the historical specificity of particular instances of race is accounted for (Hall 1980). Not only does that mean that there will then be historically specific "racisms" rather than some singular ahistorical form, but that ideas and practices connected to the social fact of race will articulate with other social phenomena differently. Thomas Holt has argued that "the idea that race is socially constructed implies also that it can and must be constructed differently at different historical moments and in different social contexts" (2000: 21). Holt refuses to be pinned down to a definition of race, insisting instead that we must "adopt a conception of historical transformation, in which we recognize that a new historical construct is never entirely supplanted by the new. Rather the new is grafted onto the old. Thus racism, too, is never entirely new. Shards and fragments of its past incarnations are embedded in the new. Or, if we switch metaphors to an archaeological image, the new is sedimented onto the old, which occasionally seeps or bursts through" (2000: 20).

In 1997, Ann Stoler published an article which has since become a widely read and important text in the field of race studies. She took account of the state of the field and observed that contemporary scholarship on racism acknowledges that there is no single object called racism, but instead a plurality of racisms which are not rehearsals of one another but distinct systems of practice and belief. "Within this frame, historically different meanings are attached to the concept of 'race' and the racisms they entail. Recognition of plurality in part stems from the attribution of racisms' condition of origin in different events and different contexts" (Stoler 1997: 184). Stoler's intervention was most notable, in my opinion, for its insistence on the "polyvalent mobility" of racism (a term she takes from Foucault), which refers to the ways that racism "may vacillate and be embraced by those opposed to and beleaguered by the state at one moment and become an integral part of the technologies of state rule at another, then the fact that racial discourses contain and coexist with a range of political agendas is not a contradiction but a fundamental historical feature of their non-linear, spiraling political genealogies" (1997: 191). Stoler uses Foucault's discussion of discourse in the *Archeology of Knowledge* as "a field and set of conditions in which it becomes impossible to talk about sexuality, class membership, morality, and childrearing without talking about race" (Foucault 1972: 144).

In a critique of Stoler, Wacquant argues that she overlooks non-discursive practices and institutions. Stoler's arguments tend to autonomize discourse and endow it with the capacity to act on its own impulses.

> But the conditions of possibility that make up an épistémè do not guarantee its effectiveness. Just as the "conditions of felicity" of performative utterances are institutional factors residing outside of language, discourses do not contain within themselves the social mechanisms that endow them with potency. The most limiting assumption of Stoler's research program, then, is that we can elucidate "racism" by scanning and probing its discourse, as if some transparent, stable, and immediately elucidable connection obtained between discursive instantiations of "race" and the systems of concrete practices and organizations through which it materializes itself (Wacquant 1997: 228).

Wacquant is right to insist on an analytics of race that includes its materiality in concrete practices and institutions. But he argues that the term "racism" no longer plays a useful analytical role, and instead argues for the following corrective:

> These basic mechanisms of ethnoracial subordination enter into mobile combinations in different societies and during different periods with the same society so that at any point each group is confronted with a particular profile of racial domination. These profiles in turn tend to get locked into

systems of racial ruling endowed with their own internal coherence, logic, and inertia. To explain a given racial formation, then, requires that we break it down into its constituent mechanisms and uncover the linkages between them. Such linkages, for example, between stigma and segregation or between idioms of exclusion and discriminatory practices, have to be empirically parsed and analytically reconstructed: they can neither be assumed nor grasped at the level of discourse. Indeed, by properly differentiating its interlocking forms, we will find out that "tactical mobility" is a property not of racial discourse but of the whole complex of relations and technologies through which racial domination operates (1997: 231).

The historical profession has plenty of room for different approaches, some focused on intellectual history and others on social history. But historians of race should heed Wacquant's directive and better connect intellectual histories of racial ideas with the materiality of race in different contexts.

We are a long way from having to justify the possibility of finding racial formations in non-western contexts, and can instead identify race in all its manifestations as polyvalent, historically specific, and bound up in practice and institutions. This clearer set of analytic tools allows us to move away from analogies with ideas and situations in the more obviously racially inflected West. Over the last two decades, an increasingly wide range of scholarship has been published which uses race as a key feature in histories of Asia and Africa. Some follow a more established path of showing the role of race in the exercise of imperial power in the non-western world. Others have sought to identify non-western traditions of racial thought and practice. The most interesting work, at least in my eyes, are those studies which seek to unravel the complex interplay of ideas and practices around race that have multiple authors, borrow from western and non-western sources alike, which constitute the ground for important political struggles across the world.

HISTORIES OF RACE

The role of race in twentieth-century European and American imperial projects is well known, even if the details of that history sometimes are not. The strand of literature drawing inspiration from Michel Foucault's nexus of knowledge and power and Edward Said's *Orientalism* (1978) is still influential. On India, a well-developed literature chronicles the colonial construction of knowledge about south Asia in ways that rendered the subcontinent more governable. Ronald Inden's *Imagining India* (1990) attempts to do for south Asia what Said did for the Middle East. Thomas Trautmann has traced the intellectual history of the development of Indology and the idea of Aryanism (Trautmann 1997, 2006; Ballantyne 2002). Bernard Cohn (1987) and Nicholas Dirks (2001) each chronicled ways in which, they argued, British tools to render India legible and hence governable resulted in the invention or increasing importance of distinctions such as those of caste. As Cohn put it in a widely read article on the Indian census, "[c]oncern with counting the characteristics of the Indian population, which may have started as the intellectual concerns of a few British officials or the administrative necessity of knowing the 'natives', had become an object to be used in the political, cultural and religious battles at the heart of Punjabi politics which have been crucial down to the present" (Cohn 1987: 250). The question in this literature is not so much whether caste in India had taken on a racial dimension, but how to understand the history of that fact and the role of the British colonial state in it. According to Peter Robb, "the issue is not whether there are 'race theories' in India today. Clearly there are; and they are Indian in the sense of being peculiar to the subcontinent, albeit combining Western with indigenous influences . . . The debate concerns the nature of this mix and its origins, in particular whether there were long-standing Indian theories of race which preceded and merged with imported ones" (1995: 43).

European racial denigrations of Africans have a long history. Philip Curtin's *The Image of Africa* (1964) and Abdallah Laroui's *History of the Maghrib* (1977), originally published in French in 1970, are two early works which detail some of the ways in which different parts of Africa were constructed as places with inferior people in need of European presence. But it was Valentin Mudimbe's publication of *The Invention of Africa* (1988) that really grappled with the epistemological implications of the ways in which race was bound up with the development of the idea of Africa. Others have described the history of racialized anthropology and its use in colonial projects in Africa (Asad 1973; Dubow 1995; Lorcin 1995; Trumbull 2009; Conklin 2013). But racial discourse was so ubiquitous in colonial rule in Africa that it hardly constitutes a sub-field of its own. Mahmood Mamdani's *Citizen and Subject* (1996) provides a nice overview of how race was used by the British in Africa, and by settler colonial states like South Africa, to construct a neotraditional native "personality" that was legally incapable of exercising the rights of full citizenship. Comaroff and Comaroff's (1991, 1997) two-volume history of the encounter between Christian missionaries and Tswana people along the South African frontier is a well-known treatment of the racial implications of the impact of European modernity in Africa. While Chloe Campbell has demonstrated settler engagement with eugenics in interwar Kenya (Campbell 2007). In places like Sudan, Heather Sharkey (2003) has shown how race was used as a tool in building the colonial regime; many others have shown how the consequences of this were a postcolonial history of racial conflict and ultimately division of the country (see also Johnson 2003; Idris 2005; Vazzadini 2015). Eve Troutt Powell's (2003) work describes the ways in which Egyptian intellectuals used race in their treatment of Sudan. More recently, she has written about enslaved

Sudanese women in Egypt (Troutt Powell 2013; see also Lewis 1990; Walz and Cuno 2011; El Hamel 2013).

Another well-known aspect of imperial rule in Africa, Asia, and parts of Latin America where the United States imposed its control formally and informally, is the extent to which violence was used in conquest and to put down any challenges to colonial power. While the fact of the violence is well known, many publications over the last two decades have revealed the hitherto unknown extent of violence, or have shown much more clearly than was known before how much of a role race played in motivating and justifying colonial violence. The publication of Adam Hochschild's *King Leopold's Ghosts* (1998) brought a well-known story of colonial violence in late nineteenth-century central Africa to a much wider audience. Yet this account of the systematic violence of forced labor in infrastructure-building and collection of wild rubber in King Leopold's Congo Free State offers little analysis of the history of racialized violence in Africa, and offers little connection to the wider story of systematic violence in the early decades of colonial rule in Africa, which was repeated across the continent to varying degrees. Mass—even genocidal—violence accompanied colonial conquest in Tanzania and what is today Namibia, Niger, South Africa, Algeria, and parts of equatorial Africa (see Bley 1971; Brower 2009; Taithe 2009; Adhikari 2010). A more provocative popular book centered on the same violence in central Africa is the Swedish writer Sven Lindqvist's *"Exterminate All the Brutes"* (1996), which is part travel narrative and part meditation on the meaning of the violence in late-nineteenth-century Africa, and the extent to which violence of this type was didactic and led directly to the Nazi crimes and the Holocaust. This issue, suggested by Hannah Arendt, has been taken up by German academic historians as well (Madley 2005; Malinowski and Gerwarth 2009; Langbehn and Salam 2011; Kundrus 2014).

Paul Kramer's work on racialized violence in the American-occupied Philippines in the first decade of the twentieth century extends Lindqvist and Arendt's logic to another colonial setting where race has long been recognized as an important dimension of colonialism, arguing that "the intersections of race and empire were contingent, contested, and transnational in scope. Race was the site of intense struggle in Philippine-American colonial history, between Filipinos and Americans, between actors in metropole and colony, between actors inside and outside the colonial state" (Kramer 2006: 4). By emphasizing that it was around the issue of race itself that much of the meaning of the conflict in the Philippines took place, Kramer makes a convincing argument about how race was made and re-made in imperial contexts, and how contingent this making and re-making were/are. Instead of a static racial denigration of those targeted by imperial violence, Kramer's is a dynamic model that is both historical and multivalent. It is made material in the exercise of violence in military conflict and colonial control, and institutionalized in the imperial state.

One of the imperial sites where race was made and re-made in contingent, contested, and transnational ways was around the issue of sex and intimacy. Ann Stoler (2002) argued in her book about the policing of sex and race in the Dutch Indies that the intimate domain figured very prominently in the way that colonial rule worked. Not only was it a preoccupation of those who exercised power in colonial settings, but it was also a domain where the micropolitics of the colonial project played out. Boundaries of intimacy were important and policed, so that intimate relationships, marriage, children, schools, and domestic spaces were all sites at which race played out (Briggs 2002; Levine 2003). As Emmanuelle Saada's (2012) work on so-called "mixed-race" children in the French empire suggests, however, sexual boundaries were often transgressed in practice and different French colonies managed the results in widely varying ways. While the "problem"—from the point of view of the colonial state—emerged in all colonies, it was in France's south-east Asian territories that the issue first arose about what the metropolitan responsibility should be for "mixed-race" children, and it was likewise for "mixed-race" children from this region—but not from others such as the African colonies—that French nationality was eventually offered. Saada tells a complex story, but one that is highly contingent and contested. A number of studies have appeared recently of so-called "mixed-race" populations in parts of sub-Saharan Africa, focused especially on the political mobilization of these "mixed" groups in the last few decades of colonial rule (Jones 2013; Jean-Baptiste 2014; Lee 2014; Duke Bryant 2015; Ray 2015).

Another theme that has received sustained attention in recent decades is the role of race in the political imaginary of anticolonial nationalist movements in Africa. One of the best studies of this sort is Jonathon Glassman's *War of Words, War of Stones: Racial Thought and Violence in Colonial Zanzibar* (2011), which seeks to explain how it was that the Arab sultan of Zanzibar on the east African coast, and his elected constitutional government, were overthrown in a bloody revolution one month after independence from Britain in 1964 by forces that claimed to represent the island's African racial majority, fighting to redress what they called the centuries-old injustice of Arab rule. The coup was accompanied by pogroms that took the lives of thousands of the islands' Arab minority (Figure 8.3). Glassman sees the origin of this violence in the development of competing racial narratives of political identity in the decades before independence. Although he traces the history of some of the central ideas that intersect in the competing racial narratives of mid-twentieth-century Zanzibar, the book is focused analytically on explaining how these forces came together in the specific context of mid-century Zanzibar, and how they influenced political and social organization in that place. Glassman shows just how integral racial thought was to Zanzibari intellectuals in the middle of the twentieth century. It was not a case of mimicry of colonial discourse, as he shows by his detailed reconstruction of conversations and debates from which racial thought emerged.

Such a reconstruction reveals that indigenous intellectuals spoke to one another more than they addressed the colonial state or responded to its demands and that their impact on the emergence of racial thought was arguably greater, and certainly more direct, than that of colonial educators ... To understand the etiology of racial thought, then, we must abandon the cliché of colonial encounter. It is just as misleading to speak of two discrete spheres of discourse—one colonial, the other indigenous—as it is to speak of the colonial state's domination of its subjects' consciousness (Glassman 2011: 17–18).

Glassman places a lot of importance on schooling and school teachers as the intellectuals who helped to fashion racial politics in Zanzibar. He traces the development of the ideological foundations of Zanzibari Arab nationalist thought by examining the writing of the island's intelligentsia, which celebrated the role of Arabs and Muslims in bringing civilization to the East African region. This intellectual and political project also included justifications for slavery as an educational and civilizing institution for "backward" blacks. Explicit racial nationalism in Zanzibar arose from a group of subaltern intellectuals connected to mainland black laborers on the island. It drew on pan-African rhetoric from

FIGURE 8.3: An Arab prisoner being questioned and jailed in camps during the Zanzibar revolution by local African revolutionaries led by John Gideon Okello, January 12, 1964. Credit: STRINGER/AFP/Getty Images.

elsewhere on the continent and in the African diaspora, but combined in the Zanzibari context to form a distinctly racialized anti-Arab politics in which the Arabs represented alien outsider oppressors. The book traces the flow of events and conflict between these political forces, culminating in the violent overthrow of the elected postcolonial government and the bloody pogroms against the island's Arab population. Glassman attempts to use the racial history he has traced in the intellectual and political realm as a means of understanding the violent actions of mobs in the acts of racialized violence themselves. And as such, it draws on literature about violence that tends to focus on the more and more microscale of the event itself. What is most interesting about Glassman's book is that it insists on a racial history constructed in the specific context of Zanzibar, but without an overlong focus on the origins of ideas. What matters is how ideas are reconfigured and inhabited to meet particular ends in a place and time. As such, we have a local racial history in a non-western context which refuses to play the genealogical card, refuses to investigate the origins of these ideas, refuses the logic of the trial, and refuses nominalist and diffusionist models of intellectual history. This is in stark contrast to much of the literature on the Rwandan genocide that attributes most of the explanatory power of the genocidal violence there to lessons in colonial schoolhouses decades earlier about the racial-civilizational disparities between Hutus and Tutsis (Mamdani 2001), or downplays the importance of the history of race as a factor leading to the genocidal violence (Strauss 2006: 9).

James Brennan's history of racial nationalism in the urban setting of Dar es Salaam in Tanzania is an example of a study which seeks to ground the production of racial ideas and practices in the colonial configuration of urban space and the role of an intermediary Asian group in becoming scapegoats for an emerging black African Tanzanian nationalism after independence in 1961. Brennan shows that a kind of organic, even subaltern, African nationalism emerged in Dar es Salaam that was aimed primarily at eradicating exploitation. It took as its targets, Asian merchants and landlords who were seen to be exploiters of Africans, even as political leaders preached a multiracial ideology of African Socialism. According to Brennan,

> African nationalists throughout this period understood nationalism first and foremost to mean the elimination of exploitation. Although the dominance of this discursive theme is partially beholden to international socialist ideology, in Dar es Salaam the discussions of exploitation emerged equally out of idioms of parasitism and witchcraft eradication. Defining exploitation was also a way to define who was a good citizen and who belonged to the nation. At its root, the ideal national citizen was someone who was "African"; someone who was an urban laborer or preferably a rural farmer; and someone who not only refrained from but actively fought exploitation (2012: 160).

The power of this racialized nationalism eventually led the Tanzanian government to nationalize housing in 1971, which was aimed at appropriating Asian property, and this accelerated the emigration of Asians from the country (see also Aminzade 2013).

In the cases discussed by both Glassman and Brennan, local intellectuals built racialized ideologies around the salience of memories of slavery. They did so with accusations directed at groups who were identified as former slaveholders, or in the Asian case in Dar es Salaam, as exploiters of poor black Tanzanians. The violence in Zanzibar was directed at people identified with the slaveholding class/race, even if many of the victims of the violence were not themselves slaveholders in reality. The accusation of a slaveholding past has also become a powerful mobilizing device in racialized postcolonial conflicts along the African Sahel, from Mauritania to Sudan. In Baz Lecocq's (2010) work on Tuareg irredentist politics and rebellions in Mali and Niger, he has shown how the accusation of being an inveterate slaveholder has been used by "black" Malian and Nigerien intellectuals and media to delegitimize the political claims made by Tuareg political groups. Conversely, Tuareg intellectuals have consistently seen "black" Malian and Nigerian state administrators as little more than slaves in disguise. This case makes it especially clear that whatever role European colonial rule played in transforming this region of the world, and whatever racial ideas flowed to Sahelian intellectuals from western sources, the core content of the racialized ideas in these conflicts are local, drawn from a long (and continuing) history of inequality and exploitation within this region. The ideas and the way that they are mobilized is contingent and contested to be sure, but they draw a good part of their strength from the existence of institutional material inequalities that survive changes in political regime and environment (Hall 2011).

CONCLUSION

This chapter has sought to explore some of the ways in which historians in the last several decades have written about race in non-western cultural contexts in the twentieth century. The choice was made to revisit some of the conceptual debates over the use of race in such contexts, as a way of showing how these historians have engaged with colleagues in sociology and anthropology in developing more sophisticated frameworks for their work. What remains to be seen is whether this work will have much influence on historians working in more traditional "race" fields of US and European colonial histories.

NOTES

Introduction

1. My thanks to Patrick Wiltz for locating the cover image to the volume.
2. The treaty was signed on June 28, 1919.
3. "A free, open-minded and absolutely impartial adjustment of all colonial claims based upon a strict observance of the principle that in determining all such questions of sovereignty, the interests of the populations concerned must have equal weight with the equitable claims of the government whose title is to be determined." *8 January, 1918: President Woodrow Wilson's Fourteen Points*, Lillian Goldman Law Library, The Avalon Project, documents in Law, History, and Diplomacy, http://avalon.law.yale.edu/20th_century/wilson14.asp, accessed July 1, 2016.
4. The Sykes-Picot Agreement was signed by Lord Grey for the British and Paul Cambon for the French.
5. There is no space in this introduction to engage with the debates about the similarities and differences between nation-states and imperialism, which have recently preoccupied scholars. For more on these issues, see Burbank and Cooper (2010) and Alessio and Renfro (2016). Nor is it possible to revisit debates about Germany's Nazi period and the quest for *lebensraum*.
6. Singapore gained independence from Malaysia in 1965.
7. Britain had installed the Greek royal family in place.
8. SCOA was dissolved in 1998; CFAO was bought out in 2012 and UAC functioned until 1987.

Chapter 1

1. Rumsfeld spoke along these lines on many occasions during his time as Secretary of Defense under President George W. Bush (2001–6). This quotation is from a press briefing on October 9, 2001: see http://www.washingtonpost.com/wp-srv/nation/

specials/attacked/transcripts/rumsfeld_100901.html. See also a 2002 speech at NATO headquarters in Brussels: http://www.nato.int/docu/speech/2002/s020606g.htm.

Chapter 2

1. Baumgart, it should be added, finds the term "informal imperialism" too broad as to be useful, but notes the history of the term's usage (1982: 5–7, 10).
2. Anecdotal evidence for the race to the bottom abounds, but most investment does not flow to the least regulatory governments. In most years, most investment flows between developed countries, which tend to have more stringent environmental, health and safety, and labor laws. Additionally, more globalized countries are apt to have higher rates of government spending than less globalized countries, as economist Dani Rodrik, who is wary of unregulated globalization, has found. This evidence is strongly against the race to the bottom argument but does not negate the many specific instances of corporations successfully negotiating with developing country governments to relax regulations as a condition of investment.
3. Adam Hochschild's *King Leopold's Ghost: A Story of Greed, Terror, and Heroism in Colonial Africa* (1998) and Sven Beckert's *Empire of Cotton, A Global History* (2015) are good examples, respectively, of the forced nature of economic relations and the importance of primary products from colonial countries to metropole economies.
4. Trade in Europe became more open with the 1860 Treaty of Commerce between France and Great Britain and the subsequent rush of other European countries seeking to be included in an increasingly integrated European market through a network of trade agreements (Lazer 1999: 447–8).
5. More specifically, oil was discovered in commercially viable amounts in Bahrain in 1932, Iraq in 1934, and in Kuwait and Saudi Arabia in 1938 (Yergin 1991: 300; Ahram 2017: 258; Crystal 2017: 362).
6. Average tariffs can be calculated with various methods, so there are different numbers cited for the impact of Smoot-Hawley. The tariff rate on "dutiable items" excludes any items imported with zero duties in calculating the average. Under Smoot-Hawley this rose to just over 47 percent in 1930, according to Douglas Irwin. He further notes that this number rose to 60 percent in late 1932 because the prices for the underlying goods dropped dramatically and some of the tariffs were specific tariffs (a specific tariff places a dollar amount per unit of imports), not just *ad valorem* tariffs (a tariff charged as a percentage of the imported product's value) (Irwin 1998: 327). Because prices dropped substantially during the Great Depression, any specific import tariff would increase as a percentage of the price of the product. This part of the tariff increase after Smoot-Hayley would have taken place with or without Smoot-Hawley for specific tariffs (1998: 327).
7. The ITO's inability to get through the US Congress is due to those that thought it too protectionist and insufficiently protectionist. There were also fears in Congress that a supranational organization would infringe on US sovereignty (Toye 2012: 86, 97).
8. The elements that include him saving capitalism from its worst excesses include the establishment of the Bretton Woods institutions, which created both stability and access to capital, at least for a time, and Keynesianism, using government to counter-

cyclically simulate (or dampen) markets. Keynesianism has provided a rationale for governments to intervene in markets to stabilize them, but the so-called Great Recession was a sobering demonstration that policymakers are not particularly capable of taming "irrationality" out of markets.

9. In fact, the first ruling by the WTO's dispute resolution body was over this very issue. The US Clean Air Act included rules regarding fuel formulations, ostensibly for environmental reasons, and treated imported and domestically produced fuels differently. Venezuela and Brazil took the United States to the WTO dispute resolution mechanism and a WTO legal panel ruled that this was a violation of the non-discrimination principle and the US should change it (or face further legal challenges that could grant Venezuela and Brazil compensation). The US complied with the ruling (WTO 2010).

10. As with all things trade, there are exceptions: members may grant better than MFN treatment if they are in a bilateral or multilateral reciprocal free trade agreement or members may grant better than MFN treatment to least developed countries through preferential trade agreements (PTAs), also called unilateral preferential trade agreements. The primary program for this at the WTO is the General System of Preferences (GSP), with more recent versions tending to have catchier names such as the EU's Everything But Arms Initiative or the United States' Africa Growth and Opportunity Act. These programs let in specific products at reduced or tariff-free levels for poorer WTO countries that meet a given program's criteria, but not for other WTO members. They are less helpful to poor WTO members than they sound. For instance, the EU's Everything But Arms Initiative would be more accurately named Everything But Arms and Agriculture. The programs tend to include more primary products than finished goods so as to not compete with domestic production in the importing country. Should any category of imports grow uncomfortably large, the importing country can, of course, unilaterally alter the program including what countries are granted the preferences and how much.

11. There are other GATT principles that scholars have identified, but there is no one identifiable official list. Richard Baldwin's schema is useful. He identifies one general overarching principle—that trade should be rules-based not results-based—and five specific principles: nondiscrimination (at the border, it is manifested as MFN and behind the border as national treatment), transparency, reciprocity, flexibility (i.e., safety valves), and consensus decision-making.

12. The top four agricultural sales per capita states are, in descending order, Nebraska, South Dakota, North Dakota, and Iowa. The four most populous states are California, Texas, Florida, and New York. Population is from US Census Bureau estimates for 2016 and the farm data is based on 2015 gross receipts. National population figures used for calculations include only those populations with representation in the US Senate (i.e., Washington DC and Puerto Rico were excluded from the data).

13. As it turned out, this was of little help to countries that were so poor so as not to have the capability to produce needed medicines, emergency or not. Thus, developing nations and activists began to push for another weakening in IPR provisions to allow off-patent production in a country other than the one facing the emergency and then export those medicines to the country with the medical emergency without

punishment for violating the WTO's IPR provisions. At one point the entire WTO membership except the US had agreed to the change. After much pressure, the US conceded. It had been worried that the medicine could easily be diverted to third countries where there was not an emergency and purchases there would undermine royalty-based sales. With what the US considered to be adequate institutional checks on third-party sales, the US agreed to the IPR exceptions. Critics charge that the institutional checks—including onerous paperwork to get the rules waiver and the requirement that a government control the importation—make the provisions far less useful.

Chapter 3

1. The cyclone flooded the rice fields with salt water from the Bay of Bengal, ruining the crop. It was also responsible for the deaths of nearly 15,000 in Bengal alone. See, for example, Sen (1977).
2. Saro-Wiwa's assassination by the legal apparatus of the Nigerian states speaks to the ways in which environmentalists have emerged as targets for their work. Currently, South America has had one of the highest, if not the highest, number of environmental activists killed (see Fonseca Q 2016). While Latin America was not ostensibly an imperial space in the twentieth century, its relationship to networks of global capital and political power reflect similar positions in more recently decolonized spaces in Asia and Africa
3. See also the history of the Cahora-Bassa Dam in Mozambique. Like the Egyptian example, Cahora-Bassa was initially a Portuguese colonial-era project of environmental "improvement" that not only displaced native peoples but also provided electricity to apartheid South Africa. It was later celebrated by FRELIMO as necessary for the development of postcolonial Mozambique. See Isaacman and Isaacman (2013).
4. Kenya's southern neighbor, Tanzania, saw state interventionism in the natural world as a critical component of advancing Julius Nyerere's "African Socialism" agenda. See, for example, Schneider (2014).

Chapter 5

1. Antigua became independent in 1981.
2. Notably, the United Kingdom and the Republic of Ireland always opted out of the agreement, choosing to control their own borders, well before England's 2016 Brexit vote to leave the European Union.
3. Scholarship shows that colonial migrants did not come to the Netherlands *en masse* from the Dutch East Indies until after the Second World War, although Gloria Wekker (2016) has argued that circulation of racialized discourse about Dutch colonial subjects before their arrival in the Netherlands has fundamentally shaped understandings of contemporary Dutch identity.
4. One estimate suggests there were no more than 8,000 "Asians" (typically meaning south Asians in this context) living and working in England in the early 1930s, within a population of 44 million (see Visram 2002: 254).

5. While there were Jewish settlements in Palestine prior to 1897, Herzl articulated Zionism as a political movement that continues into the present day.
6. The *pieds-noirs* had origins in various areas of Europe, including France, Spain, Germany, Italy, Malta, and Jewish persons from various regions who had settled in Algeria to take advantage of the 1870 Crémieux Decree that granted Jews in Algeria the rights of French citizenship. Naturalization laws passed in 1889 and 1893 similarly gave French citizenship to all Europeans of Algeria and their descendants.
7. For more on #NODAPL and the situation at Standing Rock, see Chrisler *et al.* (2016).

Chapter 6

1. The Dutch in Indonesia also tried to repress child marriage (Locher-Scholten 2000).
2. Even after she rejected surgical interventions for European women, Bonaparte remained interested in the effects of clitoridectomy on African women's sexuality. In her 1953 study of female sexuality, Bonaparte argued that clitoridectomy had the goal not of reducing women's sexual pleasure, but rather of shifting it toward the mature vaginal orgasm. Thus, she believed, African women were "more frequently, and better, 'vaginalized' than their European sisters" (quoted in Frederiksen 2008: 40).
3. Critics of her approach suggest that she relies too heavily on linguistic data (arguing, for instance, that the absence of gendered pronouns in the Yoruba language indicates an absence of gender in the culture more broadly) and for overgeneralizing about western scholarship on gender (see, for example, Geiger 1999; Manicom 2001; Bakare-Yusuf 2004).
4. At home in the Antilles, nationalist men argued that the victimization of female migrants in France represented the continuation of colonial conditions. However, Germain contends, this portrayal of migrant women as victims of French racism "failed to acknowledge how gender relations within the Antillean community victimized women" (2010: 493).
5. Taubira was also a prominent supporter of same-sex marriage in France, and made headlines in 2016 when she resigned as minister of justice in protest of President François Hollande's proposal to revoke French citizenship from convicted terrorists with dual nationality.
6. As Jordanna Bailkin has noted, experts in the postwar period argued "that a relatively benign trickle of migrants of color was being replaced by a 'flood' that threatened Britain's historic tolerance, that these migrations were qualitatively and quantitatively unprecedented, and that their impact on British identity was more important than that of any other movement of peoples in the 1950s and 1960s" (2012: 23).
7. Todd Shepard has argued that the figure of the "gay Arab" played a central role in both far-right and gay liberationist discourses in France in the 1960s and 1970s. Orientalist discourses reemerged in the arguments of French sexual liberation, while what Shepard terms "sex-talk" "created a site where many French people could and did speak about race, empire and Algeria (Shepard 2012: 83; see also Shepard 2008).
8. This parallel in conservative and progressive rhetoric has also been observed by the authors of this study of GLBT issues in Cameroon, Senegal, South Africa, and Uganda (Awondo *et al.* 2012).

9. Marc Epprecht has argued forcefully against such interpretation, claiming that it is homophobia, not homosexuality, that is the western import (Epprecht 2008).
10. See the African Queer & Social Justice Organisations and Activists Statement on the threats by UK government sanctions, originally posted October 15, 2011, reposted on several blogs including blacklooks.org, October 28, 2011, http://www.blacklooks.org/2011/10/statement-of-african-social-justice-activists-on-the-decision-of-the-british-government-to-%E2%80%9Ccut-aid%E2%80%9D-to-african-countries-that-violate-the-rights-of-lgbti-people-in-africa/.
11. She accused black American, Caribbean, and British lesbians of using "prejudiced interpretations of African situations to justify their choices of sexual alternatives which have roots and meaning in the West" (Amadiume 1987: 7).

Chapter 8

1. The Portuguese *Casa Grande e Senzala* was published in 1933.
2. For a very different, highly sympathetic take on Dalit and African American racial politics, see Pandey (2013).

FURTHER READING

Abernethy, David B. (2000), *The Dynamics of Global Dominance: European Overseas Empires, 1415–1980*, New Haven, CT: Yale University Press.
Adamson, Joni, Mei Mei Evans, and Rachel Stein, eds (2002), *The Environmental Justice Reader: Politics, Poetics, & Pedagogy*, Tucson, AZ: University of Arizona Press.
Adas, Michael (1989), *Machines as the Measure of Man: Science, Technology, and Ideologies of Western Dominance*, Ithaca, NY: Cornell University Press.
Adas, Michael (1990), *Machines as the Measure of Man: Science, Technology, and Ideologies of Western Dominance*, Ithaca, NY: Cornell University Press.
Adas, Michael (2004), "Contested Hegemony: The Great War and the Afro-Asian Assault on the Civilizing Mission," in *Decolonization: Perspectives from Now and Then*, ed. Prasenjit Duara, 78–100, New York: Routledge.
Adas, Michael (2006), *Dominance by Design: Technological Imperatives and America's Civilizing Mission*, Cambridge, MA: Harvard University Press.
Adas, Michael (2009), *Dominance by Design: Technological Imperatives and America's Civilizing Mission*, Cambridge, MA: Harvard University Press.
Aderinto, Saheed (2015), "Journey to Work: Transnational Prostitution in Colonial British West Africa," *Journal of the History of Sexuality*, 24 (1): 99–124.
Adhikari, Mohamed (2010), *The Anatomy of a South African Genocide: The Extermination of the Cape San Peoples*, Cape Town: University of Cape Town Press.
Afary, Janet (2009), *Sexual Politics in Modern Iran*, Cambridge: Cambridge University Press.
Afshari, Reza M. (2007), "On Historiography of Human Rights," *Human Rights Quarterly*, 29 (1): 1–67.
Agrawal, Arun (2005), *Environmentality: Technologies of Government and the Making of Subjects*, Durham, NC: Duke University Press.
Ahram, Ariel I. (2017), "Republic of Iraq," in *The Government and Politics of the Middle East and North Africa*, 8th edn, eds Mark Gasiorowski and Sean Yom, 235–70, Boulder, CO: Westview Press.
Aizura, Aren Z. (2010), "Feminine Transformations: Gender Reassignment Surgical Tourism in Thailand," *Medical Anthropology*, 29 (4): 424–43.

Aldrich, Robert (2002), "Homosexuality in the French Colonies," *Journal of Homosexuality*, 41 (3/4): 201–18.
Aldrich, Robert (2007), *The Age of Empires*, New York: Thames & Hudson.
Alessio, Dominic and Wesley Renfro (2016), "The Voldemort of Imperial History: Rethinking Empire & U.S. History," *International Studies Perspectives*, 17: 250–66.
Allman, Jean (1996), "Rounding up Spinsters: Gender Chaos and Unmarried Women in Colonial Asante," *Journal of African History*, 37 (2): 195–214.
Amadiume, Ifi (1987), *Male Daughters, Female Husbands: Gender and Sex in an African Society*, London: Zed Books.
Aminzade, Ron (2013), *Race, Nation, and Citizenship in Post-Colonial Africa: The Case of Tanzania*, New York: Cambridge University Press.
Amster, Ellen (2016), "The Syphilitic Arab," in *French Mediterraneans: Transnational and Imperial Histories*, eds Patricia Lorcin and Todd Shephard, 320–46, Lincoln, NB: University of Nebraska Press.
Anderson, David (2005), *Histories of the Hanged: The Dirty War in Kenya and the End of Empire*, New York: W.W. Norton.
Anderson, David M. (2011), "Mau Mau in the High Court and the 'Lost' British Empire Archives: Colonial Conspiracy or Bureaucratic Bungle?," *Journal of Imperial and Commonwealth History*, 39 (5): 699–716.
Andrew, Christopher M. and A.S. Kanya Forstner (1981), *France Overseas: The Great War and the Climax of French Imperial Expansion*, London: Thames & Hudson.
Appadurai, Arjun (1988), "Putting Hierarchy in its Place," *Cultural Anthropology*, 3 (1): 36–49.
Arendt, Hanna (1968), *Imperialism: Part Two of* The Origins of Totalitarianism, New York: Harcourt.
Arnold, David (2000), *Science, Technology and Medicine in Colonial India*, Cambridge: Cambridge University Press.
Asad, Talal, ed. (1973), *Anthropology and the Colonial Encounter*, Ithaca, NY: Ithaca Press.
Asian-African Conference (1955), "Final Communique," in *Asia-Africa Speak from Bandung*, ed. Ministry of Affairs, Republic of Indonesia, 161–9, Djakarta: Ministry of Foreign Affairs.
Augustine of Hippo ([1631] 1912), *St. Augustine's Confessions*, trans. William Watts (1631), eds T.E. Page and W.H.D. Rouse (1912), New York: Macmillan.
Austin, Gareth (2005), *Labour, Land, and Capital in Ghana: From Slavery to Free Labour in Asante, 1807–1956*, Rochester, NY: University of Rochester Press.
Awondo, Patrick, Peter Geschiere, and Graeme Reid (2012), "Homophobic Africa? Toward a More Nuanced View," *African Studies Review*, 55 (3): 145–68.
Bahba, Homi K. (1994), "Of Mimicry and Man: The Ambivalence of Colonial Discourse," in *The Location of Culture*, 85–90, London: Routledge.
Bailkin, Jordanna (2012), *The Afterlife of Empire*, Berkeley, CA: University of California Press.
Bakare-Yusuf, Bibi (2004), "'Yorubas Don't Do Gender': A Critical Review of Oyeronke Oyewumi's *The Invention of Women: Making an African Sense of Western Gender Discourses*," in *African Gender Scholarship: Concepts, Methodologies, and Paradigms*, eds Signe Arnfred, Bibi Bakare-Yusuf, Edward Waswa Kisiang'ani, Desiree Lewis, Oyeronke Oyewumi, and Filomina Chioma Steady, 61–81, Dakar, Senegal: CODESRIA.
Baldwin, Richard (2016a), *The Great Convergence*, Cambridge, MA: Belknap Press of Harvard University Press.

Baldwin, Richard (2016b), "The World Trade Organization and the Future of Multilateralism," *Journal of Economic Perspectives*, 30 (1): 95–116.
Baldwin, Richard (2016c), *The Great Convergence: Information Technology and the New Globalization*, Recorded Presentation, November 15, Peterson Institute for International Economics, https://piie.com/events/great-convergence-information-technology-and-new-globalization, accessed December 30, 2016.
Balfour, Sebastian (2002), *Deadly Embrace: Morocco and the Road to the Spanish Civil War*, Oxford: Oxford University Press.
Balibar, Etienne (1991), "Racism and Nationalism," in *Race, Nation, Class: Ambiguous Identities*, eds Etienne Balibar and Immanuel Wallerstein, 37–67, New York: Verso.
Balibar, Etienne (2004), *We, The People of Europe? Reflections on Transnational Citizenship*, trans. James Swenson, Princeton, NJ: Princeton University Press.
Ballantyne, Tony (2002), *Orientalism and Race: Aryanism in the British Empire*, New York: Palgrave.
Ballantyne, Tony and Antoinette M. Burton, eds (2009), *Moving Subjects: Gender, Mobility, and Intimacy in an Age of Global Empire*, Urbana, IL: University of Illinois Press.
Banivanua Mar, Tracey (2016), *Decolonisation and the Pacific: Indigenous Globalisation and the Ends of Empire*, Cambridge: Cambridge University Press.
Bank for International Settlements (2016), *Triennial Central Bank Survey Foreign Exchange Turnover in April 2016*, http://www.bis.org/publ/rpfx16fx.pdf, accessed December 29, 2016.
Banton, Michael (1987), *Racial Theories*, Cambridge: Cambridge University Press.
Baptiste, Nathalie and Foreign Policy in Focus (2014), "It's Not Just Uganda: Behind the Christian Right's Onslaught in Africa," *The Nation*, April 4, https://www.thenation.com/article/its-not-just-uganda-behind-christian-rights-onslaught-africa/.
Baratieri, Daniela (2014), "'More than a Tree, Less than a Woman.' Sex and Empire: The Italian Case," *Australian Journal of Politics and History*, 60 (3): 360–72.
Barber, Noel (2007), *War of the Running Dogs: Malaya, 1948–1960*, London: Cassell.
Barton, Benedict (1994), "Rituals of Representation: Ethnic Stereotypes and Colonised Peoples at World's Fairs," in *Fair Representations: World's Fairs and the Modern World*, eds Robert W. Rydell and Nancy Gwinn, 28–61, Amsterdam: VU University Press.
Basalla, George (1989), *The Evolution of Technology*, Cambridge: Cambridge University Press.
Basu, Subho (2004), *Does Class Matter? Colonial Capital and Workers' Resistance in Bengal (1890–1937)*, Oxford: Oxford University Press.
Baumgart, Winfried (1982), *The Idea and Reality of British and French Colonial Expansion, 1880–1914*, trans. Winfried Baumgart and B. Mast, Oxford: Oxford University Press.
Beckert, Sven (2015), *Empire of Cotton: A Global History*, London: Penguin Books.
Béliard, Yann (2016), "A 'Labour War' in South Africa: The 1922 Rand Revolution in Sylvia Pankhurst's Workers' Dreadnought," *Labor History*, 57 (February): 20–34.
Bell, Roger J. (1984), *Last Among Equals: Hawaiian Statehood and American Politics*, Honolulu, HI: University of Hawai'i Press.
Bender, Daniel Eric (2016), *The Animal Game: Searching for Wildness at the American Zoo*, Cambridge, MA: Harvard University Press.
Bender, Daniel E. and Richard A. Greenwald, eds (2003), *Sweatshop USA: The American Sweatshop in Historical and Global Perspective*, New York: Routledge.

Benewick, Robert and Philip Green, eds (1992), *The Routledge Dictionary of Twentieth-Century Political Thinkers*, New York: Routledge.
Ben-Ghiat, Ruth and Mia Fuller (2005), *Italian Colonialism*, New York: Palgrave Macmillan.
Berman, Bruce (1996), "Ethnography as Politics, Politics as Ethnography: Kenyatta, Malinowski, and the Making of Facing Mount Kenya," *Canadian Journal of African Studies/Revue Canadienne Des Études Africaines*, 30 (3): 313–44.
Bhagwati, Jagdish N. (2005), "A New Vocabulary for Trade," *Wall Street Journal*, August 4, www.wsj.com/articles/SB112311935638704645, accessed December 28, 2016.
Biddle, Tammi Davis and Robert M. Citino (2014), "The Role of Military History in the Contemporary Academy," *A Society for Military History White Paper*, 1–7, http://www.smh-hq.org/whitepaper.html.
Birmingham, David (1995), *The Decolonization of Africa*, Athens, OH: Ohio University Press.
Blake, Jody (1999), *Le Tumulte Noir: Modernist Art and Popular Entertainment in Jazz-Age Paris, 1900–1930*, University Park, PA: Pennsylvania State University Press.
Blake, Susan L. (2003), "What 'Race' is the Sheik? Rereading a Desert Romance," in *Doubled Plots: Romance and History*, eds Susan Strehle and Mary Paniccia Carden, 67–85, Jackson, MS: University Press of Mississippi.
Bland, Lucy (2005), "White Women and Men of Colour: Miscegenation Fears in Britain after the Great War," *Gender and History*, 17 (1): 29–61.
Bley, Helmuth (1971), *South-West Africa Under German Rule, 1894–1914*, Evanston, IL: Northwestern University Press.
Bloom, Joshua and Waldo E. Martin, Jr. (2012), *Black Against Empire: The History and Politics of the Black Panther Party*, Berkeley, CA: University of California Press.
Boittin, Jennifer Anne (2010), *Colonial Metropolis: The Urban Grounds of Anti-Imperialism and Feminism in Interwar Paris*, Lincoln, NB: University of Nebraska Press.
Bonilla-Silva, Eduardo (1996), "Rethinking Racism: Toward a Structural Interpretation," *American Sociological Review*, 62: 465–80.
Bonilla-Silva, Eduardo (2014), *Racism without Racists: Color-Blind Racism and the Persistence of Racial Inequality in America*, 4th edn, New York: Rowman & Littlefield.
Booth, Anne (2012), "Measuring Living Standards in Different Colonial Systems: Some Evidence from South East Asia, 1900–1942," *Modern Asian Studies*, 46 (5): 1145–81.
Booth, Anne and Kent Deng (2016), "Japanese Colonialism in Comparative Perspective," London School of Economics and Political Science, *Economic History Working Papers #254*, http://eprints.lse.ac.uk/68883/?from_serp=1.
Borgwardt, Elizabeth (2005), *A New Deal for the World*, Cambridge, MA: Harvard University Press.
Boulle, Pierre H. (2003), "François Bernier and the Origins of the Modern Concept of Race," in *The Color of Liberty: Histories of Race in France*, eds Sue Peabody and Tyler Stovall, 11–27, Durham, NC: Duke University Press.
Bourdieu, Pierre (1994), "Identity and Representation: Elements for a Critical Reflection on the Idea of Region," in *Language and Symbolic Power*, trans. Gino Raymond and Matthew Adamson, Cambridge, MA: Harvard University Press.
Bourdieu, Pierre and Loïc Wacquant (1999), "On the Cunning of Imperialist Reason," *Theory, Culture, Society*, 16 (1): 41–58.

Braithwaite, Rodric (2011), *Afgantsy: The Russians in Afghanistan, 1979–89*, New York: Oxford University Press.
Brennan, James (2012), *Taifa: Making Nation and Race in Urban Tanzania*, Athens, OH: Ohio University Press.
Breuilly, John, ed. (2013), *The Oxford Handbook of the History of Nationalism*, Oxford: Oxford University Press.
Bricmont, Jean (2006), *Humanitarian Imperialism: Using Human Rights to Sell War*, New York: Monthly Review Press.
Briggs, Laura (2002), *Reproducing Empire: Race, Sex, Science, and U.S. Imperialism in Puerto Rico*, Berkeley, CA: University of California Press.
British National Archives (n.d.), "Jungles Today are Gold Mines Tomorrow," http://www.nationalarchives.gov.uk/education/empire/g2/cs1/g2cs1s4.htm, accessed February 6, 2017.
Britton, Sarah (2010), "'Come and See the Empire by the All Red Route!': Anti-Imperialism and Exhibitions in Interwar Britain," *History Workshop Journal*, 69 (1): 68–89.
Brower, Benjamin ([2009] 2011), *A Desert Named Peace: The Violence of France's Empire in the Algerian Sahara, 1844–1902*, New York: Columbia University Press.
Brown, Carolyn (2015), "African Labor in the Making of World War II," in *Africa and World War II*, eds Judith Byfield, Carolyn A. Brown, Timothy Parsons, and Admad Alawad Sikainga, 43–70, New York: Cambridge University Press.
Brubaker, Rogers (1998), *Citizenship and Nationhood in France and Germany*, Cambridge, MA: Harvard University Press.
Buergin, Rainer, Jeff Black and Josh Wingrove (2017), "G–20 Drops Anti-Protectionist Pledge as Price of U.S. Assent," *Bloomberg*, March 18, https://www.bloomberg.com/news/articles/2017–03–18/g-20-drops-anti-protectionist-pledge-as-trump-stance-goes-global, accessed March 28, 2017.
Burbank, Jane and Frederick Cooper (2010), *Empires in World History: Power and the Politics of Difference*. Princeton, NJ: Princeton University Press.
Burke, Roland (2006), "'The Compelling Dialogue of Freedom': Human Rights at the 1955 Bandung Conference," *Human Rights Quarterly*, 28 (4): 947–65.
Burke, Roland (2010), *Decolonization and the Evolution of International Human Rights*, Philadelphia, PA: University of Pennsylvania Press.
Burton, Antoinette M., ed. (1999), *Gender, Sexuality and Colonial Modernities*, London: Routledge.
Burton, Antoinette (2015), *The Trouble with Empire: Challenges to Modern British Imperialism*, Oxford: Oxford University Press.
Burton, A., A. Espiritu and F.C. Wilkins (2006), "The Fate of Nationalisms in the Age of Bandung," *Radical History Review*, 95: 145–8.
Bush, Barbara (1999), *Imperialism, Race and Resistance: Africa and Britain, 1919–1945*, New York: Routledge.
Butalia, Urvashi (1993), "Community, State and Gender: On Women's Agency during Partition," *Economic and Political Weekly*, 28 (17): 12–24.
Butalia, Urvashi (1998), *The Other Side of Silence: Voices from the Partition of India*, New Delhi: Penguin India.
Butler, Larry and Sarah Stockwell, eds (2013), *The Wind of Change: Harold Macmillan and British Decolonization*, London: Palgrave Macmillan.
Byrne, Jeffrey James (2016), *Mecca of Revolution: Algeria, Decolonization, and the Third World Order*, Oxford: Oxford University Press.

Cairns Group (n.d.), "Background on the Cairns Group and the WTO Doha Round," http://cairnsgroup.org/Pages/wto_negotiations.aspx, accessed January 22, 2017.

Callwell, Charles E. ([1896] 1906), *Small Wars: Their Principles and Practice*, 3rd edn, London: General Staff, War Office.

Camiscioli, Elisa (2009), *Reproducing the French Race: Immigration, Intimacy, and Embodiment in the Early Twentieth Century*, Durham, NC: Duke University Press.

Campbell, Chloe (2007), *Race and Empire: Eugenics in Colonial Kenya*, Manchester: Manchester University Press.

Carbaugh, Robert J. (2015), *International Economics*, Boston, MA: Cengage.

Carey, Jane and Jane Lydon, eds (2014), *Indigenous Networks: Mobility, Connections and Exchange*, London: Routledge.

Castells, Manuel (2009), *Communication Power*, Oxford: Oxford University Press.

Césaire, Aimé ([1950] 2000), *Discourse on Colonialism*, trans. J. Pinkham, New York: Monthly Review Press.

Chakrabarty, Dipesh (1989), *Rethinking Working-Class History: Bengal, 1890–1940*, Princeton, NJ: Princeton University Press.

Chakrabarty, Dipesh (2010), "The Legacies of Bandung: Decolonization and the Politics of Culture," in *Making a World After Empire: The Bandung Moment and its Political Afterlives*, ed. Christopher Lee, 45–68, Athens, OH: Ohio University Press.

Chandavarkar, Rajnarayan (1994), *The Origins of Industrial Capitalism in India: Business Strategies and the Working Classes in Bombay, 1900–1940*, Cambridge: Cambridge University Press.

Chang, Ha-Joon (2008), *Bad Samaritans; The Myth of Free Trade and the Secret History of Capitalism*, New York: Bloomsbury Press.

Chanock, Martin (1982), "Making Customary Law: Men, Women, and Courts in Colonial Northern Rhodesia," in *African Women and the Law: Historical Perspectives*, eds Margaret Jean Hay and Marcia Wright, 53–67, Boston, MA: Boston University, African Studies Center.

Charby, Jacques (2004), *Les Porteurs d'espoir: Les Réseaux de Soutien au FLN Pendant la Guerre d'Algérie*, Les Acteurs Parlent, Paris: Découverte.

Chase, Paul Wilder (1992), "The Politics of Morality in Weimar Germany: Public Controversy and Parliamentary Debate over Changes in Moral Behavior in the Twenties," PhD dissertation, State University of New York at Stony Brook.

Chatterjee, Partha (1989), "Colonialism, Nationalism and Colonized Women: The Contest in India," *American Ethnologist*, 16 (4): 662–83.

Chaudhuri, Nupur and Margaret Strobel, eds (1992), *Western Women and Imperialism: Complicity and Resistance*, Bloomington, IN: Indiana University Press.

Chi-Minh, Ho (1970), "The Path that Led Me to Leninism" (April 1960), in *Selected Articles and Speeches, 1920–1967*, ed. Jack Woddis, 156–8, New York: International Publishers.

Chomsky, Aviva (2008), *Linked Labor Histories: New England, Colombia, and the Making of a Global Working-Class*, Durham, NC: Duke University Press.

Chow, Karen (1999), "Popular Sexual Knowledges and Women's Agency in 1920s England: Marie Stopes's 'Married Love' and E. M. Hull's 'The Sheik,'" *Feminist Review*, 63 (1): 64–87.

Choy, Catherine Ceniza (2003), *Empire of Care: Nursing and Migration in Filipino American History*, Durham, NC: Duke University Press.

Chrisler, Matt, Jaskiran Dhillon, and Audrey Simpson (2016), "The Standing Rock Syllabus Project," October 21, http://www.publicseminar.org/2016/10/nodapl-syllabus-project/.

Chua, Amy (2007), *Day of Empire: How Hyperpowers Rise to Global Dominance—and Why They Fall*, New York, Doubleday.
Citino, Robert M. (2007), "Military Histories Old and New: A Reintroduction," *American Historical Review*, 112 (4): 1070–90.
Clancy-Smith, Julia and Frances Gouda (1998), *Domesticating the Empire: Race, Gender, and Family Life in French and Dutch Colonialism*, Charlottesville, VA: University Press of Virginia.
Clark, Hannah-Louise (2013), "Civilization and Syphilization: A Doctor and His Disease in Colonial Morocco," *Bulletin of the History of Medicine*, 87 (1): 86–114.
Clark, Nancy L. and William H. Worger (2004), *South Africa: The Rise and Fall of Apartheid*, London: Routledge.
Clavin, Patricia (2005), "Defining Transnationalism," *Contemporary European History*, 14 (4): 421–39.
Clavin, Patricia (2011), "Introduction: Conceptualising Internationalism Between the World Wars," in *Internationalism Reconfigured: Transnational Ideas and Movements Between the World Wars*, ed. D. Laqua, 1–14, London: Palgrave.
Clayton, Anthony (1992), "The Sétif Uprising of May 1945," *Small Wars and Insurgencies*, 3 (1): 1–21.
Clayton, Anthony (1994), *The Wars of French Decolonization*, London: Routledge.
Coates, Ken S. (2004), *A Global History of Indigenous Peoples: Struggle and Survival*, New York: Palgrave Macmillan.
Cohen-Hattab, Kobi and Yossi Katz (2001), "The Attraction of Palestine: Tourism in the Years 1850–1948," *Journal of Historical Geography*, 27 (2): 166–177.
Cohn, Bernard S. (1987), *An Anthropologist among the Historians and Other Essays*, Delhi: Oxford University Press.
Colby, Jason M. (2011), *The Business of Empire: United Fruit, Race and U.S. Expansion in Central America*, Ithaca, NY: Cornell University Press.
Coleman, Kevin (2016), *A Camera in the Garden of Eden: The Self-Forging of a Banana Republic*, Austin, TX: University of Texas Press.
Collett, Nigel (2006), *The Butcher of Amritsar: General Reginald Dyer*, London: Bloomsbury.
Comaroff, John and Jean Comaroff (1991), *Of Revelation and Revolution, Vol. 1: Christianity, Colonialism, and Consciousness in South Africa*, Chicago, IL: University of Chicago Press.
Comaroff, John and Jean Comaroff (1997), *Of Revelation and Revolution, Vol. 2: The Dialectics of Modernity on a South African Frontier*, Chicago, IL: University of Chicago Press.
Conklin, Alice L. (1997), *A Mission to Civilize: The Republican Idea of Empire in France and West Africa, 1895–1930*, Stanford, CA: Stanford University Press.
Conklin, Alice (2013), *In the Museum of Man: Race, Anthropology, and Empire in France, 1850–1950*, Ithaca, NY: Cornell University Press.
Connelly, Matthew (2002), *A Diplomatic Revolution: Algeria's Fight for Independence and the Origins of the Post-Cold War Era*, Oxford: Oxford University Press.
Cooper, Frederick (1987), *On the African Waterfront: Urban Disorder and the Transformation of Work in Colonial Mombasa*, New Haven, CT: Yale University Press.
Cooper, Frederick (1996a), "'Our Strike': Equality, Anticolonial Politics and the 1947–48 Railway Strike in French West Africa," *Journal of African History*, 37 (1): 81–118.

Cooper, Frederick (1996b), *Decolonization and African Society: The Labor Question in French and British Africa*, New York: Cambridge University Press.
Cooper, Frederick (2002), *Africa Since 1940: The Past of the Present*, Berkeley, CA: University of California Press.
Cooper, Frederick (2008), "Possibility and Constraint: African Independence in Historical Perspective," *Journal of African History*, 49: 167–96.
Cooper, Frederick (2014), *Citizenship between Empire and Nation: Remaking France and French Africa*, Princeton, NJ: Princeton University Press.
Cooper, Frederick, Thomas C. Holt, and Rebecca J. Scott (2000), *Beyond Slavery: Explorations of Race, Labor, and Citizenship in Postemancipation Societies*, Chapel Hill, NC: University of North Carolina Press.
Cooper, Nicola J. (2009), "Gendering the Colonial Enterprise," in *Empires and Boundaries: Race, Class, and Gender in Colonial Settings*, eds Harald Fischer-Tiné and Susanne Gehrmann, 129–45, New York: Routledge.
Cronon, William, ed. (1995), *Uncommon Ground: Rethinking the Human Place in Nature*, New York: W.W. Norton.
Crosby, A. (1986), *Ecological Imperialism: The Biological Expansion of Europe*, Cambridge: Cambridge University Press.
Crystal, Jill (2017), "Eastern Arabian States: Kuwait, Bahrain, Qatar, United Arab Emirates, and Oman," in *The Government and Politics of the Middle East and North Africa*, 8th edn, eds Mark Gasiorowski and Sean L. Yom, 337–376, Boulder, CO: Westview Press.
Curless, Gareth (2016), "Introduction: Trade Unions in the Global South from Imperialism to the Present Day," *Labor History*, 57 (1): 1–19.
Curtin, Philip D. (1964), *The Image of Africa: British Ideas and Action, 1780–1850*, Madison, WI: University of Wisconsin Press.
Curtin, Philip (1992), "Medical Knowledge and Urban Planning in Colonial Tropical Africa," in *The Social Basis of Health and Healing in Africa*, eds Steven Feierman and John M. Janzen, 235–255, Berkeley, CA: University of California Press.
Dahm, Bernhard (1969), *Sukarno and the Struggle for Indonesian Independence*, Ithaca, NY: Cornell University Press.
Davey, Eleanor (2015), *Idealism Beyond Borders: The French Revolutionary Left and the Rise of Humanitarianism, 1954–1988*, Cambridge: Cambridge University Press.
Davin, Anna (1978), "Imperialism and Motherhood," *History Workshop*, 5: 9–65.
Davis, Diana K. (2007), *Resurrecting the Granary of Rome: Environmental History and French Colonial Expansion in North Africa*, Athens, OH: Ohio University Press.
De Costa, Ravi (2006a), *A Higher Authority: Indigenous Transnationalism and Australia*, Sydney, NSW: UNSW Press.
De Costa, Ravi (2006b), "Identity, Authority, and the Moral Worlds of Indigenous Petitions," *Comparative Studies in Society and History*, 48 (3): 669–98.
Degler, Carl (1971), *Neither Black nor White: Slavery and Race Relations in Brazil and the United States*, New York: Macmillan.
De Grazia, Victoria (2005), *Irresistible Empire: America's Advance through Twentieth-Century Europe*, Cambridge, MA: Harvard University Press.
Derrick, Jonathan (2008), *Africa's "Agitators": Militant Anti-Colonialism in Africa and the West, 1918–1939*, New York: Columbia University Press.
Dikötter, Frank (1992), *The Discourse of Race in Modern China*, Stanford, CA: Stanford University Press.
Dikötter, Frank (1997), "Racial Discourse in China: Continuities and Permutations," in *The Construction of Racial Identities in China and Japan: Historical and

Contemporary Perspectives, ed. Frank Dikötter, 12–33, Honolulu, HI: University of Hawai'i Press.

Dimier, Véronique (2009), "Recycling Empire. French Colonial Administration at the Heart of European Development Policy," in *The French Colonial Mind: Mental Maps of Empire and French Colonial Policy Making*, ed. Martin Thomas, 251–74, Lincoln, NB: University of Nebraska Press.

Dinius, Oliver J. and Angela Vergara, eds (2011), *Company Towns in the Americas: Landscape, Power, and Working-Class Communities*, Athens, GA: University of Georgia Press.

Dirks, Nicholas (2001), *Castes of Mind: Colonialism and the Making of Modern India*, Princeton, NJ: Princeton University Press.

Dower, John W. (1986), *War without Mercy: Race and Power in the Pacific War*, New York: Pantheon.

Drache, Daniel (2000), "The Short but Significant Life of the International Trade Organization: Lessons for Our Time," Warwick University's Centre for the Study of Globalisation and Regionalisation, *CSGR Working Paper #62/00*, November 2000, http://wrap.warwick.ac.uk/2063/, accessed December 26, 2016.

Draper, Alfred (1985), *The Amritsar Massacre: Twilight of the Raj*, London: Buchan & Enright.

Dubow, Saul (1995), *Scientific Racism in Modern South Africa*, Cambridge: Cambridge University Press.

Dubow, Saul (2014), *Apartheid 1948–1994*, Oxford: Oxford University Press.

Dueck, Jennifer M. (2010), *The Claims of Culture at Empire's End: Syria and Lebanon under French Rule*, Oxford: Oxford University Press.

Duke Bryant, Kelly (2015), *Education as Politics: Colonial Schooling and Political Debate in Senegal, 1850s–1914*, Madison, WI: University of Wisconsin Press.

Dutta, Aniruddha (2012), "An Epistemology of Collusion: Hijras, Kothis and the Historical (Dis)continuity of Gender/Sexual Identities in Eastern India," *Gender and History*, 24 (3): 825–49.

Eichenberg, Julia and John Paul Newman, eds (2010), "Aftershocks: Violence in Dissolving Empires after the First World War," *Contemporary European History*, 19 (3): 183–274.

Eichengreen, Barry (1986), "The Political Economy of the Smoot-Hawley Tariff," *NBER Working Paper #2001*, http://www.nber.org/papers/w2001.

Eichengreen, Barry (2015), *Hall of Mirrors, The Great Depression, the Great Recession and the Uses—and Misuses—of History*, New York: Oxford University Press.

Eldridge, Claire (2013), "Returning to the 'Return': *Pied-noir* Memories of 1962," *Revue Européene des Migrations Internationales*, 29 (3): 121–40.

El Hamel, Chouki (2013), *Black Morocco: A History of Slavery, Race, and Islam*, New York: Cambridge University Press.

Elkins, Caroline (2005a), *Britain's Gulag: The Brutal End of Empire in Kenya*, London: Jonathan Cape.

Elkins, Caroline (2005b), *Imperial Reckoning: The Untold Story of Britain's Gulag in Kenya*, New York: Henry Holt.

Ellena, Liliana (2004), "Political Imagination, Sexuality and Love in the Eurafrican Debate," *European Review of History*, 11 (2): 241–72.

Elliot-Lynn, Sophie C. (1927), "Private Flying in Africa," *Flight*, June 2: 354–5.

Elshakry, Marwa (2014), *Reading Darwin in Arabic, 1860–1950*, Chicago, IL: University of Chicago Press.

El Shakry, Omnia (2007), *The Great Social Laboratory: Subjects of Knowledge in Colonial and Postcolonial Egypt*, Stanford, CA: Stanford University Press.

El-Tayeb, Fatima (2011), *European Others: Queering Ethnicity in Postnational Europe*, Minneapolis, MN: University of Minnesota Press.

El-Tayeb, Fatima (2012), "'Gays Who Cannot Properly Be Gay': Queer Muslims in the Neoliberal European City," *European Journal of Women's Studies*, 19 (1): 79–95.

Emerson, Rupert (1962), *From Empire to Nation*, Boston, MA: Beacon Press.

Enloe, Cynthia H. (2014), *Bananas, Beaches and Bases: Making Feminist Sense of International Politics*, 2nd edn, Berkeley, CA: University of California Press.

Epprecht, Marc (2008), *Heterosexual Africa? The History of an Idea from the Age of Exploration to the Age of AIDS*, Athens, OH: Ohio University Press.

Estienne-Mondet, Arlette (2005), *Ligne de Hoggar*, Paris: PC Editions.

European Commission (2017), *Schengen Area*, https://ec.europa.eu/home-affairs/what-we-do/policies/borders-and-visas/schengen_en.

European Initiative on Global Markets (2016), "Trade in Europe," *European IGM Economic Experts Panel*, http://www.igmchicago.org/surveys/trade-within-europe, accessed December 30, 2016.

Evans, Martin (2008), "Opening up the Battlefield: War Studies and the Cultural Turn," *Journal of War and Culture Studies*, 1 (1): 47–51.

Fall, Bernard (1964), *The Two Viet-Nams: A Political and Military Analysis*, New York: Praeger.

Fanon, Frantz (1952), *Peau noire masques blancs*, Paris: Seuil.

Fanon, Frantz (1974), *Les damnés de la terre*, Paris: Maspero.

Fanon, Frantz ([1961] 2004), *The Wretched of the Earth*, New York: Grove Press.

Feith, Herbert and Lance Castles, eds (1970), *Indonesian Political Thinking, 1945–1965*, Ithaca, NY: Cornell University Press.

Ferguson, Niall (2003), *Empire: The Rise and Demise of the British World Order and the Lessons for Global Power*, New York: Basic Books.

Finch, Michael P.M. (2013), *A Progressive Occupation? The Gallieni-Lyautey Method and Colonial Pacification in Tonkin and Madagascar, 1885–1900*, Oxford: Oxford University Press.

Fleming, Melissa (2015), "Crossings of Mediterranean Sea Exceed 300,000, including 200,000 to Greece," http://www.unhcr.org/en-us/news/latest/2015/8/55e06a5b6/crossings-mediterranean-sea-exceed–300000-including–200000-greece.html, accessed September 17, 2017.

Flores, Alfred Peredo (2015), "No Walk in the Park: US Empire and the Racialization of Civilian Military Labor in Guam, 1944–1962," *American Quarterly*, 67 (3): 813–35.

Fogarty, Richard S. and Michael A. Osborne (2010), "Eugenics in France and the Colonies," in *The Oxford Handbook of the History of Eugenics*, eds Alison Bashford and Philippa Levine, 332–46, Oxford: Oxford University Press.

Fonseca Q, Pablo (2016), "Latin America is the World's Deadliest Region for Environmental Activists," *Scientific American*, June 24, https://www.scientificamerican.com/article/latin-america-is-the-world-s-deadliest-region-for-environmental-activists/.

Ford, Caroline (2008), "Reforestation, Landscape Conservation, and the Anxieties of Empire in French Colonial Algeria," *American Historical Review*, 113 (2): 341–62.

Foucault, Michel (1972), *The Archeology of Knowledge*, New York, Pantheon.

Foucault, Michel ([1977] 1979), *Discipline and Punish: The Birth of the Modern Prison*, trans. Alan Sheridan, New York: Vintage Books.
Frank, Dana (2005), *Bananeras: Women Transforming the Banana Unions of Latin America*, Cambridge: South End Press.
Frederiksen, Bodil Folke (2008), "Jomo Kenyatta, Marie Bonaparte and Bronislaw Malinowski on Clitoridectomy and Female Sexuality," *History Workshop Journal*, 65 (1): 23–48.
Freidberg, Susanne (2004), *French Beans and Food Scares: Culture and Commerce in an Anxious Age*, New York: Oxford University Press.
French, John D. (2000), "The Missteps of Anti-Imperialist Reason," *Theory, Culture and Society*, 17 (1): 107–28.
Freyre, Gilberto (1986), *The Masters and the Slaves: A Study in the Development of Brazilian Civilization*, trans. Samuel Putnam, Berkeley, CA: University of California Press.
Friedman, Thomas (2005), *The World is Flat: A Brief History of the Twenty-First Century*, New York: Farrar, Strauss & Giroux.
Fromkin, David (1989), *A Peace to End All Peace: The Fall of the Ottoman Empire and the Creation of the Modern Middle East*, New York: Henry Holt.
Fukuyama, Francis (1992), *The End of History and the Last Man*, Toronto: Maxwell Macmillan.
G20 (2017), "Communiqué," March 17, Baden Baden G20 Conference, http://www.g20.utoronto.ca/2017/170318-finance-en.html, accessed March 28, 2017.
Gaines, Kevin Kelly (2006), *American Africans in Ghana: Black Expatriates and the Civil Rights Era*, Chapel Hill, NC: University of North Carolina Press.
Galula, David (1964), *Counterinsurgency Warfare: Theory and Practice*, Westport, CT: Praeger.
Gasiorowski, Mark (2017), "Islamic Republic of Iran," in *The Government and Politics of the Middle East and North Africa*, 8th edn, eds Mark Gasiorowski and Sean Yom, 271–306, Boulder, CO: Westview Press.
Geiger, Susan (1999), "Women and Gender in African Studies," *African Studies Review*, 42 (3): 21–33.
Gengenbach, Heidi (2010), *Binding Memories: Women as Makers and Tellers of History in Magude, Mozambique*, ACLS Humanities E-Book electronic edition, New York: Columbia University Press.
George, Abosede A. (2014), *Making Modern Girls: A History of Girlhood, Labor, and Social Development in Colonial Lagos*, Athens, OH: Ohio University Press.
Germain, Felix (2010), "Jezebels and Victims: Antillean Women in Postwar France, 1946–1974," *French Historical Studies*, 33 (3): 475–95.
Gerwarth, Robert and Erez Manela (2014a), "The Great War as a Global War: Imperial Conflict and the Reconfiguration of World Order, 1911–1923," *Diplomatic History*, 38 (4): 786–800.
Gerwarth, Robert and Erez Manela, eds (2014b), *Empires at War, 1911–1923*, Oxford: Oxford University Press.
Gide, André (1927), *Voyage au Congo. carnet de route*, Paris: Gallimard.
Gilroy, Paul (1993), *The Black Atlantic*, Cambridge, MA: Harvard University Press.
Glassman, Jonathon (2011), *War of Words, War of Stones: Racial Thought and Violence in Colonial Zanzibar*, Bloomington, IN: Indiana University Press.
Go, Julian (2011), *Patterns of Empire; The British and American Empires, 1688 to Present*, Cambridge: Cambridge University Press.

Goebel, Michael (2015), *Anti-Imperial Metropolis*, Cambridge: Cambridge University Press.
Goebel, Michael (2016), "'The Capital of the Men without a Country': Migrants and Anticolonialism in Interwar Paris," *American Historical Review*, 121 (5): 1444–67.
Goldthree, Reena N. (2016), "'Vive La France!': British Caribbean Soldiers and Interracial Intimacies on the Western Front," *Journal of Colonialism and Colonial History*, 17 (3).
Gonzalez, Vernadette Vicuña (2015), "Making Aloha: Lei and the Cultural Labor of Hospitality," in *Making the Empire Work: Labor and United States Imperialism*, eds Daniel E. Bender and Jana K. Lipman, 161–84, New York: New York University Press.
Gorman, Daniel (2008), "Empire, Internationalism, and the Campaign against the Traffic in Women and Children in the 1920s," *Twentieth Century British History*, 19 (2): 186–216.
Goscha, Christopher (2016), *Vietnam: A New History*, New York: Basic Books.
Grandin, Greg (2009), *Fordlandia: The Rise and Fall of Henry Ford's Forgotten Jungle City*, New York: Metropolitan Books.
Greenblatt, Stephen (2010), *Cultural Mobility: A Manifesto*, Cambridge: Cambridge University Press.
Greene, Julie (2009), *The Canal Builders: Making America's Empire at the Panama Canal*, New York: Penguin.
Greenhalgh, Paul (1988), *Ephemeral Vistas: The Expositions Universelles, Great Exhibitions and World's Fairs, 1851–1939*, Manchester: Manchester University Press.
Gregory, Derek (2004), *The Colonial Present: Afghanistan, Palestine, Iraq*, Oxford: Blackwell.
Griffiths, Tom and Libby Robin (1997), *Ecology and Empire: Environmental History of Settler Societies*, Seattle, WA: University of Washington Press.
Grimal, Henri (1978), *Decolonization: The British, French, Dutch, and Belgian Empires, 1919–1963*, London: Routledge & Kegan Paul.
Guevara, Che (1998), *Guerilla Warfare*, Lincoln, NE: University of Nebraska Press.
Guly, Christopher (2016), "Canada Keeps Signing Free Trade Deals, and Few People Seem to Mind," *Los Angeles Times*, October 30, http://www.latimes.com/world/mexico-americas/la-fg-canada-trade-20161030-story.html, accessed December 31, 2016.
Gupta, Dipankar (2001), "Caste, Race, Politics," *Seminar #508*, http://www.india-seminar.com/2001/508/508%20dipankar%20gupta.htm.
Haas, Ernst B. (1967), "The Attempt to Terminate Colonialism: Acceptance of the United Nations Trusteeship System," in *The United Nations Political System*, ed. David A. Kay, 281–301, New York: Wiley.
Haberman, Clyde (2014), "Agent Orange's Long Legacy, for Vietnam and for Veterans," *New York Times*, May 11.
Hall, Bruce S. (2011), *A History of Race in Muslim West Africa, 1600–1960*, New York: Cambridge University Press.
Hall, Catherine (2002), *Civilising Subjects: Metropole and Colony in the English Imagination, 1830–1867*, Chicago, IL: University of Chicago Press.
Hall, Kim F. (1996), *Things of Darkness: Economies of Race and Gender in Early Modern England*, Ithaca, NY: Cornell University Press.

Hall, Rachel A. (2002), "When is a Wife not a Wife? Some Observations on the Immigration Experiences of South Asian Women in West Yorkshire," *Contemporary Politics*, 8 (1): 55–68.

Hall, Stuart (1980), "Race, Articulation and Societies Structures in Dominance," in *Sociological Theories: Race and Colonialism*, 305–45, Paris: UNESCO.

Hall, Stuart (1997), "The Local and the Global: Globalization and Ethnicity," in *Dangerous Liaisons: Gender, Nation, and Postcolonial Perspectives*, eds A. McClintock, A. Mufi, and E. Shohat, 173–87, Minneapolis, MN: University of Minnesota Press.

Hamon, Hervé and Patrick Rotman (1979), *Les Porteurs de Valises: La Résistance Française à la Guerre d'Algérie*, Paris: Albin Michel.

Hanchard, Michael (1994), *Orpheus and Power: The Movimento Negro of Rio de Janeiro and São Paulo, Brazil, 1945–1988*, Princeton, NJ: Princeton University Press.

Hannaford, Ivan (1996), *Race: The History of an Idea in the West*, Baltimore, MD: Johns Hopkins University Press.

Hardt, Michael and Antonio Negri (2000), *Empire*, Cambridge, MA: Harvard University Press.

Hardy, R. (2016), *The Poisoned Well: Empire and its Legacy in the Middle East*, Oxford: Oxford University Press.

Harper, Marjory and Stephen Constantine (2011), *Migration and Empire*, Oxford: Oxford University Press.

Harvey, David (2003), *The New Imperialism*, New York: Oxford University Press.

Hasegawa, Tsuyoshi (2006), *Racing the Enemy: Stalin, Truman, and the Surrender of Japan*, Cambridge, MA: Belknap Press.

Hatta, Mohammad (1960), *Past and Future*, Ithaca, NY: Modern Indonesia Project, Cornell University.

Heffernan, Michael J. (1991), "The Desert in French Orientalist Painting during the Nineteenth Century," *Landscape Research*, 16 (2): 37–42.

Helleiner, Eric (2014), *Forgotten Foundations of Bretton Woods, International Development and the Making of the Postwar Order*, Ithaca, NY: Cornell University Press.

Henderson, Ian (1974), "The Limits of Colonial Power: Race and Labour Problems in Colonial Zambia, 1900–1953," *Journal of Imperial and Commonwealth History*, 2: 294–307.

Henderson, Timothy J. (2011), "Bracero Blacklists: Mexican Migration and the Unraveling of the Good Neighbor Policy," *The Latin Americanist*, 55 (4): 199–217.

Hitchcock, William I. (2009), *Liberation: The Bitter Road to Freedom, Europe 1944–45*, New York: Faber & Faber.

Hoad, Neville (2000), "Arrested Development or the Queerness of Savages: Resisting Evolutionary Narratives of Difference," *Postcolonial Studies: Culture, Politics, Economy*, 3 (2): 133–58.

Hoad, Neville (2007), *African Intimacies: Race, Homosexuality, and Globalization*, Minneapolis, MN: University of Minnesota Press.

Hobsbawm, Eric and Terence O. Ranger, eds (1992), *The Invention of Tradition*, Cambridge: Cambridge University Press.

Hochschild, Adam (1998), *King Leopold's Ghost: A Story of Greed, Terror, and Heroism in Colonial Africa*, New York: Houghton Mifflin.

Hodann, Max ([1932] 1975), *Sex Life in Europe: A Biological and Sociological Survey*, trans. J. Gibbs, New York: AMS Press.

Hoffman, Stefan-Ludwig, ed. (2011), *Human Rights in the Twentieth Century*, Cambridge: Cambridge University Press.
Höhn, Maria and Seungsook Moon, eds (2010), *Over There: Living with the U.S. Military Empire from World War Two to the Present*, Durham, NC: Duke University Press.
Holt, Thomas (2000), *Problem of Race in the 21st Century*, Cambridge, MA: Harvard University Press.
Hopkins, Anthony G. (1973), *An Economic History of West Africa*, London: Longman Press.
Horak, Roman (2013), "'We Have Become Niggers!': Josephine Baker as a Threat to Viennese Culture," *Culture Unbound: Journal of Current Cultural Research*, 5 (4): 515–30.
Horne, Alistair ([1977] 2006), *A Savage War of Peace, Algeria 1954–1962*, New York: Macmillan.
Howard, Michael (1976), *War in European History*, Oxford: Oxford University Press.
Hull, Isabel V. (2005), *Absolute Destruction: Military Culture and the Practices of War in Imperial Germany*, Ithaca, NY: Cornell University Press.
Hull, Edith Maud (1919), *The Sheik*, London: E. Nast & Grayson.
Hunt, Michael H. and Steven I. Levine (2012), *Arc of Empire: America's Wars in Asia from the Philippines to Vietnam*, Chapel Hill, NC: University of North Carolina Press.
Hunt, Nancy Rose (1988), "'Le Bebe En Brousse': European Women, African Birth Spacing and Colonial Intervention in Breast Feeding in the Belgian Congo," *International Journal of African Historical Studies*, 21 (3): 401–32.
Hutchins, Francis (1973), *India's Revolution*, Cambridge, MA: Harvard University Press.
Hyde, David (2015), "East African Railways and Harbours 1945–60: From 'Crisis of Accumulation' to Labour Resistance," in *Subversions of Colonial Cultures: Commodities and Anti-Commodities in Global History*, ed. Matt Harro and Sandip Hazareesingh, 147–69, Basingstoke: Palgrave Macmillan.
Hyde, David (2016), "The East African Railway Strike, 1959–60: Labour's Challenge of Inter-Territorialism," *Labor History*, 57 (1): 71–91.
Hyslop, Jonathan (1995), "White Working-Class Women and the Invention of Apartheid: 'Purified' Afrikaner Nationalist Agitation for Legislation Against 'Mixed' Marriages, 1934–9," *Journal of African History*, 36 (1): 57–81.
Idris, Amir Hasan (2005), *Conflict and Politics of Identity in Sudan*, New York: Palgrave Macmillan.
Inden, Ronald (1990), *Imagining India*, Bloomington, IN: Indiana University Press.
Inglis, Amirah (1975), *The White Women's Protection Ordinance: Sexual Anxiety and Politics in Papua*, New York: St. Martin's Press.
Irwin, Douglas A. (1998), "The Smoot-Hawley Tariff: A Quantitative Assessment," *Review of Economics and Statistics*, 80 (2): 326–34.
Irwin, Douglas A. (2011), *Peddling Protectionism: Smoot-Hawley and the Great Depression*, Princeton, NJ: Princeton University Press.
Irwin, Douglas A. (2012), *Trade Policy Disaster: Lessons from the 1930s*, Cambridge, MA: MIT Press.
Irwin, Douglas A., Petros C. Mavroidis, and Alan O. Sykes (2008), *The Genesis of the GATT*, New York: Cambridge University Press.
Isaac, Benjamin (2004), *The Invention of Racism in Classical Antiquity*, Princeton, NJ: Princeton University Press.

Isaacman, Allen F. and Barbara S. Isaacman (1976), *The Tradition of Resistance in Mozambique: The Zambesi Valley, 1850–1921*, Berkeley, CA: University of California Press.

Isaacman, Allen F. and Barbara S. Isaacman (1983), *Mozambique: From Colonialism to Revolution, 1900–1982*, Aldershot: Gower.

Isaacman, Allen F. and Barbara S. Isaacman (2013), *Dams, Displacement and the Delusion of Development: Cahora Bassa and its Legacies in Mozambique, 1965–2007*, Athens, OH: Ohio University Press.

Jaakson, Reiner (2004), "Globalisation and Neocolonialist Tourism," in *Tourism and Postcolonialism: Contested Discourses, Identities and Representations*, eds Michael C. Hall and Hazel Tucker, 169–83, London: Routledge.

Jackson, Peter A. (1997), "Thai Research on Male Homosexuality and Transgenderism and the Cultural Limits of Foucaultian Analysis," *Journal of the History of Sexuality*, 8 (1): 52–85.

Jackson, Will (2013), "Dangers to the Colony: Loose Women and the 'Poor White' Problem in Kenya," *Journal of Colonialism and Colonial History*, 14 (2).

James, Leslie and Daniel Whittall (2016), "Ambiguity and Imprint: British Racial Logics, Colonial Commissions of Enquiry, and the Creolization of Britain in the 1930s and 1940s," *Callaloo*, 39 (1): 166–84.

Jarboe, Andrew Tait and Richard S. Fogarty (2014), *Empires in World War I: Shifting Frontiers and Imperial Dynamics in a Global Conflict*, London: I.B. Tauris.

Jean-Baptiste, Rachel (2008), "'These Laws Should Be Made by Us': Customary Marriage Law, Codification and Political Authority in Twentieth-Century Colonial Gabon," *Journal of African History*, 49 (3): 217–40.

Jean-Baptiste, Rachel (2014), *Conjugal Rights: Marriage, Sexuality, and Urban Life in Colonial Libreville, Gabon*, Athens, OH: Ohio University Press.

Jenkinson, Jacqueline (2012), "'All in the Same Uniform'? The Participation of Black Colonial Residents in the British Armed Forces in the First World War," *Journal of Imperial and Commonwealth History*, 40 (2): 207–30.

Jennings, Eric (2015), *Free French Africa in World War II: The African Resistance*, Cambridge: Cambridge University Press.

Jhappan, Radha (1992), "Global Community? Supranational Strategies of Canada's Aboriginal Peoples," *Journal of Indigenous Studies*, 3 (1): 59–90.

Johnson, Douglas (2003), *The Root Causes of Sudan's Civil War*, Bloomington, IN: Indiana University Press.

Jones, Hilary (2013), *The Métis of Senegal: Urban Life and Politics in French West Africa*, Bloomington, IN: Indiana University Press.

Jones, James A. (2002), *Industrial Labor in the Colonial World: Workers of the Chemin de Fer Dakar-Niger, 1881–1963*, Portsmouth, NH: Heinemann.

Jones, Reece (2016), *Violent Borders: Refugees and the Right to Move*, New York: Verso.

Joshi, Chitra (2003), *Lost Worlds: Indian Labour and its Forgotten Histories*, Delhi: Permanent Black.

Judd, Denis (1996), *Empire: The British Imperial Experience from 1765 to the Present*, New York: Basic Books.

Jung, Moon-Kie (2006), *Reworking Race: The Making of Hawaii's Interracial Labor Movement*, New York: Columbia University Press.

Kahin, George McTurnan (1956), *The Asian-African Conference: Bandung, Indonesia, April 1955*, Ithaca, NY: Cornell University Press.

Karnow, Stanley (1983), *Vietnam, a History*, New York: Viking Press.
Karsch-Haack, Ferdinand and René Stelter, eds (2002), *Uranos: Unabhägige uranische Monatsschrift für Wissenschaft, Polemik, Belletristik, Kunst*, Hamburg: MännerschwarmSkript Verlag.
Keegan, John ([1976] 1978), *The Face of Battle*, New York: Penguin.
Keese, Alexander (2013), "Searching for the Reluctant Hands: Obsession, Ambivalence and the Practice of Organising Involuntary Labour in Colonial Cuanza-Sul and Malange Districts, Angola, 1926–1945," *Journal of Imperial and Commonwealth History*, 41 (2): 238–58.
Kendall, Kathryn (1999), "Women in Lesotho and the (Western) Construction of Homophobia," in *Female Desires: Same-Sex Relations and Transgender Practices across Cultures*, eds Evelyn Blackwood and Saskia Wieringa, 157–80, New York: Columbia University Press.
Kennedy, Dane (1987), *Islands of White: Settler Society and Culture in Kenya and Southern Rhodesia*, Durham, NC: Duke University Press.
Keynes, John Maynard (1920), *The Economic Consequences of the Peace*, New York: Harcourt, Brace & Howe.
Khalidi, Rashid (2004), *Resurrecting Empire: Western Footprints and America's Perilous Path in the Middle East*, Boston, MA: Beacon Press.
Khalidi, Walid (2006), *All That Remains: The Palestinian Villages Occupied and Depopulated by Israel in 1948*, Washington, DC: Institute for Palestine Studies.
Khan, Yasmin (2008), *The Great Partition: The Making of India and Pakistan*, New Haven, CT: Yale University Press.
Khan, Yasmin (2015), *India at War*, Oxford: Oxford University Press.
Kholoussy, Hanan (2010), "Monitoring and Medicalising Male Sexuality in Semi-Colonial Egypt," *Gender and History*, 22 (3): 677–91.
Khor, Denise (2014), "Hawaii's Theaters, Labor Strikes, and Counterpublic Culture, 1909–1934," in *The Rising Tide of Color: Race, State Violence, and Radical Movements across the Pacific*, ed. Moon-Ho Jung, 102–27, Seattle, WA: University of Washington Press.
Kiernan, Victor G. (1998), *Colonial Empires and Armies: 1815–1960*, Stroud: Sutton Publishing.
Kilcullen, David (2010), *Counterinsurgency*, New York: Oxford University Press.
Killingray, David (2010), *Fighting for Britain: African Soldiers in the Second World War*, Woodbridge: James Currey.
Kincaid, Jamaica (1988), *A Small Place*, New York: Penguin.
Klose, Fabian (2013), *Human Rights in the Shadow of Colonial Violence*, trans. Dona Geyer, Philadelphia, PA: University of Pennsylvania Press.
Kramer, Paul (2006), *The Blood of Government: Race, Empire, the United States, and the Philippines*, Chapel Hill, NC: University of North Carolina Press.
Krikler, Jeremy (2005), *White Rising: The 1922 Insurrection and Racial Killing in South Africa*, Manchester: Manchester University Press.
Kristol, Irving (1997), "The Emerging American Imperium," *Wall Street Journal*, August 18.
Kuklick, Henrika (1991), *The Savage Within: The Social History of British Anthropology, 1885–1945*, Cambridge: Cambridge University Press.
Kumar, Amitava (2000), *Passport Photos*, Berkeley, CA: University of California Press.
Kundrus, Birthe (2014), "Colonialism, Imperialism, National Socialism. How Imperial was the Third Reich?," in *German Colonialism in a Global Age*, eds Bradley Naranch and Geoff Eley, 330–46, Durham, NC: Duke University Press.

Lal, Vinay (1993), "The Incident of the Crawling Lane: Women in the Punjab Disturbances of 1919," *Genders*, 16: 35–60.
Langbehn, Volker and Mohammad Salam, eds (2011), *German Colonialism: Race, the Holocaust, and Postwar Germany*, New York: Columbia University Press.
Laroui, Abdallah (1977), *The History of the Maghrib: An Interpretive Essay*, Princeton, NJ: Princeton University Press.
Lawrence, Mark Atwood (2005), *Assuming the Burden: Europe and the American Commitment to War in Vietnam*, Berkeley, CA: University of California Press.
Lazer, David (1999), "The Free Trade Epidemic of the 1860s and Other Outbreaks of Economic Discrimination," *World Politics*, 51 (4): 447–83.
Lecocq, Baz (2010), *Disputed Desert: Decolonization, Competing Nationalisms and Tuareg Rebellions in Northern Mali*, Leiden: Brill.
Lee, Christopher (2011), "*Jus Soli* and *Jus Sanguinis* in the Colonies: The Interwar Politics of Race, Culture, and Multiracial Legal Status in British Africa," *Law and History Review*, 29 (2): 497–522.
Lee, Christopher (2014), *Unreasonable Histories: Nativism, Multiracial Lives, and the Genealogical Imagination in British Africa*, Durham, NC: Duke University Press.
Legge, John David (1972), *Sukarno: A Political Biography*, New York: Praeger.
Levine, Philippa (2003), *Prostitution, Race and Politics: Policing Venereal Disease in the British Empire*, London: Routledge.
Lewis, Bernard (1990), *Race and Slavery in the Middle East: An Historical Enquiry*, New York: Oxford University Press.
Limoncelli, Stephanie A. (2010), *The Politics of Trafficking: The First International Movement to Combat the Sexual Exploitation of Women*, Palo Alto, CA: Stanford University Press.
Lindqvist, Sven (1996), *"Exterminate All the Brutes,"* trans. Joan Tate, New York: The New Press.
Lipman, Jana K. (2009), *Guantánamo: A Working-Class History Between Empire and Revolution*, Berkeley, CA: University of California Press.
Liu, Lydia H. (2004), *The Clash of Empires: The Invention of China in Modern World Making*, Cambridge, MA: Harvard University Press.
Locher-Scholten, Elspeth (2000), *Women and the Colonial State: Essays on Gender and Modernity in the Netherlands Indies, 1900–1942*, Amsterdam: Amsterdam University Press.
Logevall, Frederik (2012), *Embers of War: The Fall of an Empire and the Making of America's Vietnam*, New York: Random House.
Loh Kok Wah, Francis (1988), *Beyond the Tin Mines: Coolies, Squatters and New Villagers in the Kinta Valley, Malaysia, c. 1880–1980*, Oxford: Oxford University Press.
Lorcin, Patricia M.E. ([1995] 2014), *Imperial Identities: Stereotyping, Prejudice, and Race in Colonial Algeria*, Lincoln, NE: University of Nebraska Press.
Lorcin, Patricia M.E. (2002), "Rome and France in Africa: Recovering Colonial Algeria's Latin Past," *French Historical Studies*, 25 (2): 295–329.
Lorcin, Patricia M.E. (2013a), "Imperial Nostalgia; Colonial Nostalgia: Differences of Theory, Similarities of Practice?," *Historical Reflections/Reflexions Historiques*, 39 (3): 97–111.
Lorcin, Patricia M.E. (2013b), "*Pax Romana* Transposed: Rome as an Exemplar for Western Imperialism," in *The Routledge History of Western Empires*, eds Robert Aldrich and Kirsten McKenzie, 409–23, London: Routledge.

Lorcin, Patricia M.E. (2014), "France's Nostalgias of Empire," in *France Since the 1970s: History, Politics and Memory in an Age of Uncertainty*, ed. Emile Chabal, 143–72, London: Bloomsbury.

Lorcin, Patricia M.E. and Todd Shepard (2016), *French Mediterraneans: Transnational and Imperial Histories*, Lincoln, NE: University of Nebraska Press.

Love, Joseph L. (1980), "Raúl Prebisch and the Origins of the Doctrine of Unequal Exchange," *Latin American Research Review*, 15 (3): 45–72.

Lugard, Frederick John Dealtry (Baron) (1922), *The Dual Mandate in British Tropical Africa*, Edinburgh: William Blackwood.

Lynn, John A. (1997), "The Embattled Future of Academic Military History," *Journal of Military History*, 61 (4): 777–89.

Lynn, John A. (2007), "Breaching the Walls of Academe: The Purposes, Problems, and Prospects of Military History," *Academic Questions*, 21 (1): 18–36.

Lyth, Peter J. and Marc L.J. Dierikx (1994), "From Privilege to Popularity: The Growth of Air Travel Since 1945," *Journal of Transport History*, 15 (2): 97–116.

Maathai, Wangari (2004), *The Green Belt Movement: Sharing the Approach and the Experience*, New York: Lantern Books.

Maathai, Wangari (2008), *Unbowed: A Memoir*, New York: Knopf Doubleday.

Macharia, Keguro (2014), "African Queer Studies," *Gukira*, https://gukira.wordpress.com/2014/08/24/african-queer-studies/.

Macmaster, Neil (2004), "Torture: From Algiers to Abu Ghraib," *Race and Class*, 46 (2): 1–21.

MacMillan, Margaret (2003), *Paris 1919: Six Months that Changed the World*, New York: Random House.

MacQueen, Norrie (1997), *The Decolonization of Portuguese Africa: Metropolitan Revolution and the Dissolution of Empire*, London: Longman.

Madley, Benjamin (2005), "From Africa to Auschwitz: How German South West Africa Incubated Ideas and Methods Adopted and Developed by the Nazis in Eastern Europe," *European History Quarterly*, 35 (3): 429–64.

Malinowski, Stephan and Robert Gerwarth (2009), "Hannah Arendt's Ghosts: Reflections on the Disputable Path from Windhoek to Auschwitz," *Central European History*, 42: 279–300.

Mamdani, Mahmood (1996), *Citizen and Subject: Contemporary Africa and the Legacy of Late Colonialism*, New Haven, CT: Princeton University Press.

Mamdani, Mahmood ([1973] 2011), *From Citizen to Refugee: Uganda Asians Come to Britain*, 2nd edn, Cape Town: Pambazuka Press.

Mamdani, Mahmood (2001), *When Victims Become Killers: Colonialism, Nativism, and the Genocide in Rwanda*, Princeton, NJ: Princeton University Press.

Mamdani, Mahmood (2009), *Saviors and Survivors: Darfur, Politics, and the War on Terror*, New York: Pantheon.

Manela, Erez (2007), *The Wilsonian Moment: Self-Determination and the International Origins of Anticolonial Nationalism*, Oxford: Oxford University Press.

Manicom, Desireé (2001), "Review of *The Invention of Women: Making African Sense of Western Gender Discourses*, by Oyeronke Oyewumi," *Agenda: Empowering Women for Gender Equity*, 50: 134–5.

Manjapra, Kris (2014), *Age of Entanglement*, Cambridge, MA: Harvard University Press.

Mao, Zedong (1961), *Selected Works of Mao Tse-Tung*, Vol. IV, Oxford: Pergamon.

Mao, Zedong ([1937] 1978), *On Guerilla Warfare*, New York: Anchor.

Marsh, Steve (2002), *Anglo-American Relations and Cold War Oil: Crisis in Iran*, Basingstoke: Palgrave Macmillan.
Martin, Enrique (2012), "Clandestine Recruitment Networks in the Bight of Biafra: Fernando Pó's Answer to the Labour Question," *International Review of Social History*, 57 (S20): 39–72.
Massad, Joseph A. (2008), *Desiring Arabs*, Chicago, IL: University of Chicago Press.
Matera, Marc (2015), *Black London: The Imperial Metropolis and Decolonization in the Twentieth Century*, Oakland, California: University of California Press.
Maul, Daniel (2012), *Human Rights, Development, and Decolonization: The International Labour Organization, 1940–70*, New York: Palgrave.
Mavhunga, Clapperton Chakanetsa (2014), *Transient Workspaces: Technologies of Everyday Innovation in Zimbabwe*, Cambridge, MA: MIT Press.
Maxwell, Donald (1924), "Concrete Studies in Empire Building – At Wembley," *The Graphic*, 109 (March 8): 324–5.
Mazower, Mark (2008), *Hitler's Empire: How the Nazis Ruled Europe*, New York: Penguin.
McDonald, Judith A., Anthony Patrick O'Brien, and Colleen M. Callahan (1997), "Trade Wars: Canada's Reaction to the Smoot-Hawley Tariff," *Journal of Economic History*, 57 (4): 802–26.
McDougall, James (2008), *History and the Culture of Nationalism in Algeria*, Cambridge: Cambridge University Press.
McMeekin, Sean (2010), *The Berlin–Baghdad Express: The Ottoman Empire and Germany's Bid for World Power*, Cambridge, MA: Belknap Press.
McNeill, J.R. (2000), *Something New Under the Sun: An Environmental History of the Twentieth-Century World*, New York: W.W. Norton.
McNeill, J.R. and Peter Engelke (2016), *The Great Acceleration*, Cambridge, MA: Harvard University Press.
Mikhail, Alan (2016), "Enlightenment Anthropocene," *Eighteenth-Century Studies*, 49 (2): 211–31.
Miller, Robert and Dennis D. Wainstock (2013), *Indochina and Vietnam: The Thirty-Five Year War, 1940–1975*, New York: Enigma Books.
Mirrlees, Tanner (2006), "American Soft Power, or, American Cultural Imperialism," in *The New Imperialists: Ideologies of Empire*, ed. Colin Mooers, 199–227, Oxford: Oneworld.
Mitchell, Timothy (2002), *Rule of Experts: Egypt, Techno-Politics, Modernity*, Berkeley, CA: University of California Press.
Mitchell, Timothy (2011), *Carbon Democracy: Political Power in the Age of Oil*, New York: Verso.
Mongia, Radhika Viyas (1999), "Race, Nationality, Mobility: A History of the Passport," *Public Culture*, 11 (3): 527–56.
Mooers, Colin, ed. (2006), *The New Imperialists: Ideologies of Empire*, Oxford: Oneworld.
Morel, Edmund Dene (1906), *Red Rubber: The Story of the Rubber Slave Trade Flourishing on the Congo in the Year of Grace 1906*, London: T. Fisher Unwin.
Mort, Frank (2006), "Scandalous Events: Metropolitan Culture and Moral Change in Post-Second World War London," *Representations*, 93 (1): 106–37.
Motadel, David (2014), *Islam and Nazi Germany's War*, Cambridge, MA: Belknap Press.
Moyd, Michelle R. (2014), *Violent Intermediaries: African Soldiers, Conquest, and Everyday Colonialism in German East Africa*, Athens, OH: Ohio University Press.
Moyn, Samuel (2010), *The Last Utopia*, Cambridge, MA: Belknap Press.

Mudimbe, Valentin (1988), *The Invention of Africa: Gnosis, Philosophy and the Oder of Knowledge*, Bloomington, IN: Indiana University Press.
Mukherjee, Sumita (2006), "Using the Legislative Assembly for Social Reform: The Sarda Act of 1929," *South Asia Research*, 26 (3): 219–33.
Murphy, Cullen (2008), *Are We Rome? The Fall of an Empire and the Fate of America*, Boston, MA: Houghton Mifflin.
Museveni, Yoweri (1971), "Fanon's Theory on Violence: Its Verification in Liberated Mozambique," in *Essays on the Liberation of Southern Africa*, ed. N. Shamuyarira, 1–24, Dar es Salaam: Tanzania Publishing House.
Myers, Ramon Hawley and Mark R. Peattie (1984), *The Japanese Colonial Empire, 1895–1945*, Princeton, NJ: Princeton University Press.
Nagl, John (2005), *Learning to Eat Soup with a Knife: Counterinsurgency Lessons from Malaya and Vietnam*, Chicago, IL: University of Chicago Press.
Najmabadi, Afsaneh (2008), "Types, Acts, or What? Regulation of Sexuality in Nineteenth-Century Iran," in *Islamicate Sexualities: Translations across Temporal Geographies of Desire*, eds Kathryn Babayan and Afsaneh Najmabadi, 275–96, Cambridge, MA: Harvard University Press.
Neep, Daniel (2012), *Occupying Syria under the French Mandate: Insurgency, Space and State Formation*, Cambridge: Cambridge University Press.
Nehru, Jawaharlal ([1946] 1985), *The Discovery of India*, Delhi: Oxford University Press.
Nirenberg, David (2007), "Race and the Middle Ages: The Case of Spain and Its Jews," in *Rereading the Black Legend: The Discourses of Religious and Racial Difference in the Renaissance Empires*, eds Margaret R. Greer, Walter D. Mignolo, and Maureen Quilligan, 71–87, Chicago, IL: University of Chicago Press.
Nixon, Rob (2013), *Slow Violence and the Environmentalism of the Poor*, Cambridge, MA: Harvard University Press.
Nkrumah, Kwame (1965), *Neo-Colonialism: The Last Stage of Imperialism*, New York: International Publishers.
O'Brien, Michael (2005), *John F. Kennedy: A Biography*, New York: Thomas Dunne Books/St. Martin's Press.
OECD (2009), "Trade Rounds and the World Trade Organization," *International Trade: Free, Fair and Open?*, Paris: OECD Publishing, http://dx.doi.org/10.1787/9789264060265-6-en.
Okihiro, Gary Y. (2009), *Pineapple Culture: A History of the Tropical and Temperate Zones*, Berkeley, CA: University of California Press.
Olwig, Karen F. (2015), "Migrating for a Profession: Becoming a Caribbean Nurse in Post- WWII Britain," *Identities: Global Studies in Culture and Power*, 22 (3): 258–72.
Omi, Michael and Howard Winant (1994), *Racial Formation in the United States: From the 1960s to the 1990s*, 2nd edn, New York: Routledge.
Orwell, George (1934), *Burmese Days: A Novel*, New York: Harper.
Oxfam (2003), "Running into the Sand: Why Failure at the Cancun Trade Talks Threatens the World's Poorest People," *Oxfam Briefing Paper #53*, https://policy-practice.oxfam.org.uk/publications/running-into-the-sand-why-failure-at-the-cancun-trade-talks-threatens-the-world–114588, accessed September 14, 2016.
Oyěwùmí, Oyèrónkẹ́ (1997), *The Invention of Women*, Minneapolis, MN: University of Minnesota Press.
Paisley, Fiona (2006), "An 'Education in White Brutality': Anthony Martin Fernando and Australian Aboriginal Rights in Transnational Context," in *Rethinking Settler Colonialism*, ed. A. Coombes, 209–26, Manchester: Manchester University Press.

Paisley, Fiona (2012), *The Lone Protestor: A.M. Fernando in Australia and Europe*, Canberra, ACT: Aboriginal Studies Press.
Palmer, Colin (2014), *Freedom's Children: The 1938 Labor Rebellion and the Birth of Modern Jamaica*, Chapel Hill, NC: University of North Carolina Press.
Pande, Ishita (2012), "Coming of Age: Law, Sex and Childhood in Late Colonial India," *Gender and History*, 24 (1): 205–30.
Pandey, Gyanendra (2006), *Routine Violence: Nations, Fragments, Histories*, Stanford, CA: Stanford University Press.
Pandey, Gyanendra (2013), *A History of Prejudice: Race, Caste, and Difference in India and the United States*, New York: Cambridge University Press.
Pannikar, K.N. (2009), *Colonialism, Culture and Resistance*, Oxford: Oxford University Press.
Pappé, Ilan (2006), *The Ethnic Cleansing of Palestine*, Oxford: Oneworld.
Paret, Peter (1991), "The New Military History," *Parameters*, 21 (3): 10–18.
Parry, Marc (2016), "Uncovering the Brutal Truth about the British Empire," *The Guardian*, August 19.
Parsons, Timothy (2015), "The Military Experiences of Ordinary Africans in World War II," in *Africa and World War II*, ed. Judith Byfield, Carolyn A. Brown, Timothy Parsons, and Admad Alawad Sikainga, 3–23, New York: Cambridge University Press.
Passavant, Paul A. and Jodi Dean (2004), *Empire's New Clothes: Reading Hardt and Negri*, New York: Routledge.
Pedersen, Susan (1991), "National Bodies, Unspeakable Acts: The Sexual Politics of Colonial Policy-Making," *Journal of Modern History*, 63 (4): 647–80.
Pedersen, Susan (2015), *The Guardians: The League of Nations and the Crisis of Empire*, Oxford: Oxford University Press.
Pennell, C. Richard (1986), *Country with a Government and a Flag: The Rif War in Morocco, 1921–1926*, Ann Arbor, MI: University of Michigan Press.
Perham, Margery (1944), "The View from the Aeroplane," in *Race and Politics in Kenya: A Correspondence between Elspeth Huxley and Margery Perham*, Elspeth Huxley and Margery Perham, London: Faber & Faber.
Planche, Jean-Louis (2006), *Sétif 1945: Histoire d'un massacre annoncé*, Paris: Perrin.
Polanyi, Karl ([1944] 2001), *The Great Transformation: The Political and Economic Origins of Our Time*, Boston, MA: Beacon Press.
Pols, Hans (2010), "Eugenics in the Netherlands and the Dutch East Indies," in *The Oxford Handbook of the History of Eugenics*, eds Alison Bashford and Philippa Levine, 347–62, Oxford: Oxford University Press.
Pomeranz, Kenneth (2000), *The Great Divergence, China, Europe, and the Making of the World Economy*, Princeton, NJ: Princeton University Press.
Porch, Douglas (1986), "Bugeaud, Gallieni, Lyautey: The Development of French Colonial Warfare," in *Makers of Modern Strategy from Machiavelli to the Nuclear Age*, ed. Peter Paret, 376–408, Princeton, NJ: Princeton University Press.
Portuondo, María (2009), "Constructing a Narrative: The History of Science and Technology in Latin America," *History Compass*, 7 (2): 500–22.
Posel, Deborah (1991), *The Making of Apartheid*, Oxford: Clarendon Press.
Prashad, Vijay (2008), *The Darker Nations: A People's History of the Third World*, New York: The New Press.
Pratt, Mary Louise (1992), *Imperial Eyes: Travel Writing and Transculturation*, London: Routledge.

Price-Smith, Andrew T. (2015), *Oil, Illiberalism, and War: An Analysis of Energy and US Foreign Policy*, Cambridge, MA: MIT Press.

Proschan, Frank (2002), "'Syphilis, Opiomania, and Pederasty': Colonial Constructions of Vietnamese (and French) Social Diseases," *Journal of the History of Sexuality*, 11 (4): 610–36.

Puar, Jasbir K. (2007), *Terrorist Assemblages: Homonationalism in Queer Times*, Durham, NC: Duke University Press.

Ramnath, Maia (2011), *From Haj to Utopia: How the Ghadar Movement Charted Global Radicalism and Attempted to Overthrow the British Empire*, Berkeley, CA: University of California Press.

Ravenhill, John (2011), *Global Political Economy*, Oxford: Oxford University Press.

Ray, Carina E. (2014), "Decrying White Peril: Interracial Sex and the Rise of Anticolonial Nationalism in the Gold Coast," *American Historical Review*, 119 (1): 78–110.

Ray, Carina E. (2015), *Crossing the Color Line: Race, Sex, and the Contested Politics of Colonialism in Ghana*, Athens, OH: Ohio University Press.

Reagan, Leslie J. (2016), "My Daughter was Genetically Drafted with Me: U.S.–Vietnam War Veterans, Disabilities, and Gender," *Gender and History*, 28 (3): 833–53.

Reynolds, David (2014), *The Long Shadow: The Great War and the Twentieth Century*, New York: W.W. Norton.

Robb, Peter (1995), "Introduction: South Asia and the Concept of Race," in *The Concept of Race in South Asia*, ed. Peter Robb, 1–76, Delhi: Oxford University Press.

Rodríguez García, Magaly (2012), "The League of Nations and the Moral Recruitment of Women," *International Review of Social History*, 57 (S20): 97–128.

Rodrik, Dani (2015), "Premature Deindustrialization," Princeton Institute for Advanced Study (IAS), School of Social Science, *Economics Working Papers* #107, https://www.sss.ias.edu/files/papers/econpaper107.pdf, accessed December 30, 2016.

Roediger David R. and Elizabeth Esch (2012), *The Production of Difference: Race and the Management of Labor in U.S. History*, New York: Oxford University Press.

Rooney, David (1988), *Kwame Nkrumah: The Political Kingdom in the Third World*, New York: St. Martin's Press.

Rosenberg, Clifford (2006), *Policing Paris: The Origins of Immigration Control Between the Wars*, Ithaca, NY: Cornell University Press.

Ross, Kristin (1995), *Fast Cars, Clean Bodies: Decolonization and the Reordering of French Culture*, Cambridge, MA: MIT Press.

Rostow, W.W. (1960), *The Stages of Economic Growth*, Cambridge: Cambridge University Press.

Saada, Emmanuelle (2012), *Empire's Children: Race, Filiation, and Citizenship in the French Colonies*, trans. Arthur Goldhammer, Chicago, IL: University of Chicago Press.

Said, Edward (1978), *Orientalism*, New York: Pantheon.

Saranillio, Dean Itsuji (2010), "Colliding Histories: Hawai'i Statehood at the Instersection of Asians 'Ineligible for Citizenship' and Hawaiians 'Unfit for Self-Government,'" *Journal of Asian American Studies*, 13 (3): 283–309.

Sarraut, Albert (1923), *La mise en valeur des colonies françaises*, Paris: Payot.

Schneider, Leander (2014), *Government of Development: Peasants and Politicians in Postcolonial Tanzania*, Bloomington, IN: Indiana University Press.

Scott, James C. (1990), *Domination and the Arts of Resistance: Hidden Transcripts*, New Haven, CT: Yale University Press.
Scott, James C. (1998), *Seeing Like a State: How Certain Schemes to Improve the Human Condition Have Failed*, New Haven, CT: Yale University Press.
Sen, Amartya (1977), "Starvation and Exchange Entitlements: A General Approach and its Application to the Great Bengal Famine," *Cambridge Journal of Economics*, 1 (1): 33–59.
Sharkey, Heather (2003), *Living with Colonialism: Nationalism and Culture in the Anglo-Egyptian Sudan*, Berkeley, CA: University of California Press.
Sharpe, Jenny (1989), "Figures of Colonial Resistance," *Modern Fiction Studies*, 35 (1): 137–55.
Shepard, Todd ([2006] 2008), *The Invention of Decolonization: The Algerian War and the Remaking of France*, Ithaca, NY: Cornell University Press.
Shepard, Todd (2012), "'Something Notably Erotic': Politics, 'Arab Men,' and Sexual Revolution in Post-Decolonization France, 1962–1974," *Journal of Modern History*, 84 (1): 80–115.
Shetler, Jan Bender (2007), *Imagining Serengeti: A History of Landscape Memory in Tanzania from Earliest Times to the Present*, Athens, OH: Ohio University Press.
Shipway, Martin (1996), *The Road to War: France and Vietnam 1944–1947*, Oxford: Berghahn Books.
Shipway, Martin (2008), *Decolonization and its Impact: A Comparative Approach to the End of the Colonial Empires*, Oxford: Blackwell.
Simatei, Tirop (2005), "Colonial Violence, Post-Colonial Violations, Violence, Landscape and Memory in Kenyan Fiction," *Research in African Literatures*, 36 (2): 85–94.
Simeon, Dilip (1995), *The Politics of Labour under Late Colonialism: Workers, Unions and the State in Chota Nagpur, 1928–1939*, New Delhi: Manohar.
Simons, Geoff L. (1998), *Vietnam Syndrome: Impact on US Foreign Policy*, New York: St Martin's Press.
Sinha, Mrinalini (1995), *Colonial Masculinity*, Manchester: Manchester University Press.
Sinha, Mrinalini (2006), *Specters of Mother India: The Global Restructuring of an Empire*, Durham, NC: Duke University Press.
Sluga, Glenda (2013), *Internationalism in the Age of Nationalism*, Philadelphia, PA: University of Pennsylvania Press.
Sluga, Glenda and Patricia Clavin, eds (2017), *Internationalisms: A Twentieth-Century History*, Cambridge: Cambridge University Press.
Somerville, Siobhan B. (2000), *Queering the Color Line: Race and the Invention of Homosexuality in American Culture*, Durham, NC: Duke University Press.
Sougnenet, Leon (1918), *Le Dernier Chameau, Le Premier Pneu, La Primiere Aile*, Bruxelles: Éditions de l'Éventail.
Spear, Thomas (2003), "Neo-Traditionalism and the Limits of Invention in British Colonial Africa," *Journal of African History*, 44 (1): 3–27.
Stanard, Matthew (2014), "Belgium, the Congo, and Imperial Immobility: A Singular Empire and the Historiography of the Single Analytic Field," *French Colonial History*, 15: 87–109.
Statler, Kathryn (2007), *Replacing France: The Origins of American Intervention in Vietnam*, Lexington, KY: University Press of Kentucky.
Stein, Rebecca (2008), "Souvenirs of Conquest: Israeli Occupations as Tourist Events," *International Journal of Middle East Studies*, 40: 647–69.

Stenson, Michael R. (1970), *Industrial Conflict in Malaya: Prelude to the Communist Revolt of 1948*, Oxford: Oxford University Press.

Stoler, Ann Laura (1992), "Sexual Affronts and Racial Frontiers: European Identities and the Cultural Politics of Exclusion in Colonial Southeast Asia," *Comparative Studies in Society and History*, 34 (3): 514–51.

Stoler, Ann Laura (1995), *Race and the Education of Desire: Foucault's History of Sexuality and the Colonial Order of Things*, Durham, NC: Duke University Press.

Stoler, Ann Laura (1997), "Racial Histories and their Regimes of Truth," *Political Power and Social Theory*, 11: 183–206.

Stoler, Ann Laura (2002), *Carnal Knowledge and Imperial Power: Race and the Intimate in Colonial Rule*, Berkeley, CA: University of California Press.

Stoler, Ann Laura, ed. (2006), *Haunted by Empire: Geographies of Intimacy in North American History*, Durham, NC: Duke University Press.

Stoler, Ann Laura (2016), *Duress: Imperial Durabilities in Our Times*, Durham, NC: Duke University Press.

Stone, Dan (2001), "Race in British Eugenics," *European History Quarterly*, 31 (3): 397–425.

Stovall, Tyler (1998), "The Color Line Behind the Lines: Racial Violence in France During the Great War," *American Historical Review*, 103 (3): 737–69.

Strauss, Scott (2006), *The Order of Genocide: Race, Power, and War in Rwanda*, Ithaca, NY: Cornell University Press.

Streets-Salter, Heather and Trevor R. Getz (2015), *Empires and Colonies in the Modern World*, Oxford: Oxford University Press.

Stromberg Childers, Kristen (2016), *Seeking Imperialism's Embrace*, Oxford: Oxford University Press.

Stubbs, Richard (2004), *Hearts and Minds in Guerrilla Warfare: The Malayan Emergency 1948–1960*, Singapore: Times Academic Press.

Summers, Carol (1991), "Intimate Colonialism: The Imperial Production of Reproduction in Uganda, 1907–1925," *Signs*, 16 (4): 787–807.

Surkis, Judith (2010), "Ethics and Violence: Simone de Beauvoir, Djamila Boupacha, and the Algerian War," *French Politics, Culture and Society*, 28 (2): 38–55.

Tabili, Laura (1994), "The Construction of Racial Difference in Twentieth-Century Britain: The Special Restriction (Coloured Alien Seaman) Order, 1925," *Journal of British Studies*, 33 (1): 54–98.

Tabili, Laura (2005), "Empire Is the Enemy of Love: Edith Noor's Progress and Other Stories," *Gender and History*, 17(1): 5–28.

Taine-Cheikh, Catherine (1989), "La Mauritanie en noir et blanc. Petit Promenade linguistique en Hassaniya," *Revue du Monde Musulman et de la Méditerranée*, 54: 90–105.

Taithe, Bertrand (2009), *The Killer Trail: A Colonial Scandal in the Heart of Africa*, New York: Oxford University Press.

Tal, Alon, ed. (2006), *Speaking of Earth: Environmental Speeches that Moved the World*, New Brunswick, NJ: Rutgers University Press.

Talbott, John (1980), *The War Without a Name: France in Algeria, 1954–1962*, New York: Knopf.

Tambe, Ashwini (2009), "The State as Surrogate Parent: Legislating Nonmarital Sex in Colonial India, 1911–1929," *Journal of the History of Childhood and Youth*, 2 (3): 393–427.

Tannanbawm, Frank (1946), *Slave and Citizen, the Negro in the Americas*, New York: Knopf.

Tanzanian African National Union (TANU) (1967), *The Arusha Declaration*, Dar es Salaam: TANU.
Taraud, Christelle (2003), *La Prostitution Coloniale: d'Algérie, Tunisie, Maroc (1830–1962)*, Paris: Payot.
Taussig, Michael (1993), *Mimesis and Alterity*, New York: Routledge.
Taylor, Robert H., ed. (2002), *The Idea of Freedom in Asia and Africa*, Stanford, CA: Stanford University Press.
Teo, Hsu-Ming (2010), "Historicizing *The Sheik*: Comparisons of the British Novel and the American Film," *Journal of Popular Romance Studies*, 1 (1).
Thénault, Sylvie (2011), *Violence Ordinaire dans l'Algérie Coloniale: Camps, Internements, Assignations à Residence*, Paris: Odile Jacob.
Thomas, Lynn M. (1998), "Imperial Concerns and 'Women's Affairs': State Efforts to Regulate Clitoridectomy and Eradicate Abortion in Meru, Kenya, *c*. 1910–1950," *Journal of African History*, 39 (1): 121–45.
Thomas, Martin (2005), *The French Empire between the Wars: Imperialism, Politics and Society*, Manchester: Manchester University Press.
Thomas, Martin, ed. (2011), *The French Colonial Mind, Vol. 2: Violence, Military Encounters, and Colonialism*, Lincoln, NE: University of Nebraska Press.
Thomas, Martin and Gareth Curless, eds (2017), *Decolonization and Conflict: Colonial Comparisons and Legacies*, London: Bloomsbury Academic.
Thomas, Martin, Bob Moore, and L.J. Butler, eds ([2007] 2015), *Crises of Empire: Decolonization and Europe's Imperial States, 1918–1975*, Berkeley, CA: University of California Press.
Thompson, Elizabeth ([2000] 2013), *Colonial Citizens: Republican Rights, Paternal Privilege, and Gender in French Syria and Lebanon*, New York: Columbia University Press.
Torpey, John (2000), *The Invention of the Passport: Surveillance, Citizenship and the State*, Cambridge: Cambridge University Press.
Towle, Evan B. and Lynn Marie Morgan (2002), "Romancing the Transgender Native: Rethinking the Use of the 'Third Gender' Concept," *GLQ: A Journal of Lesbian and Gay Studies*, 8 (4): 469–97.
Toye, Richard (2012), "The International Trade Organization," in *The Oxford Handbook on the World Trade Organization*, eds Amrita Narlikar, Martin Daunton, and Robert M. Stern, 85–101, Oxford: Oxford University Press.
Trautmann, Thomas (1997), *Aryans and British India*, Berkeley, CA: University of California Press.
Trautmann, Thomas (2006), *Languages and Nations: The Dravidian Proof in Colonial Madras*, Berkeley, CA: University of California Press.
Tronchon, Jacques (1986), *L'insurrection malgache de 1947*, Karthala: Paris.
Troutt Powell, Eve (2003), *A Different Shade of Colonialism: Egypt, Great Britain, and the Mastery of the Sudan*, Berkeley, CA: University of California Press.
Troutt Powell, Eve (2013), *Tell This in My Memory: Stories of Enslavement from Egypt, Sudan, and the Ottoman Empire*, Stanford, CA: Stanford University Press.
Trumpbour, John (2002), *Selling Hollywood to the World: U.S. and European Struggles for Mastery of the Global Film Industry, 1920–1950*, New York: Cambridge University Press.
Uchida, Jun (2011), *Brokers of Empire: Japanese Settler Colonialism in Korea, 1876–1945*, Cambridge, MA: Harvard University Press.
Ulloa, Marie Pierre (2008), *Francis Jeanson: A Dissident Intellectual from the French Resistance to the Algerian War*, trans. Jane Marie Todd, Stanford, CA: Stanford University Press.

United Nations (1948), *The Universal Declaration of Human Rights*, New York: United Nations.
United Nations Department of Economic and Social Affairs (2016), *International Migration Report, United States, 2015*, New York: United Nations.
United Nations General Assembly (UNGA) (1960), *Declaration on the Granting of Independence to Colonial Countries and Peoples*, Resolution 1514, December 14.
United Nations General Assembly (UNGA) (1974a), *Charter of Economic Rights and Duties of States*, Resolution 3281, December 12.
United Nations General Assembly (UNGA) (1974b), *Declaration on the Establishment of a New International Economic Order*, Resolution 3201, May 1.
US Census Bureau (2016), *Vintage 2016 Population Estimates: Population Estimates, Related Statistics about United States Population*, http://www.census.gov/search-results.html?q=2015+state+population+&search.x=0&search.y=0&search=submit&page=1&stateGeo=none&searchtype=web&cssp=SERP, accessed December 27, 2016.
USDA Economic Research Service (2016), *Data Files: U.S. and State-Level Farm Income and Wealth Statistics*, https://data.ers.usda.gov/reports.aspx?ID=49642, data posted November 30, 2016, accessed December 27, 2016.
van der Linden, Marcel (2008), *Workers of the World: Essays Towards a Global Labor History*, Leiden: Brill.
Van de Velde, Theodoor H. ([1926] 1930), *Ideal Marriage: Its Physiology and Technique*, trans. Stella Browne, New York: Random House.
Van Galen Last, Dick (2015), *Black Shame: African Soldiers in Europe, 1914–1922*, London: Bloomsbury.
Vaughan, Megan (2004), *Curing Their Ills: Colonial Power and African Illness*, Oxford: Polity Press.
Vazzadini, Elena (2015), *Lost Nationalism: Revolution, Memory, and Anti-colonial Resistance in Sudan*, London: James Currey.
Vine, David (2015), "The United States Probably Has More Foreign Military Bases Than Any Other People, Nation, or Empire in History," *The Nation*, September 14.
Visram, Rozina (2002), *Asians in Britain: Four Hundred Years of History*, London: Pluto Press.
Vitalis, Robert (2013), "The Midnight Ride of Kwame Nkrumah and Other Fables of Bandung," *Humanity*, 4 (2): 261–88.
von Eschen, Penny M. (1997), *Race Against Empire: Black Americans and Anticolonialism, 1937–1957*, Ithaca, NY: Cornell University Press.
Wacquant, Loïc (1997), "For an Analytic of Racial Domination," *Political Power and Social Theory*, 11: 221–34.
Walia, Harsha (2013), *Undoing Border Imperialism*, Oakland, CA: AK Press.
Walker, Tim (2014), "How Uganda was Seduced by Anti-Gay Conservative Evangelicals," *The Independent*, March 14, http://www.independent.co.uk/news/world/africa/how-uganda-was-seduced-by-anti-gay-conservative-evangelicals-9193593.html.
Wall, Irwin M. (2001), *France, the United States, and the Algerian War*, Berkeley, CA: University of California Press.
Wallach, Janet ([1996] 2005), *Desert Queen: The Extraordinary Life of Gertrude Bell, Adventurer, Adviser to Kings, Ally of Lawrence of Arabia*, 2nd edn, New York: Anchor Books.

Walther, Daniel J. (2013), "Sex, Public Health and Colonial Control: The Campaign Against Venereal Diseases in Germany's Overseas Possessions, 1884–1914," *Social History of Medicine*, 26 (2): 182–203.

Walz, Terrence and Kenneth Cuno, eds (2011), *Race and Slavery in the Middle East: Histories of Trans-Saharan Africans in 19th-Century Egypt, Sudan, and the Ottoman Mediterranean*, Cairo: The American University in Cairo Press.

Wattenberg, Ben J. (1991), *The First Universal Nation: Leading Indicators and Ideas about the Surge of America in the 1990s*, New York: Free Press.

Webb, Clive (2017), "Special Relationships: Mixed-Race Couples in Post-War Britain and the United States," *Women's History Review*, 26 (1): 1–20.

Wekker, Gloria (2016), *White Innocence: Paradoxes of Colonialism and Race*, Durham, NC: Duke University Press.

Wesseling, H.L. (1997), *Imperialism and Colonialism: Essays on the History of European Expansion*, Westport, CT: Greenwood Press.

Wheatley, Natasha (2015), "Mandatory Interpretation: Legal Hermeneutics and the New International Order in Arab and Jewish Petitions to the League of Nations," *Past and Present*, 227: 205–48.

Wheeler, Roxann (2000), *The Complexion of Race: Categories of Difference in Eighteenth-Century British Culture*, Philadelphia, PA: University of Pennsylvania Press.

White, Luise (1980), *Women's Domestic Labor in Colonial Kenya: Prostitution in Nairobi, 1909–1950*, Boston, MA: African Studies Centre.

Whitehead, John S. (2004), *Completing the Union: Alaska, Hawai'i, and the Battle for Statehood*, Albuquerque, NM: University of New Mexico Press.

Wieviorka, Olivier (2010), *Normandy: The Landings to the Liberation of Paris*, Cambridge, MA: Harvard University Press.

Wilder, Gary (2015), *Freedom Time: Negritude, Decolonization, and the Future of the World*, Durham, NC: Duke University Press.

Wilkinson, R.C. (1939), *Annual Report of the Department of Labour*, Port Louis, Mauritius: Government of Mauritius.

Wilks, Jennifer M. (2015), "Revolutionary Genealogies: Suzanne Césaire's and Christiane Taubira's Writings of Dissent," *Small Axe*, 19 (3): 91–101.

Winham, Gilbert R. (2009), "The Evolution of the World Trading System—The Economic and Policy Context," in *The Oxford Handbook of International Trade Law*, eds Daniel Bethlehem, Donald McRae, Rodney Neufeld, and Isabelle Van Damme, 5–29, Oxford: Oxford University Press.

Wipplinger, Jonathan O. (2017), *The Jazz Republic: Music, Race, and American Culture in Weimar Germany*, Ann Arbor, MI: University of Michigan Press.

Wolski, N. (2001), "All's Not Quiet on the Western Front," in *Colonial Frontiers: Indigenous-European Encounters in Settler Societies*, ed. L. Russell, 216–36, esp. 218–21, Manchester: Manchester University Press.

Wood, Ellen Meiksins (2006), "Democracy as Ideology of Empire," in *The New Imperialists: Ideologies of Empire*, ed. Colin Mooers, 9–24, Oxford: Oneworld.

World Trade Organization (WTO) (2010), *Dispute DS2; United States—Standards for Reformulated and Conventional Gasoline*, https://www.wto.org/english/tratop_e/dispu_e/cases_e/ds2_e.htm, webpage updated February 24, 2010, accessed December 29, 2016.

World Trade Organization (WTO) (2016), *Statistical Review*, https://www.wto.org/english/res_e/statis_e/wts2016_e/wts2016_e.pdf, accessed December 29, 2016.

World Trade Organization (WTO) (n.d.), *Legal Texts: The WTO Agreements, A Summary of the Final Act of the Uruguay Round*, https://www.wto.org/english/docs_e/legal_e/ursum_e.htm, accessed December 27, 2016.

Wright, Helena ([1931] 1937), *The Sex Factor in Marriage: A Book for Those Who Are or Are About to Be Married*, New York: Vanguard Press [reprint, twentieth printing].

Wright, Richard (1956), *The Colour Curtain*, London: Dobson.

Yergin, Daniel (1991), *The Prize: The Epic Quest for Oil, Money and Power*, New York: Simon & Schuster.

Young, Marilyn B. (1991), *The Vietnam Wars, 1945–1990*, New York: Harper Collins.

Young, Robert J.C. (2001), *Postcolonialism: An Historical Introduction*, London: Blackwell.

Zarobell, John (2010), *Empire of Landscape: Space and Ideology in French Colonial Algeria*, University Park, PA: Pennsylvania State University Press.

Zimmerer, Jürgen and Joachim Zeller (2008), *Genocide in German South-West Africa: The Colonial War (1904–1908) in Namibia and Its Aftermath*, Monmouth: Merlin Press.

NOTES ON CONTRIBUTORS

Daniel Bender is the Canada Research Chair in Global Culture, a Professor of History, and the founding director of the Culinaria Research Centre at the University of Toronto. He is the author of *The Animal Game: Searching for Wildness at the American Zoo* (Harvard University Press, 2016), *American Abyss: Savagery and Civilization in an Age of Industry* (Cornell University Press, 2009), and *Sweated Work, Weak Bodies: Anti-Sweatshop Campaigns and Languages of Labor* (Rutgers University Press, 2004), and the co-editor of *Making the Empire Work: Labor and United States Imperialism* (with J.K. Lipman, New York University Press, 2015) and *Sweatshop U.S.A.: The American Sweatshop in Historical and Global Perspective* (with R.A. Greenwald, Routledge, 2003). He is currently working on a new book project on food, empire, and global tourism entitled *Travelling on Their Stomachs: Round the World in Search of Flavor*.

Roland Burke is a lecturer in the Department of History and Archeology at La Trobe University in Australia. He is the author of *Decolonization and the Evolution of Human Rights* (University of Pennsylvania Press, 2010) and numerous articles in edited volumes and journals. He is at present working on a project that will examine the intellectual history of the arguments made against human rights. He has been the recipient of several prestigious awards and fellowships, including the R.M. Crawford Medal from the Australian Academy of the Humanities.

Anna Clark is Professor of History at the University of Minnesota. She is the author of *Alternative Histories of the Self: A Cultural History of Sexuality and Secrets* (Bloomsbury, 2017), *Desire: A History of European Sexuality* (Routledge, 2008), *Scandal: The Sexual Politics of the British Constitution*

(Princeton University Press, 2004), *The Struggle for the Breeches: Gender and the Making of the British Working Class* (University of California Press, 1995), and *Women's Silence, Men's Violence: Sexual Assault in England 1770–1845* (Pandora, 1987), as well as articles on human rights and humanitarianism, lesbian history, domestic violence, and imperialism.

Richard S. Fogarty is Associate Professor of History at the University at Albany, State University of New York, and specializes in the histories of modern France and Europe, war in its social and cultural contexts, colonialism, and race and racism. He is the author of *Race War in France: Colonial Subjects in the French Army, 1914–1918* (winner of the Phi Alpha Theta Best First Book Prize, Johns Hopkins University Press, 2008) and co-editor, with Andrew Tait Jarboe, of *Empires in World War I: Shifting Frontiers and Imperial Dynamics in a Global Conflict* (I.B. Tauris, 2014). His current research focuses on North African Muslims in the French army and as German prisoners of war, with special attention to the place of Islam and Muslims in France and Germany, as well as in the wider military and ideological struggle in Europe and the Middle East.

Bruce S. Hall is a specialist in African history. He is currently an Associate Professor in the Department of History at the University of California, Berkeley. He previously held positions at Duke University, University at Buffalo (SUNY), and the Johns Hopkins University. His book *A History of Race in Muslim West Africa, 1600–1960* (Cambridge University Press, 2011) was the co-winner of the American Historical Association's Martin Klein Prize for best book in African history.

Patricia M.E. Lorcin is holder of the Samuel Russell Chair in Humanities and Professor of History at the University of Minnesota-Twin Cities. She is the author of *Imperial Identities: Stereotyping, Prejudice, and Race in Colonial Algeria* (I.B. Taurus, 1995) and *Historicizing Colonial Nostalgia: European Women's Narratives of Algeria and Kenya 1900–present* (Palgrave Macmillan, 2011). She has edited or co-edited five volumes and three special issues, the most recent being *French Mediterraneans: Transnational and Imperial Histories* (with T. Shepard, University of Nebraska Press, 2016), and a special issue of *Gender and History* on global war. She has published numerous articles and book chapters on different aspects of French and western imperialism. She is at present working on a project tentatively entitled *The Cold War, Art, Politics and Transnational Activism during Decolonization*.

David A. Lynch is Professor in the Department of Social Science at Saint Mary's University of Minnesota where he has taught political science since 1996. He is the author of *Trade and Globalization: An Introduction to Regional Trade Agreements* (Rowman & Littlefield, 2010) and has written over a dozen chapters on international relations, international political economy, and American foreign policy, including the chapter on trade in the UN Association of the USA's *A Global Agenda* from 1996 to 2005. He received his PhD in political science from the University of California, Santa Barbara and his B.A. in political science from Iowa State University.

Jessica Namakkal is Assistant Professor of International Comparative Studies and Gender, Sexuality, and Feminist Studies at Duke University. She works on histories of decolonization, migration, and diaspora in the twentieth century.

Robert M. Rouphail is a doctoral candidate at the University of Illinois at Urbana-Champaign. He writes on the social, cultural, and environmental history of Indian Ocean Africa. His research ranges from the history of tropical meteorology, natural disasters, and biological science across the Indian Ocean world to histories of race, gender, and development in colonial and postcolonial Mauritius.

Elizabeth W. Williams is a Visiting Lecturer in the Department of Women, Gender, and Sexuality Studies at the University of Massachusetts, Amherst. She completed her PhD in History at the University of Minnesota-Twin Cities in 2017. Her research focuses on discourses of race and sexuality in the British Empire. Elizabeth's book project, tentatively titled *Sexual Trusteeship: Constructing Race and Sexuality in Colonial Kenya, 1895–1963*, explores discourses of sexual deviance and normativity in colonial East Africa.

INDEX

Abacha, Sani 87
Abdülhamid II 127
Abidine, Baba Oueld 73–4, 76
Adas, Michael 72
Aderinto, Saheed 142
Afghan War 25
Afghanistan 17, 24, 44, 46, 116, 134
AFL-CIO 111
Africa 12–14, 69–70, 89, 122, 190
   development 32, 80
   European assumptions 72, 95
   francophone 159
   HIV/AIDS 63
   migrants 118
   independence movements 42
   political economy 87
   post-colonial 88
   race 77, 188–9
   resources 83, 96
   sexuality 148
African and Caribbean Colonies, ACP 14
African National Congress, ANC 168, 173
African Party for the Independence of Guinea-Bissau and Cape Verde, PAIGC 169
African Socialism 171, 193
African Trading Corporation 3
African Village 94
Africanization 13
Afrikanerdom 173
Agent Orange 90

agriculture 3, 60, 63
Aizura, Aren 153
Alaska 11
Aldrich, Robert 141
Algeria 40, 79, 107–8
   Adrar region 73–4
   citizenship 130
   collaborators 150
   French conquest 2, 5
   French settlers 5, 39, 73, 75, 117
   nationalists 39, 144
   pieds-noirs 74, 130–1
   race 126
   resources 15
   Sétif 33, 37
   violence 190
   War of Independence 10, 23, 39, 130, 134, 149, 158, 167
   women 145
Alien Seaman Order (1925) 122
Allende, Salvador 20
al-Qadir, Abd 2
al-Qaida 16
Alternative for German, AfD 134
Amadiume, Ifi 152
Amazon River 98
Ambedkar, B. R. 123, 185
American Indians 87
Americanization 181
Amin, Idi 131
Amritsar 24

Amster, Ellen 139
Anarchical and Revolutionary Crimes Act
    (1919) 162
Anderson, David 41, 167
Angola 42, 95–6, 100–1, 124–5, 168
anthropocene 70, 81
antibiotics 69
anti-colonialism 3, 22
anticommunism 39
Antigua 102
anti-imperialism 107, 156
anti-industrialization 82
Antilles 150
apartheid 98, 173
Appadurai, Arjun 78
Arab Emirates 15
Arabian Peninsula 54
Arabs 28, 179
Arendt, Hannah 35, 190
Argentina 14, 60
Armenia 28
Armistice Day 43
Arusha Declaration (1967) 171
Aryanism 188
Asia 8, 35, 60, 69–70, 77, 80, 83, 89,
    95–6, 122, 188, 190
Asia Minor 2
Asian-African Conference (1955) 166
Aswan High Dam 88
Aswan Low Dam 88
Ataturk, Kemal 5
Atlantic Charter 159, 163
Atlantic Ocean 14, 95, 99
Atlantic slave trade 115, 150
Atlas Mountains 73
Augustine 60
Australia 26, 56, 73, 117, 126, 130,
    164, 174
Austria 125, 127
Austro-Hungarian Empire 1, 26. 28
automobile industry 4, 78
aviation 74, 78, 117

Ba'ath Party 16
Badoglio, Pietro 31
Bahamas, the 102
Baker, Josephine 7, 145
Baldwin, Richard 66
Balfour, Arthur James 128
Balfour Declaration 128

Balibar, Etienne 118
Balkans 28
Baltic States 28
Banana Wars 14
bananas 101, 110
bananeras 111
Bangladesh 37, 60, 111, 128, 171
Banivauna Mar, Tracey 155
Banton, Michael 177–8
Barbados 102
Basalla, George 71, 78
Bastille Day 43
Battle of Adwa 31
Battle of Annual 29
bauxite 102
Belgian Congo 4, 124, 133, 139, 165
Belgium 1, 26, 32, 123–4, 133, 161
Belize 102
Bell, Gertrude 18, 133
Bengal Cyclone (1943) 81
Berber peoples 29, 75
Berlin Wall 12
Biafra 171
Biafran War 16
Biko, Steve 173
biopolitics 138
Black Consciousness Movement 173
Black Shame 27
Blair, Tony 14, 16–17
Blumenbach, Johann Frederick 179
Blum-Violette Bill 5
Boas, Franz 145, 183
Bolivia 60
Bolshevik Revolution 101
Bonaparte, Marie 147
Bonilla-Silva, Eduardo 185–6
Botswana 171
Bouhired, Djamila 149
Boupacha, Djamila 149
Bourdieu, Pierre 23, 180–3, 185
Bourguiba, Habib 124
Bracero program 118
Brazil 48, 60, 98, 180, 183, 185
Brazzaville Declaration 159
Brennan, James 193–4
Bretton Woods Conference 8, 57–8, 61
Brexit 14, 66
Bricmont, Jean 20
British Colonial Office 103
British Commonwealth 14

British East Africa 108–9
British East Africa Protectorate 3
British Empire Exhibition (1924) 26–7
British Empire Marketing Board 54
British Honduras, *see* Belize
British India 24–5, 33
British National Health Service 130
British Riots (1919) 27
British School 24
British West Africa 3
Brower, Benjamin 76
Buddhists 128
Bugeaud, Thomas-Robert 24
Bulgaria 28
Burma 8, 34, 69, 81, 93, 165
Burton, Antoinette 71, 155
Bush, George W. 14, 16–17
Bustamante, Alexander 102–3

Cabral, Amilcar 123, 159
Cairns Group 60
Cairo Conference (1921) 2
Callwell, Charles 23–4
Cambodia 12, 43, 172
Cameroon 28, 143
Campbell, Chloe 139, 189
Camus, Albert 159
Canada 56, 67, 73, 117, 119, 123, 126, 130
Cape Verde 124, 168
capitalism 9, 17, 94, 96, 100, 103, 109
capitulations 5
Caribbean 6, 96, 100–1, 122
Caribbean Basin Initiative 111
Caribbean Labor Revolt 102
Caribbean Sea 89
Casa dos Estudantes de Império 123
Caucasus 15–16
Central America 126
Central Intelligence Agency, CIA 19
Césaire, Aimé 35, 107–8, 123, 126, 160
Césaire, Suzanne 123
Ceylon, *see* Sri Lanka
Chad 14
Chakrabarty, Dipesh 88, 101
Cheney, Dick 17
Cheysson, Claude 14
Chilcott Report 17
Chile 60

China 5, 35, 67
  intellectuals 179
  laborers 97
  manufacturing 65
  migrant labor 104
  race 177–8
  revolution (1911) 104
  sexuality 152
  war 41–3
  workers 104
Chiquita Banana 110–11
Chirac, Jacques 15
Christians 128
Churchill, Winston 29, 37
citizenship 79, 91
Civil Rights Movement 10, 186
Clemenceau, Georges 2
Clifford, Sir Bede 82
coal 15, 104
Coca-Cola 6
cocoa 105
coffee 96
Cohn, Bernard 188–9
Cold War 9, 12, 16–18, 37, 39, 58, 61, 89, 94, 100, 111
Colombia 60
colonialism 18, 21, 50
  culture of 22
  violence 23, 25
Columbia 111
Comaroff, John & Jean 189
Commonwealth of Nations 14, 132
communication 52, 117
communism 5, 10, 18, 28, 37, 39, 44, 58, 101, 104, 124
Communist Party of South Africa 97
Compagnie Française de l'Afrique Occidentale, CFAO 3, 13
Companie General de Transport Transsaharienne 73
Comprehensive Anti-Apartheid Act, CAAA 12
concentration camps 37
concubinage 140
Congo 32, 105
Congo Free State 190
Constantine, Stephen 117
consumerism 12, 15, 49
consumption 49
Contagious Diseases Acts 142

Convention People's Party (Ghana) 167
Cooper, Frederick 79, 87–8, 103, 109
copper 96
Corsica 124
Costa Rica 60
cotton 53, 96
Council of Women in Kenya, NCWK 85
Cox, Percy 18
Crosby, Alfred 73
Cuba 12, 56, 105–6, 123
Cuban Missile Crisis 12
Cubism 145
cultural imperialism 17
currency market 49
Curtin, Phillip 77, 189
Cuvier, Georges 179
Cyclone Nargis 69

Dakota Pipeline 134
Dalit 183–4
Dance, Charleston 7
Darwin, Charles 179
de Andrade, Mario 123
de Beauvoir, Simone 149
de Gaulle, Charles 15, 105, 159
de Grazia, Victoria 6, 13, 49
Debray, Regis 159
Declaration on Colonialism (1960) 167
decolonization 8, 9, 21, 23, 34–5, 37–42, 44, 94, 117, 130, 149, 170
Defense of India Act (1915) 162
deforestation 84
Delbrück, Hans 22
democracy 2, 19, 20
Democratic Party, PDG 165
dependency theory 83, 170
d'Estaing, Valéry Giscard 58
development colonialism 72, 79, 87
Điện Biên Phủ 8, 39
Dikötter, Frank 177–8
Dimier, Véronique 14
Dirks, Nicholas 188–9
Dirty War 38
Doha Development Agenda, DDA 61, 63–4
Dole Pineapple Company 96–7
dominions 27, 34
Dos Santos, Marcellino 123
Dreyfus Affair 127

Dubois, W.E.B. 107, 156
Dutch East Indies 124, 140, 165
Dyer, Reginald 25–6

Earth Summit 174
East Africa 34, 74, 77, 84
East African Standard 74
East Timor 42, 172
Eastern Europe 44
Eastern Trading Corporation 3
Economic Commission for Latin America, ECLA 61
economic liberalization 48
education 3, 32, 157
Egypt 10, 34, 88, 143–4, 162, 179, 189
Eichengreen, Barry 57
Eiffel Tower 95
Eisenhower, Dwight D. 10–11
El Salvador 12
Eldridge, Claire 131
Elkins, Caroline 167
el-Krim, Abd 29
Ellis, Havelock 145
Elshakry, Marwa 179
Enlai, Zhou 123
Enloe, Cynthia 100
environment 70–1, 176
Epprecht, Marc 147
Eritrea 134, 140
Estado Novo 42
Estienne, Georges 73–4, 76
Ethiopia 31, 162, 172
eugenics 138, 177
Europe 34, 35, 49, 51, 79
European Coal and Steel Community 9
European Commission 14, 117
European Development Policy 14
European Economic Community, EEC 14–15
European Union, EU 9, 14, 15, 57, 66, 117, 134
Evans Pritchard, E.E. 145
Evian Accords 130
Export Processing Zone, EPZ 113
Exposition Internationale des Arts et Techniques dans la Vie Moderne 95

Faisal, King 31
Falklands Crisis (1982) 14, 43
Fall, Bernard 41

Fanon, Frantz 21–4, 32, 42, 107, 123, 149, 159, 167
farming 55
fascism 6, 31, 55, 94, 107, 162
Fédération des Travailleurs Africains 108
Ferguson, Niall 18
Finland 28
First Peoples 175
First World War, *see* World War I
Ford II, Henry 99
Ford, Henry 98
Fordlandia 98–100
forestry 88
Fort Kidal 73
Foucault, Michel 187–8
fourteen points 2
Françafrique 14, 43
France 3, 10, 13–17, 26–9, 32–4, 36, 38–9, 41, 44, 47, 54, 56, 59, 67, 78, 91, 121–4, 127, 130–2, 134, 142, 150, 158–9, 161, 165, 168, 181–2
   citizenship 120
   civilizing mission 20
   DOM/TOM 11
   empire 26, 28, 36, 39–40, 43, 45, 70, 72, 75, 79–80, 89, 101, 108–9, 121–2, 133, 138, 143, 173, 191
   mandate 28, 31
   military 31, 34, 39, 121, 134
   surveillance 122
   values 15
Franco, Francisco 30
Frederiksen, Bodil Folke 147
Free France 34, 105, 108
Free Trade 2, 55, 64, 135
Freedom Charter (1955) 173
French Communist Party, PCF 107
French Equatorial Africa 28, 73
French India 121
French West Africa 32, 34, 73, 101, 105, 108, 111, 117, 121, 142
Freud, Sigmund 145, 147
Frevre, Gilberto 183
Friedman, Thomas 135
Fromentin, Eugene 75
Front National de Libération, FLN 10, 144, 149, 159, 167
Fukuyama, Francis 12

G7 66
Gallieni, Joseph 24, 45
Galula, David 41
Gandhi, Indira 172
Gandhi, Mahatma 5, 32, 124, 162–3
Gandhi, Mohandas 123
Gap 111
General Agreement on Tariff and Trade, GATT 57–60, 62
General Labour Union 104
Georges-Picot, François 2
German East Africa 3, 139
German Southwest Africa 138
Germany 28, 57, 67, 123, 125
   anti-Semitism 127
   empire 1, 7, 26, 35–6, 47, 54, 96
   military 33
   settlers 77
   war 27, 34–5
   war reparations 52–3, 58
Getz, Trevor 155
Ghadar Party 123
Ghana 10, 108, 123, 141, 169
Ghosh, Aurobindo 123
Gide, André 4
Gikuyu 77, 148–9
Glassman, Jonathon 191–3
globalization 48, 50, 52, 61, 65–7, 116
Goebbels, Joseph 6
gold 97
Gold Coast, *see* Ghana
gold standard 8
Golden Dawn 134
Gonzalez, Vernadette Vicuña 97
Goodman, Amy 134
Gorbachev, Mikhail 12
Gore, Al 56
Government of India Act (1919) 162
Great Britain 3, 8–9, 10, 13–17, 26–8, 33–4, 36–7, 43, 47, 50–2, 54, 56, 58–9, 67, 74, 80, 121–2, 124, 132, 151, 158, 161, 163–4, 168, 172, 178, 191
   colonial officials 95
   empire 26, 34, 36–7, 40, 70–2, 79–80, 88–9, 94–5, 99, 104, 108, 123, 133, 138, 149, 165
   empire exhibition (1924) 94
   industry 95

military 29, 37, 41, 121
   settlers 93
Great Convergence 67
Great Depression 3, 52, 55–8, 101, 103–4
Great Divergence 67
Great Recession 57, 65
Great War, *see* World War I
Greece 9, 28, 118, 133–4
Greece, civil war 9
Greenbelt Movement, GBM 84–5
Greenblatt, Stephen 115
Group of 20 57
Guam 11
Guantanamo 105–6
Guatemala 60
Guevara, Che 42, 159
Guiana 102
Guillame, Gustave 75
Guinea 108, 165
Guinea-Bissau 42
Gulf War 16
Gupta, Dikankar 183–4
Gurkhas 25

Hadj, Messali 123
Hall, Stuart 132, 178
Halliburton 17
Hanchard, Michael 180, 183
Harding, Warren 53
Hardt, Michael 17
Harper, Marjory 117
Harvey, David 18
Hatta, Mohammed 124, 165
Hawai'i 11, 97
Heffernnan, Michael 75
Herero 138
Herzl, Theodor 127
hierarchy 6, 35
Hindus 128, 142
Hitler, Adolph 6, 16, 35, 56, 126
HIV/AIDS 63
Hoad, Neville 152
Hobson, John 96
Hochschild, Adam 190
Hodann, Max 145
Hollywood film industry 6
holocaust 138, 190
Holt, Thomas 186
homosexuality 147, 151–2
Hong Kong 43, 142, 175

Horak, Roman 145
Horne, Alistair 159
Houphouet-Boigny, Felix 14, 108–9
Howard, Michael 22
Hull, Edith Maud 145
human rights 16, 19–20, 156–7, 163, 166, 173, 175
human trafficking 115
humanitarian imperialism 17
humanitarianism 24
Hungary 118
Hussein, Saddam 16
Hutchins, Francis 164
Hutus 193
Huxley, Elspeth 75
Hyslop, Jonathan 141

Iceland 117
Igbo 16, 152
Imperial Airway 74
imperialism 3, 18, 35, 41, 47
Inden, Ronald 188
India 5, 34, 37, 50, 54, 67, 88, 101, 104, 107–8, 127–9, 142, 150, 152, 162, 164, 172, 176, 183, 188
   caste system 183–4, 189
   decolonization 37
   independence 37, 127, 165
   laborers 82
   partition 126, 165
   race 185
   settlers 78
   soldiers 121
Indian Congress Party 167
Indian National Congress 5, 124, 162, 164
Indian National Liberation Army 164
Indian Ocean 34, 40, 81–2
indirect rule 79
Indochina 4, 8, 12, 28, 38–40, 80, 88, 117, 121, 140, 158–9, 191
Indo-Mauritians 81–2
Indonesia 3, 5, 42, 48, 59–60, 67, 108, 140–1, 158, 164, 171, 180
Indonesian Nationalist Party, PNI 5
industrial production 47
industrialization 15, 48, 65, 67
inflation 9
infrastructure projects 80
Intellectual Property Rights, IPR 62–3

International Bank for Reconstruction and Development, IBRD, *see* World Bank
International Labor Organization, ILO 170
International Monetary Fund, IMF 9, 57–8
International Trade Organization, ITO 57, 61–2
interwar period 3, 16, 27, 99, 122, 138
Iran 16–17, 34, 54, 136, 144
Iraq 12, 15–17, 28–9, 34, 46, 89, 134, 136
Ireland 28, 162
Irish Free State 28
Irish Republican Army, IRA 163
Irrawaddy Delta 69
irrigation 82
Islam 16, 36, 130, 144
Israel 9, 127–9
Italy 31–2, 56, 67, 105
Ivory Coast 14, 108–9

Jains 128
Jallianwala Bagh 24–5, 33
Jamaica 101–3, 106
Jamaica Labour Party 103
James, C.L.R. 107
Japan 7, 15, 26–7, 33–5, 37, 41, 67, 69, 104–5, 123, 164
  empire 39
  Fukushima Prefecture 69
  laborers 97
  military 164–5
Jean-Baptiste, Rachel 148
Jefferson, Thomas 158
Jews 28, 34, 127–8
Jim Crow Laws 151
Jinnah, Muhammad Ali 123
Johnson, Lyndon B. 49
Jung, Carl 147
jus sanguinis 119
jus soli 119

Kahn, Yasmin 128
Kant, Immanuel 179
Keegan, John 22
Kendall, Kathryn 152
Kennedy, John F. 10, 12, 49
Kenya 3, 40–1, 73–4, 77, 79, 84–5, 88, 91, 107–9, 148–9, 158, 189
  eugenics 139
  independence 85
  settlers 167
  women 84
Kenyatta, Jomo 149, 167
Keynes, John Maynard 52, 58
Khaled, Emir 2
Khaled, Leila 159
Khalidi, Rashid 17–18
Khama, Seretse 171
Khmer Rouge 12, 43
Khrushchev, Nikita 12
Kidd, Benjamin 2
Kiernan, V.G. 25
Kikuyu 41, 75, 149
Kincaid, Jamaica 115
King Kong 6–7, 95
Korea 10, 100, 106
Korean War 10, 100
Kramer, Paul 190
Kristol, Irving 1
Kuklick, Henrika 145
Kuwait 16, 89

Labor 93
  colonial 96
  forced 32, 96, 108
  mobilization 100
  race 98
  recruitment 100
  rights 104
  solidarity 94
  wage 96
Laird, MacGregor 77
Lake Victoria 74
land 41, 84
Laos 12
Lara, Lucio 123
Laroui, Abdallah 189
Latin America 42, 45, 89, 126, 183, 190
Lausanne Treaty 5
Lawrence, T.E. 18, 133
Le Bon, Gustav 179
League of Nations 2, 26, 31, 54, 99, 142, 161, 163
Lebanon 28, 34, 165
Lecocq, Baz 194
Lee, Christopher 120
Lenin, Vladimir 101
Leopold II of Belgium 32, 190

Lesotho 152
Levant 54
liberalization 50, 59, 65
Libya 15, 31, 134, 136
Lichtenstein 117
Lindqvist, Sven 190
Livingston, David 133
Lloyd George, David 2
Lugard, Lord Frederick 3, 19
Lumumba, Patrice 124
Lyautey, Hubert 24, 30, 45

M'zab 78
Maathai, Wangari 72, 84, 87–8, 91
Macau 42–3, 175
Macharia, Keguro 147
Machel, Samora 159
Macmillan, Harold 8
Madagascar 34, 40, 121
Maendeleo ya Wanawake Organization, MYWO 85
malaria 82
Malawi 120
Malay Peninsula 37
Malaya 4, 8, 34, 38, 80, 98, 103–4, 108
Malayan Communist Party 37
Malaysia 37, 48, 59–60
Malcolm X 10
Mali 14, 194
Malinoski, Bronislaw 145
Mamdani, Mahmood 131–2, 148, 189
mandate system 2, 26
Mandela, Nelson 168
Mangoenkoesoemo, Tjipto 124
Manley, Norman 103
Maori 87
Mariam, Haile Mengistu 172
marriage customs 141
Marshall Plan 9, 58
Marx, Karl 101
Marxism 104
Marxism-Leninism 101
masculinity 25
mass consumption 49
mass culture 6
mass migration 120
mass mobilization 6
Massad, Joseph 152
Mau Mau 41, 77, 85, 108–9, 149, 167
Mauritania 194

Mauritius 81
Maxwell, Donald 94
May, Teresa 14
Mayhunga, Clapperton 72
Mayo, Katherine 142
Maysalun 31
Mazower, Mark 36
Mazzini, Giuseppe 158
Mboye, Tom 109
McDonalds 13
McNeill, John 69–70
Mediterranean Sea 8, 73
Mexico 48, 56, 118, 123, 130
Middle East 1, 9, 16–18, 27, 31, 45, 54, 89, 107, 118, 122, 128, 152, 175, 188
migration 115–16
Mines and Work Act (1924) 98
Minh, Ho Chi 5, 101, 123, 159
Miranda, Carmen 110
miscegenation 121, 191
mise en valeur 32
Mitchell, Timothy 83, 88–9
Mitterrand, François 15
mobility 115
modernity 20, 117
modernization 99
Mohammed V, Sultan of Morocco 124
Mondland, Eduardo 123
monetary policy 49
Mongia, Radhika Viyas 120
Mongols 17
Montenegro 28
Moon, Seungsook 100
Morel, Edmund D. 4
Morocco 12, 29–30, 34, 73, 139, 143
Most Favored Nation Status, MFN 59
Mount Cameroon 77
Moyne, Lord 103
Mozambique 42, 141, 168
Mozambique Liberation Front, FRELIMO 124, 169
Mudimbe, Valentin 189
Murphy, Cullen 17
Muslims 36, 128, 141
Mussolini, Benito 31, 162
Myanmar, *see* Burma

Namibia 174, 190
Napalm 90

Nasser, Gamal Abdel 10, 88, 166
National Front, FN 134
National Liberation Front, *see Front National de Libération*
National Party, GNP 141
National Party, South Africa 173
nationalism 50, 109, 116, 158
Nazis 33–5, 37, 125, 138, 190
    architecture 95
    empire 36
    expansionism 35
    ideology 57, 94, 105
    New Order 36
    racial policy 36
Negri, Antonio 17
negritude 107
Nehru, Jawaharlal 108, 123–4, 166
neocolonialism 43, 170
Neo-Destour Party 124
neoimperialism 43
Netherlands 3, 33, 35, 59, 108, 132, 161, 165, 180, 173
Netherlands Indies 191
Neto, Agostinho 123–4
new imperialism 17
New Zealand 26, 56, 117, 126, 130
NGO 175
Niger 190, 194
Niger Company 3
Niger Delta 84–5
Niger River 74
Nigeria 3, 16, 85, 87–8, 99, 103, 151–2, 171
Nigerian National Petroleum Organization 86
Nike 111
Nile River 88
Nirenberg, David 179–80
Nkrumah, Kwame 108, 123–4, 169
Noble Peace Prize 84
Non-Aligned Movement 126, 170
Non-tariff Barriers, NTB 62
North Africa 12, 34, 75, 121, 139, 143, 159, 164
North American Free Trade Agreement, NAFTA 56–7, 66, 111
North Atlantic Treaty Organization, NATO 9, 10, 15
North Vietnam 89
Northern Rhodesia, *see* Zambia
Norway 117

Nyasaland 120
Nyerere, Julius 171

O'Keefe, Georgia 96
Ogoni Bill of Rights 86
Ogoni people 85–7
Ogoniland 87
oil 15–16, 54, 88–9, 102
Okinawa 18, 100, 107
Omi, Michael 186
Operation Barbarossa 16
Opium Wars 5, 13
Organization of the Petroleum Exporting Countries, OPEC 16
orientalism 74, 144–5, 147, 151, 153, 188
Orwell, George 93–4, 99, 112
Ottoman Empire 1, 16, 26, 28, 54, 75, 143–4
Oyěwùmí, Oyèrónkẹ́ 148
ozone layer 70

Pacific Ocean 6, 33–4, 89, 100, 107
pacification 29
Pakistan 37, 60, 127–9, 150, 165, 171
Palestine 2, 9, 28, 127–9
Pan-African Congress 107
Pan-Africanism 156, 173
Panama Canal 96
Pappé, Ilan 127
Paraguay 60
Paris Colonial Exposition (1931) 26–7
Paris Peace Conference (1919) 161
passport 119–20
Pax Americana 18
Pax Britannica 18
peanuts 96
Pearl Harbor 8, 11, 35, 164
Pedersen, Susan 149
People's Movement for the Liberation of Angola, MPLA 124
People's National Party 103
Perham, Margery 75
Permanent Mandates Commission 161
Perot, Ross 56–7
Persian Gulf 46, 89
Peru 60
Pétain, Philippe 30
Philippines 60, 97, 100, 106–7, 158, 165, 190
Poland 28, 67, 125, 127

Polanyi, Karl 80
polar ice 70
polygamy 142
Pomeranz, Kenneth 51
Popular Movement for the Liberation of
    Angola, MPLA 169
Portugal 32, 42, 56, 124, 168–9
    empire 32, 42–3, 70, 79–80, 89, 95,
        123, 168
    laborers 97
    military 32
Powell, Enoch 132, 151
Pratt, Mary Louise 116, 133
Prebish, Raúl 49, 61
Profintern 104
prostitution 141, 143
protectionism 57, 66
Puar, Jasbar 151
Puerto Rico 11, 106
Punjab 24, 132

Quit India Campaign (1942) 164

race 78
    exclusion 93
    hierarchy 94, 97, 102
    materiality 187
    purity 140
    superiority 94
racism 36, 156, 185–6
Radcliffe Brown, A.R. 145
Radio Cairo 10
railroads 108–9, 117
Ranch Hand 90
Rand Revolt 97
Ravenhill, John 54
Ray, Carina 141
Reciprocal Trade Agreements Act of 1934
    59
Red Terror 172
Regan, Leslie 90
Regional Trade Agreements, RTA 66
Renan, Ernest 179
reproduction 138
resistance 155
resistance, laborers 100
resistance, non-violent 33
Rhineland 27
Rhodesia 167
Rif Region 29–30

Rivera, Diego 4
Robb, Peter 189
Rodrik, Dani 67
Roman Empire 17, 75
Ross, Kristen 13
Rostow, W.W. 49
rubber 4, 53, 80, 96, 98, 104
Rumsfeld, Donald 45
Russia 27, 36, 123, 127
    civil war 28
    empire 1, 26, 28, 35
    navy 164
    revolution 6
Rwandan genocide 193
Rwanda-Urundi 1

S Campaign 174
Saada, Emmanuelle 191
Sahara Desert 73, 75–6, 78–9, 91
Sahel 73
Said, Edward 188
Saigon 43
Salazar 32, 169
salt 163, 176
São Tomé and Principe 42
Sarda Act (1929) 142
Sarkozy, Nicolas 14
Saro-Wiwa, Ken 72, 84–9, 91
Sartre, Jean-Paul 149, 159, 167
Saudi Arabia 15–16
Schengen Agreement 117–19
Schutzstaffel, SS 36
Scott, James 79
Second Indochinese War, see Vietnam
    War
Second World War, see World War II
self-determination 2, 54, 96
Senegal 103, 108–10, 171
Senghor, Léopold Sédar 109–10, 123,
    160, 171
Senussi Sufi Order 31
Serbia 28
settler colonialism 72–3, 177
sex
    brothels 99
    colonization 147
    interracial 140
    regulation 137, 148
    violence 149
    workers 99, 106

Sharkey, Heather 189
Shell Oil 86
Shepard, Todd 130, 149
Sikhs 128, 132
Simatei, Tirop 75
Singapore 34, 48, 104, 164
slavery 177
Smith, Ian 167
Smoot-Hawley Tariff Act 55–7, 59, 65
Smuts, Jan 97
socialist movements 93
Société Commerciale de l'Ouest Africain, SCOA 3, 13
soft imperialism 13, 17
Soldier Settlement Scheme 3
Somalia 116, 136
Sougnenet, Léon 78
South Africa 12, 26, 43, 95, 97–8, 119, 126, 141, 162, 168, 173, 183, 185, 189–90
South African National Party 98
South America 6
South Korea 67
South Vietnam 44
Southeast Asia 15, 43
Southern Rhodesia, *see* Zimbabwe
sovereignty 47, 160
Soviet Union 9, 11–12, 16, 27–8, 34–5, 39, 107, 163
  construction 95
  demise of 44
  empire 33, 44
  military 44
Spain 29, 56
  civil war 30
  military 29–30, 105
  nationalist forces 30
Spanish Republic 30
Sparticist Revolt 6
specialization 49
Spencer, Herbert 179
Sri Lanka 8, 165
St. Kitts 102
St. Lucia 102
St. Vincent 102
Stanard, Matthew 133
Stanley, Henry Morton 133
Stein, Rebecca 129
Stoler, Ann Laura 134, 180, 186–7, 191
Stovall, Tyler 122

Straits Settlements 142
Streets-Salter, Heather 155
strikes 97, 102–4, 107–9
Sub-Saharan Africa 1, 12, 34
Sudan 136, 189, 194
Suez Canal Crisis 10
sugar 55, 81–2, 101
Sukarno 5, 108, 124, 172
Sukarno, Ahmed 164
surveillance 122
sweatshops 112
Switzerland 56, 117
Sykes, Mark 2
Sykes-Picot Agreement 16, 54
symbolic violence 23
Syria 15, 28, 31, 34, 116, 118, 133–4, 136, 143, 165

Tang China 17
Tanganyika 77, 108–9
Tannenbawm, Frank 183
Tanzania 88, 103, 132, 171, 190, 193
Tariff Act of 1930, *see* Smoot-Hawley Tariff Act
tariffs 47, 56, 62
Tarzan 95
Taubira, Christiane 150
tea 96
teak 96
technology 49, 67
  advancements 91
  change 71
  culture 117
  development 69
  expertise 70
  governance 70
  knowledge 87
  power 69, 71
  transportation 119
textiles 48, 60, 63
Thailand 67, 152
Thatcher, Margaret 12, 14
The Movement of the Survival of the Ogoni People, MOSOP 87
theory of unequal exchange 49
Third Anglo-Afghan War 24
Third World 88, 166
Thomas, Martin 23, 42, 139
tin 104

Torpey, John 119
Touareg 73–4, 76
Touré, Ahmed Sékou 165
tourism 97, 112, 116, 128–9, 134–5
Traction Company Employees' Association 104
trade unions 101, 104, 107, 109
trade
  liberals 50
  liberalization of 48
  protectionism 55, 60
transgender 152
Transjordan 28
transportation 15, 52, 117
Trautmann, Thomas 188
Trinidad 102–3
Troutt Powell, Eve 189–90
Truman Doctrine 9
Truman, Harry S. 62
Trump, Donald 14, 66, 118, 136
Trusteeship Council 163
Tuareg 194
Tunisia 124
Turkey 9, 28
Tutsis 193

Uganda 77, 109, 127, 131–2, 151
Umkhonto we Sizwe 168
Unilever 4
unions 95, 103, 111
United Africa Company, UAC 3, 13
United Democratic Front 174
United Fruit Company 110–11
United Kingdom, *see* Great Britain
United Nations 10, 14, 17, 84, 116, 125, 135, 156, 163, 170, 183
United Nations Declaration of Human Rights, UNDR 125
United Nations Environmental Program, UNEP 84
United Nations High Commissioner on Refugees 125
United Nations Relief and Rehabilitation Administration, UNRRA 125
United Nations World Tourism Organization, UNWTO 116
United Party (South Africa) 141
United States 1, 2, 6, 10, 12, 14–18, 27, 33–4, 39, 42–4, 46–7, 49–50, 55, 58, 60–1, 64, 67, 73, 84, 89, 96, 100, 105, 111, 118–19, 123, 126, 130, 132, 134, 151–3, 158, 163, 183, 185–6, 190
  capitalism 37
  Civil Rights Movement 180–1
  Commerce Department 6
  Congress 10–12, 55, 57, 59, 61
  consumerism 13, 15
  Department of Defense 18
  empire 42, 70, 105, 194
  imperialism 2, 18
  military 41, 101, 105–6
  policies of 43
  press 10
  race 181, 183–4
  Refugee Admissions Program 136
  Senate 61
  State Department 6
  tariffs 50
  technology 99
Universal Declaration of Human Rights, UDHR 157, 165–6
uranium 105
Uruguay 60
Uruguay Agreement 63
USSR, *see* Soviet Union

Valentino, Rudolph 145
Van de Velde, Theodore 147
venereal disease 139
Versailles Peace Conference (1919) 27
Vichy France 105, 108
Vietnam 8, 12, 23, 39, 41, 43, 59–60, 100, 106–8, 111
Vietnam Syndrome 12
Vietnam War 12, 38, 43–5, 89
Vine, David 18
violence
  colonial 21, 23
  cultural 22
  genocide 73
  resources 83
  structural 23, 31–2, 34–5, 37, 44
Virgin Islands 11

Wacquant, Loïc 180–3, 185, 187
Walia, Harsha 136
war 21–4, 30, 34
war on terror 46
Washington Conference (1922) 5

Wattenberg, Ben 1, 18
Webb, Clive 151
Wehrmacht 36
Weimar Republic 6, 57
Wesseling, H. L. 23
West Africa 10
West Indies 103
West Papua 171
wheat 55
White Highlands 79
white supremacy 93, 97, 186
Wilhelm II 36
Wilhelm, Kaiser 127
Wilson, Woodrow 1, 26, 161
Winant, Howard 182, 186
wine 15
women
  colonial settlers 137
  ecology 84
  resistance 155–6
  rights of 176
  sex workers 99
  South Asian 127
  veil 144
Wood, Ellen 18–19
working class 101, 103, 107–9
World Bank 9, 57
World Trade Organization, WTO 57–9, 61–3, 65

World War I 1, 3, 12, 16, 23–4, 26–8, 30–2, 34, 36, 50, 52, 54, 58, 69, 77, 94–6, 120–2, 144, 161–3
World War II 7, 11–12, 16, 21, 23, 31, 33–6, 40, 52, 55, 57–9, 61, 72. 79, 81, 87, 99, 103, 107, 110, 125, 127–8, 163, 165
world's fairs 95, 110–11
Wright, Helena 147
Wright, Richard 10

Yankee culture 6
Yemen 136
Yên Bái Revolt 5, 28
Yom Kippur War 16
Yoruba 148
youth movements 32

Zambezi River 96
Zambia 95–6, 148
Zanzibar 191–4
Zedong, Mao 41–2
Zimbabwe 72, 96, 151
Zimbabwe African National Union, ZANU 168
Zimbabwean African People's Union, ZAPU 168
Zionism 127
Zoroastrians 128